# HOW MUCH FOR A LITTLE SCREW?

Tales from

Behind the Counter

## GRAHAM HIGSON

First published in 2014

This print edition published by
CreateSpace Independent Publishing Platform
2014

© Graham Higson 2014

Cover images © Graham Higson 2014
Cover concept by Fred Higson

www.grahamhigson.com

All rights reserved. No part of this book may be reproduced,
stored or introduced into a retrieval system, or transmitted
in any form or by any means (electronic, mechanical,
photocopying, recording or otherwise) without the
prior permission of the author.

The moral rights of the author have been asserted.

Cat 0210917

ISBN-13: 978-1503096974
ISBN-10: 1503096971

*To the memory of
the MD
1921-2010*

This book is a fictionalised memoir based on some true events. Names, places and some of the timings have been changed.

## THANKS

A big thank you goes to my beta readers:

Julie Haigh
A M Rothery
S J Bradford

for their interest, time, professionalism, and comments for which I am grateful.

## **EXTRAS**

For extra information and features relating to

How Much for a Little Screw?
**please visit**
www.grahamhigson.com

# 1
## THE EARLY 1990s

*The pipe dream*

THAT MORNING THERE WERE two women in my life—no, scratch that because one of them had left. Months before, when I come to think of it. But when the phone woke me up, I turned over in bed and reached out to feel her. And she wasn't there. Because she'd gone. Old habits and all that. So yes, two women: one of them a memory, the other calling me at this ungodly hour, and the phone was on a short lead across the other side of the bedroom, which meant I had to get my freezing butt out of bed to go and answer it.

"Good morning, Sir. This is your happy hardware wake-up call. And how are you today?" The voice was an unfamiliar educated early-20s and sounded like she would be too good even for a posh airport announcer.

"Sharon? That is you, isn't it?" No answer. "Sharon?" Then I heard the tell-tale intake of breath. "It is you! Crikey! That was fantastic!" I'd not heard that voice before.

"Ah, do you fink so?" The accent had slipped back to the default Cockney of about 48, give or take. But her accent was never consistently Eastender, and depended on her mood. "Still got a few voices up my sleeve, my love. You never forget how to do it, not once you've had the training."

"It was very good. BAFTA-winning. You almost had me fooled."

1

"I did have you fooled. I used that one in an Agatha Christie in Wolverhampton many years ago. I was taught by some of the best, you know. But they're all gone now."

Sharon woke me up six days a week. Alarm clocks were rubbish since they'd invented the snooze button, and I relied on her for getting me out of bed, even if remotely. I didn't know what I'd do without her.

"I don't know what you'd do wivout me," she said, giving me a bit of a start. "At least you're out of bed."

"Yes and it's bloody freezing," I said, getting intimately frisked by the frigid air. I so wanted to get back under the covers.

And she knew what I was like. "Hmm, I can tell this isn't going to be one of your best days, is it? What's the matter, love? Come on, you know you can tell me."

It's strange, but when I got out of bed I'd had no idea that I was a bit down in the spirits' department, and Sharon picked up on it just like that (snap fingers!).

"I don't know ... it's just," I sighed, "there just doesn't seem to be anywhere left to go—at the shop, I mean. We need to be bigger, don't we? The place is minute compared with the bloody sheds, but we can't expand because we're sandwiched between two other shops."

Sheds was the technical trade term for the huge DIY stores that were systematically blitzing the independently-owned shops, taking our trade, putting us in the dole queue. They claimed their prices were lower than ours, but they lied. And they got away with it. That's the power of advertising. Was it any wonder that I was down?

"Hey—the ess has gone and dropped off All Tools' sign again!" She sounded ecstatic.

"Really?" The day was getting better already.

"They just can't keep that ess on, can they? Not a good advert for a DIY shop." Yes, so maybe there was such a thing as divine intervention. Ha! But things were never as simple as that, and I was back to thinking about how our business was snookered.

Sharon interrupted my thoughts. "What about going up in the world? Expanding upwards, eh? A few years ago that's what you had in mind, remember?"

"Ah, yeah," I remembered okay. Another pipe dream—quite appropriate for a shop selling plumbing stuff, don't you think? "Yeah, my bright idea to build on the flat roof." Come to think of it, it hadn't been such a bad plan. I fancied building it like a huge conservatory, in white uPVC, with the whole roof in clear glass. "It would be a cold day in hell before we could afford something like that."

"But it's something to work towards, eh? I think that's what you need—a plan, one of them goal things. Just take it one day at a time, then see how far you got at the end of the week."

"A load more debt?"

She grunted. "First you need some more staff. That shop might not seem big enough for all the stuff in it, but it's no good if there's only you and the old man to flog it."

"If we could afford more wage money, I'd talk you into working for us full-time."

"Ooh, don't know if you could afford that much, my love," she laughed. "Anyway, ain't got time to stand here chatting. You'd better get on yer way."

"It's so cold the car probably won't start," I said, hoping for snow.

"Hey—then we might get to shift some of that rock salt the old man bought in—"

"When he shouldn't have—"

"When he shouldn't, yeah. And there's all that de-icer to get rid of."

"I'll try squirting some under my arms."

3

"It's your arse I'm bovvered about."

"Why, what's up with it?" I tried to see.

Sharon knew everything, and what she didn't know she could work out.

"If you don't hurry up and get it covered, you'll catch cold," and she put the phone down.

See what I mean?


## *Jobs for old ladies*

The old lady stepped out from the pavement, arm outstretched as if catching a bus. I slammed on the brakes to miss her and she never flinched. The next second she was tapping on the passenger window. When I leaned over to wind it down the bloody handbrake spiked my guts like a blunt javelin. Looking at her, I could tell what was coming, and I made an audible groan.

"Excuse me, love," she said in her frail voice.

I thought I'd seen her somewhere before, then I remembered: she had been thrown out of the amusement arcade last pension day for banging the fruit machines.

She went on, as if butter wouldn't melt. "But do you know anyone can help an old woman change a light bulb?"

See? I told you. Roughly translated it means: "Would you come into my house and use your skill and expertise to fit a light bulb for me free of charge?" I hated working in people's houses. The people on the estate had been trying to get me to stop off and hang pictures and put catches on cupboard doors, and anything else you can think of, for years. So to prevent my being late for work I had taken to setting off really early so that my adoring public would be fooled into thinking I'd not passed through just yet. I imagined them all shuffling out into the street, watching the horizon for signs of my approach, then arguing with each other as to who would be the first to get sorted. But instead they just got up sooner themselves.

I followed the old dear as she staggered along the garden path in her granny boots—you know the ones: black, fleece-lined, with zips up the front.

"It's this one," she said, once the pair of us had staggered into the living room. She pointed vaguely upwards. I assumed there was a ceiling up there somewhere. It was so bloody tall it was in shadow and cobwebs and about half a century's worth of soot and other muck.

"Have you got anything for me to stand on?" That sort of request always took them by surprise. "Like a stepladder?" I ventured.

"What—a stepladder! Ooh, no," she said, shocked at the thought. "I've no need for steps. I can't do steps. Not at my age."

Ten minutes later I had roped together a motley collection of dining chairs, and it didn't look very safe. I'd used the old lady's shiny washing line to lash them together and you couldn't get tight knots with that stuff because it always slipped. I looked around. At least if I fell I'd have a soft landing because the floor seemed to be covered with four-foot high totem poles of spent pot noodle containers, lurking around like stalactites, so at least there'd be a film stuntman's landing for me. Hang on a minute—didn't they use cardboard boxes? She passed me the bulb. Just another sec—it's mites that go up, isn't it, so tights can come down? That's probably where I was going wrong in my non-existent love life: not got enough mites.

"Oh, dear," I said to her, holding the bulb like it was a dead mouse.

"Oh, isn't it the right one?" She knew damn well that it was.

"Probably yes, but you didn't buy this from my

shop, did you?"

She took a second or two to reply. "Oh I think I did, love. Next door to the Post Office? That's you, isn't it?"

Once again I looked at the Tesco packaging, and with a deep breath I took the first step into the unknown, probably uncharted since World War 2.

*Drive my car*

Now twenty-five minutes late, I drove through the housing estate (that wasn't meant to rhyme). Even at this time, the same bloke was waiting at the bus stop. He was there every day. I wondered if he ever caught a bus. I slowed down to get a better look at him. Surely he hadn't ... well, died standing up? Yes, that was him, alright, with a fawn overcoat that was forty years out of date, and his most distinguishing feature—a Russian fur hat that must have increased his height by a good nine inches.

I was about to speed up when some git behind blew his horn at me. Panicking, I jumped on the brake and the car stalled. I hurriedly turned the starter, but the engine didn't even cough. His horn sliced through me again. I didn't usually have starting problems—well, not every day. It was Sod's Law. Opening the door, balancing the feeling of embarrassment with the fact that I was causing an obstruction, I pushed the car into the side of the road so the git behind could pass. He pulled up alongside, smiling and waving. It was Gerry in his new Merc. He owned All Tools—the other hardware shop in town with the fallen S—and it could not have been a worse person to witness my degradation. He lowered the window very smoothly. Needless to say, it was electric. The winding handle on mine had dropped off long ago.

"How are you doing, Pal?"

"Fine, thanks," I said, bristling at the vulgar familiarity whilst trying to stop the car rolling away.

"You need any help with that?"

It was tempting. Maybe he would call the AA, but he went for the kill:

"One of the scrap merchants has an account with us. If I put in a good word he might give you twenty quid for it."

The bastard! He went on:

"I mean, look at this beauty, eh? I knocked the dealer down in price. Got it for forty-four K. A snip with all the extras. Beautiful automatic box, barely feel it change, so smooth. Two hundred and sixty-odd gee-gees under the bonnet, air con, electric sunroof—I could be here all day telling you what it's got—split rear seat—"

"That sounds painful—"

"—nought to sixty in under six seconds."

I'd be lucky to reach sixty miles an hour in six weeks. I looked at his shiny black chariot—I mean, I just had to, there was no choice; it drew your attention. Were those ... leather seats? Black leather seats ...?

"All leather," he said, watching me. "And heated."

It didn't look much like a hardware man's car to me. I mean, where would he put the grow-bags and tree stakes?

"Take you for a ride in it, if you like."

"No, I'm okay, thanks."

Mine was rolling away so I jumped in and stabbed the brake pedal but it was too late. When the wheel hit the kerb edge the tyre began to hiss like a steaming kettle.

"I'm just on my way to the shop. These are busy times."

I nodded, the fixed smile beginning to make

my face ache.

"Would you like me to phone yours and tell them you're taking your car for a walk?" He laughed, and sped away, with a smooth whirring noise.

# 2

*Late*

I NEVER LIKED ARRIVING at the shop when the shutters were already open because it felt like I wasn't in control. Being the one to take off the covers, so to speak, was a bit like unveiling a Formula 1 car that's just roaring to go ... Okay, you don't need to call the doctor; I was under no illusion that our little hardware store was some sort of sleek selling machine—in fact it was more like a rickety old bike with square wheels. But the paintwork and decals were mine.

Inside I found the MD lurking up the aisle where we kept the sink plungers. He had one hand in his smock pocket while making little disapproving gasps at the choice of stock and the way we—not *he*—had laid it out. He was dead set against the silly modern concept of self-service, so he grumbled. Then I realised that I was *never* in control. Yes, as far as he was concerned the paintwork and decals were all his.

He removed a decommissioned paperclip from his ear and tried to hide it from me.

"Ha—so that's where you are!" he called out, as if I was a hundred yards away. "You've missed the rush, you know."

That's what he said whenever I was late.

*There's been scores of 'em ...*

"There's been scores of them! There has that."

*Queuing down to the Post Office ...*

"And because there was only me to serve them all, they've been queuing out the door right down to the Post Office."

I closed my eyes. "And I suppose you've served them all by yourself."

"Course I have. Well, *someone* had to." I'd heard it a thousand times before—or at least that's how it felt. "We can't be doing with letting all that money go somewhere else to get spent. We should be keeping customers away from that cheeky bugger across town, Mister All Tool."

There I had to agree with him. So I opened the till to see just how much cash was in there. *A tenner!* That wasn't much to show for a News Year's Day Sales-type rush, was it?

"I worked all them damned years by myself, single-handed, building up goodwill," He went on chuntering about being the last man standing holding the fort. And he was annoying me. I slammed the till drawer.

"Right then, I might as well go back home," I told him.

"What for? You've only just got here." He looked worried.

" You've served them all. There's no point in me hanging around if you can do it all by yourself."

It took a second or two until it occurred to him that just maybe I was serious.

"Well ... well, you weren't here so I thought, now then—I'd-I'd better get serving, and sharpish like. You can't make money by staying in bed, you know."

"I *didn't* sleep in—have you got that? I got ... never mind, just remember that I don't sleep in."

*Thanks to Sharon, that is.*

Then his expression changed. Somehow he knew.

"Oh, you didn't, did you?" He shook his head and sighed. "I don't know, you young 'uns never learn. Yes, I know what you've been doing."

And I knew that he knew. He gave his customary cynical laugh. "So what sort of job was it, then? More important, *how much did you take?*"

That meant: did I sell anything from the shop? He caught my hesitation. "Ah! So it was another freebie! Oh dear, oh dear, you'll never learn. You'll have us sleeping in shop doorways, catching coins from folks passing by if all you can do is jobs for flighty pieces—I see them when I come to work, you know, standing on their doorsteps in their negliments—"

"Their *what?*"

"Well, I don't know what they call them things. I just hope they don't cost much if they're so thin."

So, he thought I'd been on the pull. Ha! The only thing I'd pulled was the bathroom light cord.

"It was for an old lady," I said. *And she's about your age.*

"Old ladies? My god! Whatever will you think of next?" His speech began to hesitate. He did that when his thought processes needed clearing with a set of drain rods. "Old women, young women—it's all the bloody same. They see mugs like you coming and they think, 'Oh look, here's that silly young bugger from the hardware shop. I'll flash whatever I've got and he'll come running all right'."

"There was no flashing—"

"No flashing?"

"The bulb had gone."

"Oh, aye—that'll be one that she bought from Tesco, I'll bet."

He was as old as the hills but still as sharp as an axe—well *sometimes*.

"And a tap washer."

"Oh—" he seemed to perk up. "So did you make up for the bulb, then, on the tap washer job?" I said

10

nothing. "So did you or didn't you get owt from the mean old bat?"

That was rich, coming from *him*.

"Yes!"

"How much?"

"I got some breakfast."

"Ha! Well, it's better than nowt."

"But I had to clean the crud off the frying pan. It was hard and crusty."

"Not like that young girl from the newsagent, eh? There's another of 'em. She wants you to go round with a gas bottle, by the way, soon as you're in."

"Careful what you're saying! Don't go calling her a young girl—you'll have me in bother. She's twenty-six if she's a day."

"Well, she's very young to me—"

"So is everybody."

"At least she won't be hard and crusty."

"I was talking about the frying pan."

"Crusted frying pans ... crusted ... Hmm, let's see, we'll have something on the shelves for that ..."

## *Maggie's News Den*

Leaving him with his yonderly trek along the aisles looking for long-lost miracle products, I set off along the high street with the gas bottle resting on my shoulder. It had little to do with strength, more a question of balance, but it impressed the hell out of Maggie Newsprint (as we called her), and I was aware of this. But I just had to do it and I didn't know why. It wasn't like I was trying to get off on some romantic assignation with her; I just wanted to ridicule that pillock of a boyfriend of hers. He was over six feet tall, with broad shoulders and ... well, you'll see when I point him out to you.

Along the high street, members of the public made sudden darts to one side or the other, not wanting to collide with me. It reminded me of the parting of the Red Sea. Okay, it was the gas bottle they were wary of, but that minute or so was the only feeling of power I seemed to get those days. A hundred yards further and I stepped into the narrow confines of Maggie's News Den.

She called to me from the counter at the far end. Her shop was long and narrow, with reading material lining the sides, and with the confectionary down by the counter where she could keep a close eye on it.

"Oh, Graham, you're a life-saver. You are—you're an absolute darling."

I had no doubt that she meant every word of it, and I swung the bottle down to the floor.

"Oh, Graham, you *are* strong. I wish my bloody Steve was as strong as you."

See what I mean? Now Maggie's bloody Steve, as she called him, had a number of inches (of height, that is) on me, so I couldn't quite understand what his problem was. Maggie told her mother—who could have successfully done impressions of Old Mother Riley (a comic drag act from the 1940s)—that she'd be in the back room if needed, and I couldn't help but detect the note of warning in her tone. It said: *You disturb me and there'll be bother.* The trouble, you see, was that Maggie also wanted me to be in the back room with her. She motioned me to bring the bottle behind the counter, and to mind that I didn't catch my leg on the sticking-out shelf, and she closed us both in the tiny room. You'd have had all on getting four people standing in there—make that three plus the gas fire: an ancient cabinet heater that should really have been dropped into a rubbish skip years ago.

"Right then, my love, what can I get you to drink? You'd better hurry 'cos me mum can't go long without asking me summat. I'm trying to train her, for god's sake ..."

It made no difference when I told her that I didn't have time for one. She wanted me to change the gas bottle for her and I might as well enjoy a cup of instant coffee whilst I did it. I tell you, changing the bottle would take less than one minute. That was a job Maggie was adamant she couldn't do because she wasn't good with her hands—not like *I* was, she said. Sliding out the old bottle into the tight space between us, I stopped.

"Maggie, this bottle isn't empty."

So had it been a wasted trip? Would I be carting the damned thing back along the high street?

"Yes it is, love—it *is*, honest." She was most insistent. "I know when it's about to fizzle out and I can't do with being cold. It's like a bloody fridge in the back here. I have to rub my arms to get some circulation going. No, you just leave me with a full one to keep me warm and I'm happy. You can crank it up, if you like. Me mum knows not to disturb us, but god knows for how long. Maybe you can rub my arms while we're waiting for the kettle to boil."

*Brad the plumber*

A small number of our customers were tradesmen and Brad Hall was one of them. Tall, 19 stones, bald, spotty complexion and fat fingers, he wasn't an excellent choice for doing intricate jobs or fitting himself into confined spaces like into cylinder cupboards or under people's kitchen sinks. As far as I was concerned, he was welcome to it. Although a joiner by trade, his workmanship could be rough and, like many other tradesmen of the time, he considered himself also to be an expert at everyone else's trade.

"What a waste of 'kin time," he grunted. He always did his nervous head-twitch when he did the apostrophe before *kin*.

"Really?" It was part of my job to appear sympathetic.

"Complete 'kin waste. You wouldn't want to know some of the shite I've to put up with." Maybe not, but no doubt he would tell me anyway. "I were called out this morning. Up the estate. Get there. What does the old bird tell me? Only that some tosser's already done the job."

"That's awful," I said, only too familiar with having one's time wasted.

"Too 'kin right it is. 'Kin cowboy poaching on my patch—*my patch!* I'll whip his 'kin arse off when I get my hands on him."

"Sounds like you lost a lot of money. What sort of job was it?"

"Tap washer."

*Don't swallow! He might spot it!*

"I know it doesn't sound much, but I'd have bumped the job up, like, and sold the old girl a new tap."

"But she didn't need a new tap—"

"What? How do *you* know?"

"... Because you just said—"

"Ah, but I'd have made it worthwhile. I mean, you've got to. When you're in this 'kin game you can't be getting out of bed just to do pissing little jobs like that. I've got me overheads."

"And how is your wife? Seen her lately?"

"Aye, Saturday night I saw her."

"Oh, that's good. So is there any chance of you two getting back—?"

"You what? She was outside the Black Bull fighting with a gang of lads."

"So you stepped in, then, to help?"

"Kept well 'kin out of it. They were in a right

state, the poor buggers. She didn't need any help from me."

The MD made me jump by opening the till. He did that every half hour or so just to see how sales were doing. Mind you, come to think of it, so did I.

"And *you've* lost out too, you know," Brad chipped in, making the MD's ears prick up.

"Really? Oh, you mean you'd have bought the tap from us?"

"No, not the tap. I don't get me taps from here, not anymore. I mean the sink plug—I'd have conned her into buying one of them, too."

"Great. That would've been another thirty pence in the till."

"I charge them five quid, but you'd have got the thirty pence, so you'd have been that much better off. It all adds up."

"Cheers."

"Less the trade discount."

"Yes, every little helps."

When he'd finished grumbling, the MD came up to me.

I told him, "Don't say anything. Don't even think about saying anything."

"I don't know what's wrong with you. You seem to forget that we're here to make a damned living—"

"Not give money away", I finished for him.

"Not give money away. But all I see is you running this place into the ground."

"Well, we do sell gardening stuff. Seriously, we need to expand."

"Rubbish, we don't at all. We're just fine as we are."

"We're not! We are treading water—and it's stagnant."

The MD prodded me on the shoulder—not a good sign.

"And don't go on about needing more staff.

We've enough with that what's-her-name—"

"You mean Sharon?"

"Aye, her. We've enough expense without having to pay the likes of that one—and she's only here afternoons."

"We can only afford her for afternoons ..."

# 3

*Cutting concerns*

ABOUT LUNCHTIME, I WENT out into the yard to sharpen a customer's pair of haircutting scissors. But it wasn't just down to running their blades across a grinding wheel; my secret weapon (an old technique known by few) was to finish off by running the blades around the neck of a beer bottle. That was how I'd achieved my reputation for being the sharpest sharpener in town. When I came back inside my way was blocked by the woman who snatched the scissors from my hand and proceeded to give her son a short back and sides hair cut, right there on the shop floor. Some people liked a trial run before parting with the one pound that I charged, and this one left us a bonus in the form of a pile of the lad's hair clippings on the floor. Mind you, I have to admit to a sense of professional satisfaction and pride when I watched the lad's hair fall away as cleanly as if those scissors were brand new. In fact they were better than brand new. *I* would have been more than satisfied with them.

But she tutted, roughly pushing the lad's head this way and that, obviously dissatisfied.

"So they're okay, then?" I ventured, trying to sound optimistic.

"They should be better than okay, especially for what you're charging," she said, throwing the pound coin at me and dragging the lad down the aisle to the door, whose bell jangled angrily.

"So that's another satisfied customer, then," said Sharon. "What was that she said to you?"

"Just the same as last time. And the time before that. Do you know, I don't think that lad of hers ever gets any older."

"That's because he daren't," and she scurried off to get the sweeping brush, stopping to look down the aisle where we displayed the tools.

Rushing straight back she looked at me from across the counter. I could tell that whatever was up was serious because she didn't lean forward (How I wished that she wouldn't do that).

"While you were out back doing the scissors, there was a couple of dodgy types lurking down there."

"So?"

"So now they've gone and I didn't hear them go out."

That was suspicious, and usually meant that they'd silenced the jangly doorbell so they could sneak away.

"Whereabouts were they?" Already I had an idea what was coming.

"The tools—where else?"

I leapt over the counter, skittling leaflets and a display of WD40, and joined Sharon. The tools aisle was the proverbial Aladdin's cave to tradesmen and committed DIYers. And thieves. Sharon—with eyes like a hawk's—went straight to an item of discarded packaging. It's an old trick that works like this: if the nicked item doesn't bear a wrapping label—or better still, a price—then, psychologically, the thief can pretend it's theirs. The fact that such stuff looks too new to be true doesn't occur to them. That's the trouble with thieves: they don't think far enough into the future; a bit like politicians.

She didn't need to show me the packaging; the printed cardboard was too distinctive. I didn't want to go any further and pick it up from the floor. My stomach felt like it had been kicked, my knees wanted to buckle. I asked what size it was.

"Seventeen," she said.

"Bloody seventeen inches—the biggest!"

"Yeah, but keep your voice down."

There wasn't much change out of two fifty pound notes for a seventeen inch brass-backed tenon saw with rosewood handle. Not in the mid-90s, there wasn't.

I rushed out into the street in a stupid frenzy of menace. Pathetic, I know. There were just the usual suspects: a mix of the town's growing number of senior citizens (it was a Thursday, pension day, so nothing strange there). From different sides of the street a couple of single young women, with babies in pushchairs, both waved at me. What frightened me even more was that the young children also raised their arms in recognition, or maybe it was just my imagination. Who else was there?—oh yes, a couple of gangs of truanting school kids, and a recklessly obese father staggering up the street, eating a huge cream bun, and his son, a smaller version of him, doing the same. Everything was normal. The thieves had been assimilated into the crowd.

Back inside the shop, the MD staggered out of the office as I rushed past, almost knocking him over.

"What's all the flapping going on?" he asked.

"Some stock has walked," I said. That was how we described stuff that had been nicked.

There wasn't time to tell him off for spending most of the day hiding away. It was time for action: we would implement the town's early warning system (sounds a bit nuclear, doesn't it?). Sharon and I called it Operation Stock Shifter and we would put it into, well, *operation*. She knew what to do.

"What's going off? Will somebody just tell me?" The MD was pretending to be all set for action.

"Graham's just calling the Co-op," she told him.

"The Co-op? Why, what can he be wanting from there?"

I picked up the phone and dialled.

"Good luck," Sharon said.

I'd need all the luck there was. Ringing the Co-op was like going back in time.

"I don't know where vey get their women from? They're all out of the ark," she muttered.

And didn't I know it. The system we had to catch town-centre thieves was a carefully devised communication plan: we phoned the Co-op—the biggest of the town centre stores—with details of what had been nicked and a description of the perpetrators. They would pass on the details to the next shop on the list, which passed on the message to the next, and so on through the network. This had been devised by Police Constable Skipper, and although only a few years older than me, his posture and indeed attitude were of the type borne by policeman of my youth, in the good old days when the local bobby knew everyone and the world was a safer place. No disrespect to him, but Sharon and I had nicknamed the band of crusading shopkeepers as the Little Sniffingham No Nickers Group, and those who could be bothered used to meet with him after closing time on the second Thursday of every month, so long as there wasn't a bank holiday that particular week in which case it would be, er ... some other time.

Now the phone was ringing at the Co-op switchboard. And it wasn't being answered.

"Better write the description down while we're waiting," I said.

"I only got a look at one of them."

"It's a start. Male?"

"Male, all right."

"What did he look like?"

"Jack Dawson." Like a shot, Sharon had matched the suspect to an established film or television character.

"Height?"

"Tom Cruise."

"Five foot three, then. Okay, make that five-four. Hair?"

She thought for a second. "Curly Watts."

"Medium length, dull and lifeless," I wrote. "Wearing?"

"*Hawaii Five-O*."

"Flowered shirt?"

"And jeans."

"Flowered jeans," I added.

"No, green jeans. Like in *M\*A\*S\*H*. That should be it."

"I bet he wasn't wearing handcuffs like Jack in *Titanic*."

"Nah, but wiv any luck he soon will be."

The woman's tone was pure ice. "Little Sniffingham Co-operative Society. Can I help?"

As soon as I said "shop watch" she fired back at me:

"Well, I hope you've got all your details to hand. Name?" She went on mute, probably to make an aside comment to the other woman.

Now I knew who they were: it must be Fiona's day for the phone, and Bea would be doing the typing and accounting. Fiona clicked back on and fired the questions as fast as she could, fervently hoping to trip me up. That way she could refuse to relay the message and it would give her some job satisfaction that day. But she hadn't reckoned on my preparation.

"And what's been stolen? Full description and

value, please ... Seventeen *what?* You'll have to repeat that ... Oh, I can't take *inches*. Certainly not. It's against the rules ... I don't care—I have strict instructions that only metric currency is allowed in this store ... No, it's more than my job's worth. I don't know what inches are anymore ..."

This time she didn't put me on mute, and I heard her tell Bea that by now I was getting very shirty with her, which, of course, I wasn't.

"Ooh, is he shouting at you?"

"No," she said, sounding disappointed. "He's not shouting."

"Is he using bad language?"

The idea seemed to excite her. "No, I'm afraid not." Pause. "But I could *say* that he is—"

I put the phone down.

Sharon looked at me. "What's wrong?"

"The Co-op's gone metric."

"That's so ridiculous! They're thirty years behind everyone else."

"They didn't believe me when I said they don't make tenon saws in metric sizes."

"Vem bitches are only up to date when it comes to being awkward. Or getting shagged. Ha! I bet they don't buy their bras in centimeters. So what now?"

"By this time it's likely our saw's been turned into a couple of ounces of wacky weed."

"You're not allowed to mention ounces, dear."

"It could even be speeding down the motorway. We should be after it."

"*Cutting* to the chase, eh?"

"Yeah. Cutting, alright." I tried to see the funny side.

"Let's hope they don't fall and break their *teeth*."

"Let's hope they don't fall and break the teeth on our saw."

The puns had run out. There's not a lot you can

do with saws.

"Let's just hope someone *saw* 'em running, eh?"

That was one I'd missed.

"It's no good. We can't just stand here doing potty puns while our stock's out there getting laundered."

"You're right. We've got to do something—get a *handle* on things?" she said.

"Would that be a rosewood handle, by any chance?"

"Only if we're lucky. That way you'll get yer *brass back*."

Brass: Yorkshire slang for money. Top-quality tenon saws have a thickened piece of brass called the *back* on the top of the blade to keep it straight and add weight so it cuts ... but you don't really want a woodwork lesson, do you?

She shuffled her shoulders, preparing for the kill.

"Leave it with me. *I'm off, Geoff!*" She called out to the MD, projecting her voice—a technique she learned when she was in the theatre. His hearing aid had been making disjointed whistling noises again.

"Aye, that's a bit better," he said, turning his little finger in his ear before looking around startled. "Have I missed something?"

"That's sixty-odd quid's worth of tackle at cost that's just been nicked."

"Never! When?" He didn't wait for an answer, and set off towards the storeroom. "I know what I'm going to do. Bloody walk-round stores! I told you this sort of thing would happen. This is no way to run a shop."

By the time Sharon had reached the door she had cast off her overall and bounded out into the bright winter sunshine. I desperately wanted to go with her but one look at the MD shuffling around carrying a heavy reel of chain and sundry packets and brackets (no rhyme intended) made me stay put. If I left him alone in the shop he would likely begin constructing some crude Heath Robinson-type anti-theft contraption.

"We don't need to fence stuff off," I called out to him. "What we need is more staff." There was no response. I spoke louder. "*More staff!*"

He rattled the chain. "This here doesn't cost as much. And we don't have to give it paid holidays."

"You silly old bugger," I said. He wouldn't have heard that.

"I heard that," he said. "Pardon?"

"I can't believe those hearing aids are so duff."

"Ya what?" came the reply and then, once my words had been received, went on: "Nay, just after t' war I used to use peroxide to clean out my ears. That used to work a treat. Difficult to get hold of now."

My mind began to go fuzzy. What was he on about? We'd just lost a piece of stock that was worth a day's takings and he was telling me about pouring chemicals with questionable-sounding names in his ears? That couldn't be right.

"You mean you cleaned hearing aids with peroxide? Didn't it melt them?"

"No! I put the peroxide *in* my ears, you chump. It used to bubble and froth up real."

I shook my head in disbelief—no, come to think of it, I didn't; I stood there feeling traumatized.

"Aye, and it did a grand job."

# 4

*Sharon's story*

SHARON TOLD ME WHAT happened. She marched along the high street towards Maggie's Newsprint's shop, no doubt calm and in full control, her nose poised to detect any suspicious movements. She would have gone inside to ask Maggie to watch out for the offending pair of tool thieves, but something made her look across the road to where, in the Oxfam shop's window, was a scrawny, tired dummy, suffering chronic backache like they do. And it was wearing only a Hawaiian hula skirt.

A couple of minutes later she stepped out of the charity shop, determinedly striding back along the high street, away from the Maggie Newsprint end. In the cheese shop she excused herself, passing the queue of customers until she got eye contact with the owner. It was all to do with posture, as Sharon called it: it's how to stand, how you put your shoulders, your general demeanor—all of this can make people notice you (to say nothing about the neckline of the dress she was wearing). All she needed to do was raise her eyebrows. It was every bit as good as shouting, "Have you seen anyfing suspicious?"

He motioned to the other side of the road where a young woman was standing with the youth in the offending shirt, looking as out of place as a sex maniac in a convent. There seemed to be some heated exchange between them.

Sharon stopped herself marching straight for him. They were probably arguing over whether to quit town now or snaffle some more stuff. They would need somewhere to stash it (or put it "to sleep") until they were finished—that was one drawback with the early warning system: it was difficult to detain the thieves if they didn't actually have the nicked stuff on their person, so they would hide it somewhere and return for it later. Sharon reached the other side just as the Hawaiian shirt's accomplice attacked him, grabbed the saw and ran off, with the shirt in pursuit. And Sharon in pursuit of the shirt.

When she called out for them to stop, the two of them shot down the narrow alley towards the precinct, bumping into people, whisking a newspaper from one reading man and leaving others gazing into space and wondering what day of the week it was. Sharon followed, throwing out token pardons and excuses, cutting a beautiful line through the shoppers in her dark dress with low neckline and grim determination.


Back in the shop the doorbell jangled. I checked the CCTV monitor and there was the monochrome top-down view of Sharon as she steered a young bloke by his elbow into the shop. Stepping out from behind the counter as they rounded the polythene stand, I looked him straight in the eye. That was the way to intimidate them—force eye contact. But this lad looked straight back at me, the cheeky little sod, then looked at Sharon.

"Go on, ven," she said. "Give it to him. He don't bite."

But give it time, I thought, and I just might.

"This young man has something for you, Graham."

"Really," I said, the upper hand firmly holding up my resolve. "And would that be some pathetic attempt at an apology, perhaps, closely followed by some sob story about your father running off, a

25

broken home, an insecure childhood, nurturing an obsession with grasping for attention? Is that it? Well, I don't like to have to deal with nickers—*thieves*, I mean—so I can save you the—"

I'd been aware of Sharon frantically motioning at me, but I'd ignored it, wanting this lad to be in no doubt that as far as I was concerned he was pretty well down on the social scale, and well off the pecking order of life. What stopped me turning the screw any further was when a brand new shiny tenon saw, with gleaming brass back and beautifully polished handle, appeared on the counter. It sort of slid there every bit as reverently as if it were Excalibur.

The young bloke looked speechless, and rather bewildered. Then his expression turned to one of panic.

"I ... *I* didn't nick it, honest! It was a girl just round there. She took it and I followed her. And when she dumped it in a bin ..." His voice trailed off, faltering. I'd seen this all before.

"It's all right," nudged Sharon, "you'll be right. Just tell him," She began stroking his arm like some alien grooming ritual (alien to me, that is). He was shaking. I thought next she might begin stroking his hair.

The MD passed on his way to find a clean paper clip and gave a token growl at Sharon's new friend, who began to tremble even more.

"So is this the thieving bugger who can't keep his fingers off other people's property, is it?"

I'd never seen the MD look so menacing.

"It's alright, darling," she soothed, and began to stroke the lad's head. This was embarrassing, so I leaped in with some meaningful conversation.

"Hang on a minute—you say *you* chased the shopkeeper?"

The look from Sharon was the exact opposite. "You mean *shoplifter*," she prompted.

"Shoplifter, yes. That's what I said."

"And this young lad—the proper little hero what he is—he retrieved our stock. *Your* stock, vat is." She sounded a touch defensive. "Or *his*," she added, nodding towards the MD.

I grovelled a bit—not too much, mind—and thanked him most profusely for his very commendable and responsible attitude. I wasn't certain if it was legal to wear a shirt like that, though. Perhaps a reward was in order? Sharon obviously knew what I was thinking and her expression said it all. We might even go as far as to not charge him at all for whatever it was he had originally come in to buy—hopefully not a seventeen inch tenon saw.

"So what was it you came in for?" My question was met with a blank stare. I tried again. "You came into this shop to buy something. So what was it? Come on, I'm in a good mood. We can sort something out for you."

He shuffled, and he coughed, and prepared himself and, looking to Sharon for some guidance, he put on his best smile and said, "I've come about a job. My name's Greville."

## *At the Post Office*

The Post Office was just down the street from us. It had five tills, with three of them permanently closed, meaning that on Mondays (benefits day) and Thursdays (pensions day) you could go through a lot of thinking time just shuffling along the two queues, wondering if you would live long enough to see daylight again. It didn't help when customers preferred to queue for half an hour just to buy one single postage stamp instead of buying a 50p book of stamps from the machine outside.

"How's it going, Pal?"

I cringed and almost lost my place. It's not the best place to close your eyes because it's so easy to lose your place to a queue jumper.

"Great, thanks." I sort of half-glanced over my shoulder. I would have sworn that Gerry was stalking me if it had been invented back then.

"Oh, really?" There was a cynical tone in his voice.

"Yeah, fantastic." *Honest, just believe me and shut up.*

"Hmm. That's not what I heard."

"Well, you can't believe—"

"I've been told your place is a shoplifter's paradise."

That was when I made the conscious effort to turn and stare at him. Gerry was smirking as he spread the dirt.

"A shoplifter's—?"

"Aye, you're getting all sorts of stuff nicked. It's because your security's all to pot."

The Post Office queue moved down another place.

"Sl-oppee," he said in one of those extra-loud whispers.

"Go on, then, seeing as you know more about what goes on in—"

"Oh, I do, Pal, I really do."

When he tapped the side of his nose I so wanted to punch it for him.

"So tell me—what have we had nicked?"

"Oh, let's see ... how about a seventeen inch tenning saw?" The way he said it, it might as well have been the Crown Jewels.

"Don't you mean *tenon* saw?"

"Whatever. Just a bloody saw. They don't hang around long enough in my shop to read the labels." He laughed, as if adding some sort of endorsement.

"And how did you find out about that?"

He tapped his nose. "I have my sources. There's not much goes on in this trade that I don't find out about."

I nodded. "At least we got it back." Then I faced forwards again.

"And there's more."

I spun round, maybe a little too quickly because I had to apologise to the woman standing behind me. "Like what?"

He shook his head. "It's okay, doesn't matter. "

"Go on, spit it out."

"There's no point in upsetting you."

*The cheek!* We moved forwards. That bugger called himself a hardware man when he didn't even smell of creosote. It went quiet for a few seconds. That was when I realised that everyone in the Post Office had been taking some interest in the exchange. Well, there was nothing else in there to entertain them.

"Losing stock at them levels," he said, his voice echoing, "you can't be expected to stay in business for much longer."

I don't know what it was, but I felt like he was pressing me into the ground. I liked to think that I could remain cool, detached even, especially when it came to suffering verbal attacks. But at that moment something in me snapped or went ping or whatever, and there was no way I was going to let Mr Bloody All Tool get away with this.

He went on: "Too much time undressing the ladies instead of dressing your shelves."

Where did he get that from? I wanted to throttle him.

"And how are things out in the sticks?" I spat back. That would be like poking him with a sharp one.

There was just a split second of hesitation, then he tried to make out that I was insane.

"You what? I don't know what you're on about."

"Well, there can't be much call for a DIY shop out on the edge of a moor, can there?"

His expression of ridicule dropped like a stone. "We're not out in the country. We're just across town—just over there."

"So how long is it from here—ten minutes? Fifteen? Not exactly town centre, is it? Still, it'll mean cheaper overheads for you."

"We do very well. We've a damned good turnover."

He was serious, almost frightening. But there was no way that I could leave it there.

"A hundred grand'll take some getting, though, won't it? All the way out there?"

He returned fire so fast I didn't have time to turn forwards.

"A hundred grand! Is that what impresses you?"

That was when I knew—I mean *really knew*—what I'd done. And in front of all those people. He went on:

"Pah! That's pocket money, it's a fraction of what we take."

Now there was something about his tone that sent a cold shiver down my back.

"Eh—that's not your turnover, is it? *It is! Ha!* Well, what a bloody joke. I can't wait to tell 'em back at the shop."

I found myself staring at my feet, waiting for the ground to open up and swallow me whole. If Gerry could have seen the look on my face he'd have realised he'd hit the nail on the head, well and truly—which was quite commendable for someone who didn't know one end of a hammer from the other.

"It is, isn't it? Well, I never. Bloody hell ..." He couldn't believe his luck. I didn't see the queue move forwards and he shot past me, laughing all the way to the counter.

*Sharon's welcome*

"Sharon!" I called out to her. "Am I glad to see you."

My prayers had been answered! Since opening the door that morning the place had been thronged with eager faces all wanting mirrors to be hung, draughts to be sealed, pottery to be repaired, lights to switch on, paths to be swept, and any manner of other problems to be solved. And they wanted *me* to make it so. If only there weren't so many of them, all piling in at once. And as if I'd rubbed the magic lamp (what did I say about this being an Aladdin's cave?) my salvation had miraculously appeared.

But something was wrong; I could tell by the look on her face as she made her way up the aisles to get to the top. The "let's make 'em happy" factor was missing, replaced with a tinge of begrudging reluctance. Maybe I was imagining it.

"It's been like this since I opened the door," I said.

"Oh, I can't stay, my love. I just wanted to see him."

"Oh, right."

I continued serving. And in all fairness, many of the customers had chosen their own stock and simply wanted to pay.

"So where is he?"

"In there," I nodded towards the office, "fighting with some tax return or other. Totally stumped as usual," and I finished laying out a selection of nails.

"I mean *the boy*."

"*The boy?*"

"I wanted to welcome him. I come in special." As if this was the most usual thing.

I felt my shoulders give. Still, though, just

work through them one at a time, I reminded myself. My woman customer was about to speak when, without waiting his turn, a man pushed through and plonked three pairs of rusty garden shears on the counter, complete with hanging bits of slimy grass, and sending the nails firing in all directions.

"I'll be back in ten minutes for 'em," he grunted.

Just like that and he was gone. *He'll be lucky.*

"That one is four inches," I said to the nail woman.

She laughed. "That's never four inches," she grumbled, looking around for support. "It's bigger than any four inch."

Like flicking a switch, everyone instantly broke off from their impatient grunting and looked towards the counter all defiant. That apparently, from their collective vast experience of such things practical, was *not* a four-inch nail.

"Yes, that's four inches," Sharon put in, impatient to get off.

"Welcome *him?*" I whispered.

"That's what I've always been taught is six inches," the nail woman said, picking up the nail and brandishing it threateningly. "And my husband knows about these things—"

*I'll bet he's an engineer.*

"He's an engineer."

In this town if you were an engineer, that was it: end of argument.

Once more Sharon stepped in. "That might be what your husband wants you to believe is six inches, but take my word for it, love, it's four." She turned to me. "So then, where is he?"

"I told him not to come in until ten. Just for today. Then I'll pack him off to see his Uncle Arthur at the man's shop."

"Not the protective clothing!"

"Of course. Regulations."

"Regulations my arse. He'll need a nuclear fallout suit when Arthur's in licking distance."

With two of us it didn't take long for us to serve everyone. And just as the last one left that's when the MD came out of the office and picked up one of the shears, lifting his glasses to his forehead to peer at the rusted blades.

"Not been looking after these, have they? Just look at all this rust. Sacrilege."

I inspected another pair. The edges were rounded, the pivot bolt was loose and one of the wooden handles dropped on to the floor. "I'd bin them," I said.

"Ya what? These were lovely shears when they were new, all tight and shining."

"And what about the state of the steel? Look—pitted, rounded edges, everything about them is shot."

"No, you're wrong. They can be fettled. We'll have something on the shelves for that."

"Or we could try selling them a new pair," I called after him. He chose to ignore me, the contrary old bugger.

# 5

WHEN SHARON GOT BACK just after lunch (not that there had been time to eat) she found the Bird & Sons' van parked outside. The driver walked into her as she came in, so she called him an uncomplimentary name. He called her one back.

The pile of delivered boxes was as massive as ever, and it would take us hours to get that lot priced up and put on the shelves—or *merchandised*, to use the new term for getting stock off the floor. Or even *dressing*, to use Gerry's term. Breathing in as she squeezed past, she poked the topmost box with her finger to see if it was in danger of collapsing to the floor. Past experience with this particular driver had made us wary of his inability to grasp the finer points of common sense. He liked to precariously balance cartons of bottled liquid right at the top: things like turpentine, methylated spirits, linseed oil—in fact anything that would smash as soon as it hit the floor, and make the most mess.

"I've come for the boy," she said. "He needs measuring up for an overall."

My expression should have frightened her—I mean, she was about to abscond with the recently-acquired apprentice, leaving me single-handed to shift this mountain of sweeping brush heads and hazardous chemicals.

"You can't," I said. "Look at that lot—it's right in the middle of the main aisle."

Sharon motioned to the boy to get around to her side and before I could do anything to stop her she took hold of his hand to march him round to see Arthur at the man's shop.

"And don't let Arthur take his inside leg measurement," I called as they left the shop.

"Don't worry, I'll protect his inside leg for him."


## *Myrtle's pipes – Sharon's story (in her own words)*

We was on our way back. And after the boy had told me what had gone on behind the changing room curtain I was thinking, Jesus, they don't call it a *man's* shop for nothing. I asked Greville what Arthur had said to him.

"He ask me where I was from."

"So you told him you was from the hardware shop," I said.

And Greville replied, "No, I said I was from Halifax."

So that's when I asked him *why* Arthur took him into the changing room.

"I dunno. He asked me to," he said. Well, I can tell you I felt myself reddening at all this. So I asked the boy exactly what *did* Arthur say to him.

Then Greville said, "Would you just step this way, young sir?"

"*No!*" I said. "I mean when you got in there with him."

Just got to the interesting part when an old woman appeared right in front of me. We had to stop. There she is, immaculate permed hair, bright red lipstick, ill-fitting teeth and a face like a contour map of the bleedin' Himalayas. It was Myrtle.

Of course, we all know Myrtle. She's been cleaning the ladies' toilets in The Square for years—decades, even, because your mother remembers her there in the early 1960s. She's a bit like an unwelcome spirit because the old dear can turn up at the most unexpected moment and tell you what she's managed to pick up in the toilet—gossip-wise, that is.

"I'm glad I've run into you, dear," she said, her teeth clicking away with every word. "It's fate, you know."

She peered up at me just to make certain she was talking to the right person.

"It's been a bitter cold week at the doors." That's what she calls the ladies' loos. "And me fingers are red raw. Just look at 'em," Myrtle said.

I sympathised with her, but not so she would show me her fingers. They looked like something you find in the butchers' scraps bin out there in the yard.

Then Myrtle told me, "I've a message for that chap of yours."

"I ain't got a chap," I told her. A bit too quick, as it happens.

"Oh, I don't mean that one you've got at home—no, not him!" She chuckled to herself, the cheeky cow. She took in a breath so deep she nearly choked. I stepped back as she launched into a coughing spasm and began thumping her own chest. Savage, it was. She's there, springing up and down and gasping, saying, "It's ... it's ... it's the bleach, you know ... that's what's done me ... I know it's the bleach ..."

So she coughed some more, standing there shaking her head—nod, nod, nod. Greville was using sign language to ask if he should go get help. I shook my head, telling him, "No, no, no," and the old dear was going, "Yes, yes, yes ..." Eventually it was over—the coughing, that is. "Your chap," she gasped, "the one—"

"Yes, I know," I told her. "Get on with it."

And, looking a bit mysterious, Myrtle told me, "I have it on good posterity that the ..." and she checked right and left, then mouthed the next word, "*Bank*," and nodded, "wants *him* out."

Well, I couldn't think what to say. I mean, all sorts went through my mind, but then all I know is what *you* tell me, and I thought you and the bank manager was alright, so I said to her, "I don't think so, my love. Are you sure you heard it right?" I mean, of course she hadn't.

"That's God's honour," she spat. And then, like a psychic medium, she said, "I heard it on the pipes meself, I did. Plain as day. Couple of girls out buying their dinners. On the pipes—and it's *this* day, *this very day it'll happen.*"

Greville, bless him, was looking quite shocked. Goodness knows how *I* looked. I ain't seen anything as scary as that since I did Lady Macbeth in

Stratford.

But the old girl wasn't yet finished. "And there was something else," she said, "there was another voice. Now what was it? Yes, they was to force him to become *prostitute* —"

"I hope you mean destitute," I said to her.

"And today, mind—*today!*" By now old Myrtle was like wailing.

"And then what?" I asked her. I tell you, Graham, the old woman had shivers running down *my* back.

"Then I lost it. It was all gone," and Myrtle looked up to the sky with her hands together as if in prayer. "It's like that sometimes. The voices just stop, lost in the sound of the flushing and the gushing. You must tell him—he'll need to watch his arse."

Poor little Greville didn't quite hear what Myrtle had said, and he asked me if that was a lady thing?

Myrtle went on. "I miss nothing, heard it along the pipes, I did. Gospel, *gospel!*" and she nodded and winked knowingly. And that was it. The reading was all done.

Then she turned to the boy. "Ooh," she said, "I've not seen you, before," and she gave him the once over with her all-seeing eyes, then she grabbed his arm and felt his thigh with her swollen red fingers. "Yes, I think you'll do. You wouldn't believe the things I get to see in my line of work," and she coughed again. "Hazard of me job, you see. It's the bleach what's done it, I know it is. I don't care what them at the Council tell me."


Sharon snapped out of performance mode and looked around. "Where's he gone? Where's the boy?"

"Never mind *him*—what happened next?"

"What? Nothing. The old girl was off, vanished in the crowds."

She paused, gauging my reaction to the tale. "Right then, what you got to say about that?"

"So you've appeared on stage at Stratford? I had no idea. That's fantastic."

She grunted. "That's Stratford in Newham, dear. It's in London."

Oh. I thought I'd better change the subject. "Can there be anything in it—with what Myrtle's said, I mean? I know the bank manager. I service his lawnmower—that big ride-on that comes in once a year. She must be going off her nut. Yeah, that'll be it. Either that or she's got it all wrong."

"Says she definitely heard it on the pipes."

A vision of Myrtle with permed hair. pressing her head against the pipes in a toilet cubicle, flushed—I mean *flashed*—through my mind, and I shook my head to dispel the thought.

## *Greville's grand tour*

Greville and Sharon put on their overalls in the office where the MD began to snarl at him.

"We don't want any staff. Just think on that I could run this place by myself, eh?"

"Then why don't you?" Sharon grumbled, giving me a sly look.

Out in the shop, Greville stood proud in his new grey ironmonger's jacket, the bright strip lights and the massive choice of stock overloading his senses. Sharon said that she had seen the same thing happen to new barrow boys when she was working the East End, "resting" between jobs. Then she handed him over to me and it was time for a whirlwind tour of the shop.

"That's the *key hole*," I said, pointing to an

enclosed area at the top that was lined with key blanks, locks and safes. "Where we cut keys, and—"

"Can I cut one?"

"Not yet."

"Well, there can't be much to it."

"Well there is. You'll need to be trained."

"Can I pick locks?"

"Not at your age, you can't. Only the MD can pick locks and he'd never approve."

"But he said he'd teach me ..."

So the old bugger was at it again. I'd seen this happen so many times with Saturday staff: he bitterly resented the influx of new blood, and would do his damnedest to convince me that we didn't need these people, when on the quiet he would curry favour with them and get them on side. In the old days I believed he was organising some kind of mutiny against me, but I think he just wanted to cover himself from all bases.

I dragged Greville along to another area (we didn't have much time). "This here is where all the brushes are kept. Biggest range for miles around. Heads only, handles only or complete—we've got the lot including coco, bassine and umpteen different varieties—"

"Bassine? That some kind of sink?"

"No, that's basin. We'll get to that in the plumbing department."

"Coco?"

"Brown sweeping brushes."

"For floors?"

"Yes."

"I thought everyone had a vac."

"Of course they do, but they still need a brush."

"What for?"

"And beware crusty-looking old ladies with black capes asking for a *broom*. They usually wear pointy hats. You must tell us straight away if you get one of them, right?"

39

"I'll do that. I'll tell the lady. Pointy hats."

For a second there he had me worried. We moved on to an aisle lined both sides with timber and decorative beadings, with that distinctive aroma of pine.

"Look at that lot," I said. "More timber here than in Sherwood Forest."

"Wow! Really?"

"No. And out here—and we always keep this door closed in summer—"

"Why?"

"Because the butcher's blowflies are as big as crows."

"Shit!"

"Oi, don't say that word in front of the customers," I said. "And don't be alarmed when they swear at you, 'cos they will. And if it sounds like the situation is going to get out of hand, get Sharon. She's used to it. From London," I nodded knowingly.

He looked worried. "Oh, I will."

I opened the door to show him the circular saw bench and grinding wheel, but there were gasps and knocking noises coming from the butchers' toilet, some of them female. I shut the door quickly, turned and smiled at the apprentice.

"What's that noise?" he said.

"Plumbing problems," and I showed him the selection of rubber gloves.

I considered drawing him a map of the shop so he wouldn't get lost, and thought it was only fair to mention one or two points about survival behind the counter. Of course, he'd learn by experience—the hard way, that is—but at the risk of causing him information overload I thought it best to mention certain aspects that had lost me some sleep when I was his age.

"A lot of the old men are going to try picking on you," I said. "They'll think they know more than you." *And they're probably right.*

"I know. That nice lady told me."

"And they'll call you *lad*."

"Yes, the lady said."

"And they'll ask for some daft stuff just to see you make a fool of yourself. It makes them feel important."

"Yeah, I know." He sounded impatient.

"So watch out. Don't argue with anyone. Call for help if you feel the situation getting out of hand."

"That's what the lady told me."

"Sharon, right."

And our apprentice walked away. It seemed he'd had his first training session with the part-time lady and was confident that he could manage all by himself. I called after him:

"Er, Greville—what do you do if you find yourself out of your depth?"

"I call for the lady."

*Yes, I thought as much.*

"And what if it all kicks off in the morning when the *nice* lady is not here?"

That had him, the little greaser. He gave me the blank stare we would become so used to seeing over the coming months.

"Sharon doesn't do mornings," I added with a touch of smugness.

He hesitated for a couple of seconds (we'd get used to that, too).

"Sharon? She says she'll be doing mornings for the next few weeks." Now it was my turn to do the blank stare. "Just to bed me in, like." He walked away, positioning himself behind the tools counter, proudly surveying the customer-less aisles before him.

As I walked past I spat at him (not literally), "That's *settle* you in." *You dozy twerp!*

The doorbell went. I smiled to myself when I

saw him jump, and a short, white-haired man strode defiantly up to the tools counter. For a second, Greville had that rabbit in the headlamps look. The customer took a scathing look at the apprentice. I knew his sort.

"Now then, sonny, what have you got in files?" That meant that he knew exactly what he was after but he wanted to play silly beggars.

Hesitation, then, "Files. Oh, hang on," and Greville turned towards the wall. His scan of its contents was soon interrupted.

"They're up there—to your left—no, your left, you daft young devil. I want a twelve inch mill bastard."

Greville froze. The next thing I saw was him running up the stairs. He'd find Sharon either half-dressed or in the toilet. Either way I didn't care. I moved through the maze of openings and staff-traffic runs and I took down a couple of large flat files and laid them on the counter.

"Now then, sir," I smiled, but with my knowing eye, "would that be a straight mill bastard or a tapered mill bastard?"

# 6

*Larry the rep*

LARRY HAD PARKED HIMSELF, as he usually did, warming his backside in front of the gas fire. He was Bird's rep, but we'd never known him turn up once a fortnight like he was supposed to do—like his employers thought he was doing, in fact—so it was anyone's guess where he went while he was supposed to be repping.

"Here she is," he called out, like some tuppenny fanfare to announce Sharon's arrival. "Had your hands on any good parts, lately?"

"Very bleeding funny," she called back, having checked the shop was clear, just in case he was determined to turn it into the sort of exchange that doesn't go down too well in front of a browsing audience.

She spoke quietly to Greville. "I've had better parts than he's got to offer."

"Who *is* the geezer with the dodgy suit?" he asked.

"Yeah, it's awful, isn't it? I've never seen him wearing anything else."

It was generally agreed that Larry's suit might have been alright in the 1960s, but thirty years later small white and black check might have better suited a circus clown.

"That's Larry," she told Greville. "Take a good look at him—he don't turn up here all that often."

"I'll not forget that suit."

The boy seemed to understand, so perhaps he might turn out better than any of the others we'd started to train. And then lost. The only little bleeder who ever did complete his apprenticeship then took his knowledge and talents to B&Q. I've never forgiven him.

Sharon heard Larry try to whisper to me—only he was like most men in that he didn't know how:

"I'm positive that's her from that dodgy bath scene in *Casanova*."

"Well, she says not," I said, trying to be discreet.

Larry took a noisy pull at his cigarette. "No, that's her, alright. I know about these things. She's a bit heavier than she was back then, mind. She had lovely tits." He straightened himself, moving half a step from the fire. "Ooh. Feels like a new gas bottle." He shook one of his legs to cool it down.

43

"Look at him," Sharon whispered to Greville. "Like a dog what's just cocked against a lamp post." Then, to Larry, "Those trousers of yours should be dry by now."

"Ooh! Bitchy. So how was the matinée?" He took a considered drag of his fag.

"Me and the boy went for coffee. I treated him to latté and cake. I thought it best to let him know what he was in for—you know, the kind of people you can get in shops—"

"Aye, you've to keep your wits about you—"

"Especially with reps what don't actually do much repping."

He looked at Greville. "Mark my words, son, never let a woman grab your balls—she can't resist digging in her pointed fingernails."

Greville, the poor lad, stood there. He was probably wondering what he should say next, but he just looked dumb. Best way, come to think of it.

"So you're the latest trainee, are you?"

"That's *apprentice*," I made a point of saying.

Larry laughed, mocking me. "Get him bloody serving. That's the best way to learn this trade. You can't take in all this stuff by sitting on your arse and reading books."

"Well, he'll be getting plenty of hands-on experience," I said. "We could do with expanding, and training some staff is the first step. We've got plans for him." I almost believed it myself.

"But does he have plans for *you?* I'm thinking about that last lad that bug—"

"Yeah, okay. Let's just say that we're looking to the future. There are big things ahead for independents like us—"

"Yes, like closing down sales."

I stopped and looked straight at him, about to ask him just whose side he was on. He must have realised that he could be in trouble, and he changed tack.

"The old man won't be happy about your expansion plans, I'll bet. I've known him a long time."

"You're right there. He believes in leaving things as they are, playing it safe."

Looking back at Larry I could see I'd lost his attention. Now he was frowning. He'd have pointed in Greville's direction but he always liked to stand with his hands in his pockets, unless he was holding a fag between his fingers.

"Hey, lad, don't I know you from somewhere?"

"No?" said Greville.

"I never forget a face," and he glanced towards Sharon. "Comes in handy when you're in my position."

I was making a quick note of which colours of varnish we wanted to order, and I couldn't help myself grunting aloud.

"I do know you," Larry persisted. "It'll come to me."

Most times he was playful, but right then, probably because Sharon had put him in his place, there was a menacing tone in his voice.

"Well, you think you've seen *me* on telly," she said, "but I say you've got the wrong show."

Greville said nothing, but again had that startled rabbit-in-the-headlamps look. Larry continued to stare at him and lit a fag from the fire's pilot light, tilting his chin back, exhaling smoke while keeping his eyes on the lad. I handed my scrap of paper to him.

"So where did you find him? Has he been on the dole since he left school?"

"No, I don't think so. He's had previous experience in, er ... something." I looked at Greville and followed Larry's third party appraisal, as if the lad wasn't actually there with us.

"And what sort of *something* is that?"

"I'm not certain, but I think it's this line ... of

things."

"What—you mean like a shed boy?"

I sprang to the lad's defence. "Oh, no, nothing like that. It might have been something like ... flat pack furniture?"

"Oh, yes?" Larry nodded. "And whereabouts would that be—not Halstead's, was it?"

"Erm ..." I looked at Sharon. There was something here that was slipping out of my control. "Y-yes, I think it might have been." Honestly, I tried to seem uncertain.

"Ha! So that's him!" Larry chuckled away to himself knowingly, taking deep drags.

When I caught Sharon's gaze she looked daggers at me—like she wanted to push the point of one into me. It didn't take much working out that she wanted Larry out of the shop as soon as possible. I watched her take a deep breath, and when she spoke she was all nice as pie with him.

"So then, my darling, where are you due next? Who's your next call? My, is that the time? You're usually out of here by now. I hear the roads are very busy ..."

Grabbing my varnish order, he paced his exit just to be awkward, extinguished his tab end between his fingers and left it on a counter.

"Has anyone asked him where you keep bubbles for spirit levels? Or where the glass hammers are?"

I shook my head. "No one's been childish enough."

He read the signs and shuffled down the shop as if trying to find fault. In fact he made a point of straightening some tins of wood filler and quickly moved on when he saw Sharon approaching. Then suddenly he turned back.

"Oh, by the way—just make sure you don't give him any ordering to do." His dramatic pause was almost as good as Sharon's. "That's the lad who was told to order five hundred flat pack cardboard boxes—five hundred, mind."

"And?"

"Why don't you ask *him?* Better still, get him to write it down for you. And if not, I'll tell you all about it next time."

And Larry was gone.

"He'll have forgotten by the next time we set eyes on *him*," Sharon spat.

We were certain we had nothing to worry about. But then we looked at each other and set off in search of the boy, who we found lurking behind a display stand where he was setting mousetraps. In the past, sundry schoolkids had come into the shop and set whole boxes of them, but I've no idea why because they were never on the premises to watch the fun and games when the traps almost took off customers' fingers.

"Hey, you! How many boxes did you order, Greville?" I needed to know exactly what I had taken on.

"I haven't ordered any boxes. This is my first day."

Sharon knelt down and put her arm around him. "Come on, Grev, it's all right, you can tell us what happened."

He looked at me, but only for a split second, then stared at the floor.

"Five hundred, like they said."

She looked up at me, and I hoped she could tell that I wasn't convinced.

"Well, as long as you did what they—"

"But they sent more than that."

"How many more?" I demanded.

He looked about to cry. "Five hundred ..." his voiced squeaked into nothingness.

"Greville, how many?"

"... thousand," he whispered.

I relaxed. "Well, it was double, but not exactly

a disaster—"

"Five hundred thousand," he said.

I felt my mouth drop open. "Five hundred ... *half a million boxes*? So I take it they misheard you?"

"No, I wrote it down."

"Oh, my God. He can't do numbers. That's all we need."

"But they were flat ones," he added.

"Oh, well, that's okay, then. I mean half a million *flat* boxes ... well, you can stick 'em behind anywhere out of the way—"

"But they still wouldn't fit in the warehouse. We'd no room for them."

"There, there," Sharon told him. "But it worked out all right, didn't it?"

"No." He was getting in a state by now. "My boss told me the boxes would have to stay out in the yard and if it rained and they got spoilt, it'd be down to me and I'd have to pay for them."

"Well, did they agree to take the boxes back? I mean, it was an honest mistake, wasn't it, Grev?"

Greville looked at me.

"It rained that night. Proper pissed it down. What's a glass hammer?"

I had begun walking away, then turned back to them. "Are you any good at making tea, or do you need a training course? It's only *one* bag per pot."

"We ain't gonna end up with a brilliant trainee with that kind of attitude, are we?" Sharon snapped. If only looks could kill, I'm sure I would have died where I stood.

"A glass hammer is a joke, right?"

Sharon told him yes.

"And a bubble for a thing—"

"A spirit level, yeah. It's a joke," she said encouragingly, and looked at me, smiling. "See, he's doing really well, isn't he, Graham?"

I closed my eyes in desperation. We had an

apprentice that was soft in the head, and an experienced sales assistant who was following him.

"They want to laugh at you. Some people can be very cruel," she soothed.

I touched her on the shoulder. "Does he know if he's got a girlfriend?"

"Why do you ask?"

"Because he's got terrible acne."

Sharon swallowed, and I heard her ask Greville if he thought he could fill the kettle and make the afternoon drinks, and he scuttled off into the office. I began disarming the mousetraps or we could end up being sued.

"At least we've found something he's good at," I told her. Then one of them went *thwack!* and I stood there shaking my hand, trying to cast the pain aside. "*Little* b*astard!*"

"Not the boy!" she said.

The shop doorbell made us nearly jump into each other's arms, the bloody thing. A young bloke in a cheap suit, unembarrassed by his sense of self-imposed importance, homed in on us. We knew by instinct that he wasn't a customer. Git or government, as Sharon called suchlike. She went towards him but, ignoring her, he came straight at me, despite me having a bruised thumb in my mouth, and held out a white A4 envelope. The natural thing is to take whatever is offered to you, but unsolicited mail wasn't on my list of priorities and the thumb won.

"Er, I've been sent to give you this."

"What is it?"

The way he shook his head told me that his employer was training him to be a liar, and he wasn't much good at it.

"So who's sent you?" (That's a translation; the thumb was still being comforted.)

"I'm from the bank," he said.

"Well, why didn't you say so? How is Mister

Canterbury? Haven't seen him for a while."

"He left before I started."

"And when was that?" I had a nagging doubt about something.

"Eleven months ago. I've nearly completed my probationary period."

See? I was right. Eleven months. And I remember him saying that we would need to review the overdraft facility by interview every six months, just to keep Regional Office happy, he'd said, nodding and winking.

"Right. Just leave it on the counter," I said between sucks.

"Oh."

"What's wrong?"

"It's important that you actually take it from me. I've to make certain it's in your hand."

I took out my thumb. "Why? Do I need rubber gloves?" I spat, taking it with my good hand. I cast a glance at the addressee. It wasn't hand written to Graham, in Mr Canterbury's scrawling style, like it used to be; this was typed and perfectly spaced. When I looked back the little banker had gone. I looked at Sharon.

"That's just how it was with Myrtle," she said.

The thumb came out of the pit lane and I opened the envelope and began reading. There weren't really that many words, but it was after the first few that the rest of them turned into some sort of blur. Try as I might, I couldn't seem to get past those first few. Sharon's voice faded in. As if from another room somewhere, she was asking what was up.

"I'm not sure ... I think it's saying that they're calling in the overdraft." There was no expression in my voice.

"Well, I've got a bit put by what I could loan you. How much they want, then?"

"What? Oh, er, just over thirty grand."

Her mouth fell open. She knew exactly how much money we took, and our approximate overall margin, and it didn't take a mathematician to realise that such a blow would finish us.

"Oh, Graham, my love, what you gonna do?"

"I suppose if it comes to it," I said, thinking on my feet, as usual, "I could work for nothing."

"Don't talk daft! You already do that sometimes. No one can expect you to do that forever."

"And forever is about how long it'll take." I could barely hear my own voice.

For some reason, I needed to sit down. My whole body weight felt like it could float away. Or did it feel extra heavy? Can't remember. If in doubt, sit down, so I did, on the floor.

Just then Greville came out of the office.

"Er," he began. "The kettle ... it-it's gone bang."

Whatever else could go bloody wrong! "How do you mean, *it's gone bang?*"

"It has! Just now! It-it's smoking."

"That means it's boiling."

"But this is black. The old man is doing a lot of coughing and stuff and waving his nail about."

Sharon put her hand on his shoulder. "Now, my darling, you did put some water in it, didn't you?" she asked.

That's when we saw the expression that we would get to know and expect.

# 7

*Into the lion's den*

WE HAVE NO IDEA what happens behind closed doors, have we? I mean, I was going into the bank every couple of days or so to get change and pay in (but mostly to get change), and I never detected that the bank had been getting its own change—in the administration. Sharon says it's because I'm not sensitive to what is going on around me. She says that when acting on stage you need to sense what the audience is doing, how they are thinking, whether they are paying attention, fully engrossed, and then fine-tune your performance accordingly to bring the audience in to the pretend world your artistry is creating for them. And I had missed it all—in the bank the grim looks on the cashiers' faces had completely escaped me.

Only a few months before, the manager's door would open into the banking hall (the public bit) and John Canterbury, late-fifties, balding, comfortable, would greet me with a cheery good morning and address me by name. In those days no one cared if others knew where you banked. In fact, it was all a bit of an advert for us all, and when the manager greeted you by first name and in such a welcoming manner ... well, all the customers waiting to be served were either already in the club, or they wanted to be. Good times.

But today it looked like a school sixth form boy who weakly pushed open the manager's door and called me by my full name, with not even a mister in front of it, and there would be no envious nodding going on in *that* queue. Not any more, there wouldn't.

"You wanted to see me," he said. There was no "good morning and how are you today?"

"No, I wanted to see a manager," I told him. *Let's not play silly buggers.*

"I am one of the management team."

"Where are the managers?"

"There's been a regional reorganisation, so we no longer have *managers* as such—not at branch level. All decisions are now taken care of at local-regional level."

"So is that local, or regional?"

The signs of brow-beating were already beginning to show. I saw a slight glazing in the eyes, and the possibility that his list of set phrases was rapidly becoming exhausted. Hopefully, *he* would soon follow.

He sighed. Bad sign. "What can I do for you?" The words were there; the respect was nowhere in sight.

"Nothing, because you're not a manager."

There was the slight expression of shock, followed by, "But I'm in charge of—"

"You're not old enough."

"I can assure you that—"

"Why have you cancelled our overdraft?"

Another sigh. "It's all explained in the letter we sent you." He sounded impatient.

"But it doesn't say *why* you've cancelled it. We've had that ..." I must have been panicking because my mind went blank.

"Overdraft facility—"

"—facility, yes, for over eight years."

"Well, that's eight years too long. It is a new principle of the bank that all such antique practises—"

"Shouldn't that be *antiquated?*"

"—running on very familiar, and unprofitable, lines, like some old pals' network, are to be outlawed. We are, after all, just like you—a business."

"I'm glad you've made that point because, you see, if you don't loan people money, then what's left for you to do?"

"I don't follow you."

"It's quite simple, you see, because if I refuse to sell my stock, then I'll lose all of my customers. If you refuse to loan money, you're in the same boat. You and I need to sell our products. Now *that's* a business."

By now he was fidgeting, touching his hair, wiping away the beads of imaginary sweat from his forehead. I had the bugger! So I carried on—in for the kill ...

"And no one in their right minds—let alone in possession of morals and any inclination of fairness—can possibly expect a thriving business to pay back such a large sum overnight. It's outrageous."

Unfortunately, I had touched upon something that he had recently been reading about in a text book, and his speech slowed, taking on an obscene patronising tone. "But that is exactly what an overdraft facility is—basically it's an overnight loan, temporary, to tide you over. It's not a *right*. And as for yours being a *thriving* business, I have to bring it to your attention that—"

"Where's John?"

"If you mean Mister Canterbury—"

"A proper bank manager—"

He sniggered. "The bank offered him early retirement—"

"You mean he was pushed."

The schoolboy gave me a steely gaze and his knuckles turned white as he gripped his shiny new Parker pen. When I walked out of the bank ten minutes later it felt like my legs wouldn't carry me the hundred and fifty yards back to the shop. But I just made it.

I asked Sharon if she had the pots ready for a drink of coffee. No, she said, because I was usually given a drink at the bank.

"That lot wouldn't cross the street to urinate on someone who was on fire," I spat.

Her expression confirmed that she'd got the message, there was no point in her asking how I had gone on, so I just ploughed in with the depressing details.

"We're not to buy any more stock. In fact, they've warned me that some of the cheques that haven't yet cleared could be returned unpaid. And as you know, when that sort of thing happens no one will deal with us again."

"No stock? So what happens if a customer places a special order," she said.

I shrugged my shoulders. That one hadn't occurred to me. You see, we were well known for being able to order in just about anything and get it for the next day—special light bulbs, for instance, that were required when the sheds bought in a job lot of imported light fittings for which they had no spare bulbs, which happened frequently. Well, that was one of our specialities and our reputation for being willing to source such rare gems, especially when the sellers of the bloody fittings could not, or would not, be bothered, had brought us a lot of extra business and goodwill. Other items were toilet seat fittings—again, to make up for the deficiencies at the likes of B&Q-it-All. In a perfect world, these new customers would have continued to shop with us for the bigger ticket items, but sadly they tended not to. But then in a perfect world the sheds would have stayed in America where they first started up and those of us with other than £ signs in our sights would still be providing the best of service.

"They'll let me pay just one more week's wages,

then that's it. I think that's only because they have to, but don't quote me on that. It all went a bit hazy in there, like a dream, with stuff floating around in mid air."

"Are you sure they didn't give you a drink with a little something in it?"

"I asked him what was supposed to happen when there was no staff left to run the place."

"And what did he say, this upstart of an office junior with his twenty-nine pound Burton's suit?"

"I don't think he's read as far as that chapter," I said.

The bell clattered and even from where we were standing we could tell by the whoosh of in-draught exactly who it was, and what would be coming next—

"Wake up! Wake up! Stand by your beds, everybody!"

It was pure instinct and habit. Despite being on the verge of bankruptcy, immediately Sharon and I pushed with each other to get to where the boxes of loose screws were neatly stacked on shelves in a concealed area behind a partition. Yes, it was easier to allow customers to choose their own woodscrews from the self-service pre-packs' stand (that the MD had bollocked me for buying, especially as we still had thousands of pounds' worth of loose screws in boxes), so when Sergeant Major Jim whooshed-in and began balling out like this—

"Twenty-four half-inch number four round-head brass. Twelve"—he was of the old school and spoke in dozens—"three-quarter sixes steel countersunk ..."

—we scurried away like busy little beavers to fulfil his requirements.

"And all slotted, mind. Don't want any o' them daft Phillips heads, the soft buggers."

Well, by the mid-90s we'd been on Pozidriv-headed screws for over twenty years, and

SuperDriv had now taken over, but it was as if most of the town couldn't handle anything more complicated than a straight screw. No idea why that was, unless it was because they couldn't bear to fork out for a new screwdriver. By the time he reached the top it was usual for us to have up to ten little paper bags of screws waiting for him on the counter. He passed the time of day with us, usually complaining about some totally useless survey he'd heard about on the radio.

"Eeee, what a cushy job them clever buggers has got, what do you think? Sitting on their arses all day thinking up daft stuff like how many starving people could be watered with all the water that would fit onto the M1 up to five inches deep. Who'd have thought of summat as daft as that?"

And we'd agree with him, and feel refreshed by his optimistic negativism.

Just then a handful of customers walked in, and we were left hoping there would be no special orders—in fact, we were hoping that someone would want one of the petrol lawnmowers that we had stacked upstairs, waiting for the following summer. Some of them were three hundred quid. Yes, I realise this was November, but the idea was for shops to buy them in big numbers, out of season, and get a bulk discount, even though it meant sitting on thousands of pounds' worth of temporarily dead stock. The little lad sitting in the bank manger's chair wouldn't be able to comprehend the intricacies of such practises. But whilst the idea of anyone wanting a lawnmower in winter was not unknown, it certainly was rare. Anyway, none of this latest influx of trade wanted anything large-ticket, and when the customers left with little packets of spare parts for their houses, Sharon and I were also left, but with a deep feeling of dread.

"Ha! I know far more about over-*draughts* than

he does!" I smiled at the rather superb display stand of draught excluders. I certainly knew how to put the *wind* up him—or rather I thought that I did.

"And how old is this neophyte?"

"Oh, maybe early-twenties—"

"You said he was like a sixth-former! That's eighteen."

"Well, he only looks eighteen, and with more spots than Greville, the poor sod. The decision's been made elsewhere, by people who have no experience of the local conditions, colour, culture even. They're clueless about what it's like down here on the shop floor. And what really gets me is that they think we can simply sell all this stuff and pay them back out of it. As if it's just a case of straight in, straight out. If only it was that simple."

"It would serve them fat-arsed bleeders right if you had a closing-down sale. You could sell the property and just bugger off." She paused and caught my look, and said the next words slowly. "Couldn't you? ... Oh, don't tell me ... you didn't ...?"

"I had to, Sharon. How else was I going to get the overdraft in the first place? Not even one of the old school like John Canterbury would give us a twenty-two grand overdraft without *some* security."

"And so you gave him the shop!" It was more statement than question.

My god, I thought, if this is how the hired help is taking it, just how bad will it be when I tell the MD? Neither of us spoke. She would normally have busied herself rearranging stock that customers invariably put back in the wrong places, or maybe done a bit of dusting (it's okay, Sharon had an eye for dust and expressly forbade me from doing it). I knew how she was feeling: was there any point in tidying a shop that would soon be having all its stock and fittings sold off cheap in a bailiff's knock-down auction? Wouldn't it be easier to shut the door now and simply go home? Then I felt guilty for thinking of Sharon as the hired help.

"Oh, Graham."

"Oh, Sharon."

"Oh, shit. Watcha gonna do, Graham?" That was the question I feared the most. "Hey—how much is this place worth, do you think, the building, I mean?"

"Don't know. But a damn sight more than what we owe the bank."

"Well," she said, brightening, making me feel like she was about to pull some miracle out of the bag, "there'll be some change then, won't there, so it's not all doom, is it?"

She thought she was doing me a favour, making me feel better, so I hated spoiling it for her. "When they put it on sale all they'll want is enough to clear the overdraft, so it's very likely it'll be sold for peanuts. That's how they work. But thanks," and I squeezed her hand.

The MD ventured out of the office and I snatched my hand away.

"Na then," he said, which translated means "now then" or simply "hello". He began winding his arm, as if urging us to get some work done. "So why aren't either of you serving customers?"

"Cos there aren't any in."

"Well ... don't we need any sweeping brushes making up? Or extension leads? There's always plenty to be getting on with."

"You can do some, if you like."

"Nay, that's your job, not mine. I'm doing the National Insurance return."

"Yes, and there's only two of us paying any National Insurance—and not for much longer. How the hell would you manage if you were a wages clerk in a big mill, with hundreds of workers?"

"Well, they keep changing the tax codes. It's very complicated, and the buggers fine you if you make a mistake. It's not like it was when I first started out. I used to go to the Post Office every Friday to buy a National Health stamp—"

"Look, if you're rubbish at doing the wages I'll tell you what you might be good at—"

"What's that?"

"Right at this very moment, this business is well and truly up to its eyeballs in the stuff of sewage systems. Okay? Have you any ideas what to do about it?"

This was my chance to tell him what an utter mess I had sort of made of things. Reckless? You bet I was. But what did I have to lose? What might he do—*sack me?* But no, when I finished he looked away and began thinking.

"Hmm, we've got something on the shelves for that ..."

The shop doorbell jangled and Sharon and I waited to see who would appear at the counter. It was Adrian Friar. Now, before I go on, I should explain that Adrian always thought that with a name like his he should either join a monastery or open a fish and chip shop. He chose the latter, not appreciating the difference in the spellings, and anyhow the idea of celibacy didn't appeal to him. His shop was exceptionally busy, and the rear wall of his restaurant (well, it was a café, really) backed on to ours. We'd often joked about knocking a serving hatch through so we could get some chips without having to walk halfway round the town for them. We sold him mops, sweeping brushes, stainless steel cleaner, dishcloths, towels, and specially-made whiteboards faced with genuine Formica for his display menus (which I made up myself so they'd last longer than the mass-produced crappy boards). Today he looked as bad as I was feeling.

"Don't suppose you do Paracetamol in bulk, do you?" He could be a bit of a joker, but not today, I suspected.

"I take it you have a massive headache."

"Headache, heartache, who cares? I'm in the shit, well and truly. If I don't finish myself off, someone's gonna do it for me."

"You're ... not serious, are you?" If so, we had a special department for this sort of thing, and she crept a little closer, listening.

He nodded, then changed his mind. "I don't know ... what a pillock of a mess I'm in ... I just can't ... can't seem to take it all in. They've sprung it on me—just like that, out of the blue. Me gut feels like it's been kicked over and over ..."

He stopped, head bowed, staring at the floor, trying to make sense of whatever was happening to him. Then he looked at me and, close to tears, he said:

"They've cancelled me loan." And he shook his head. "Just like that. And I've only just bought three grand's worth of new tables and chairs to posh-up the restaurant, and then this happens."

Sharon took his arm and began to stroke it.

"Sounds familiar, don't it, Graham?"

"Not you anawl," Adrian said, now rallying round, seeing as he wasn't alone.

I asked him which bank he used, though I didn't need to. Sharon was straight on it:

"What are vey trying to do round there—close the whole bleedin' town?"

"It sounds like it," I said, "but not every business banks at the same place, so I don't see how ..."

"Well, that's two of us out on the streets."

We were silent for a few minutes, all sorts of pictures and scenarios going through my mind, such as the MD's wife sitting on the back of a flatbed cart being pulled down the street by a donkey, surrounded by the few goods and chattels that the bailiff had allowed her to keep and take with her; the closing down sale—90% OFF,

EVERYTHING MUST GO, and crowds of people in the street pushing and clawing at the shop to get hold of the bargains, with lines of police dressed in riot gear desperately trying to keep them at bay; and the MD, now a tired and wizened old man, sitting at the door, charging an entry fee ...

"You can't let 'em do vis to you."

"They're gonna crucify us."

"You'll have to do something!"

That was pretty bleeding obvious, and not one of Sharon's more pertinent and incisive comments.

Adrian shuffled as if with a fresh burst of energy. "You know that lad I set on—the one I'm training to be a waiter?"

Yes, we had come across him. Okay, we wouldn't have dreamt of employing him ourselves, but he was, after all, Adrian's choice, so who were we to judge? Adrian's mind was ticking fast.

"Maybe—it's just a thought, mind—maybe I could train him on the Frank Ford frying range—"

"Oh, you mean and *you* do the café?" I didn't see the logic in this.

"No, I'll train him to run the *whole shop*."

"Why would you do that?"

"Just for evenings, like, 'cos I'll be there during the day, but in the evenings I'll be earning proper money."

"Where?" That was both Sharon and me. I mean, if there was *proper* money being offered, we needed to know the details, no doubt evident by our eager expressions.

"They're taking on for the night shift at Crossets Carpets."

We backed away, almost bumping our heads together. Was this as insane as it sounded, or were we missing something?

"Let me get this straight, Adrian—you'll work the shop during the day ..."

"Right! And I'll work the factory at night, yeah.

And with all that proper money I'll pay back them buggers at the bank and get 'em off me back."

I looked at Sharon. Well, he had it all sewn up, didn't he? He turned round to leave, now grinning with his cunning plan.

"Is there anything else we can do for you?" I called, unable to disguise the hint of sarcasm.

"Don't suppose you do caffeine pills in bulk, do you?"

# 8

*Operation Bounceback*

"HE CAN'T LAST," SHARON said. "He thinks he can, but he'll finish up paying the price."

"That's exactly the point—he intends to pay."

"But not with his health, the poor man."

I'd never heard of caffeine pills; they sounded quite a good idea, but Sharon warned me against using them. She had witnessed lots of instances of her fellow "dramaticals" taking such pills so they could stay up all night to learn their lines and prepare for performance, and they had "gone down with the shakes", even ending up in such deep sleep as to be unwakeable for days on end. So whatever was going off with the bank didn't only affect our livelihood, it could so easily affect our lives if we weren't careful. Between us, Sharon and I admired Adrian's devil-may-care attitude in being willing to kill himself to fight his way out of the situation. He could only last a few weeks at most, was our guess.

But what could we do here at Little Sniffingham Hardware & DIY? Maybe we should go to one of those financial specialists, the ones who hang around on street corners?

"Oh you don't want to be messing with that type," said Sharon. "Money lenders—ugh! I seen fings they do that would curl the bristles of a sweeping broom. You don't want to be getting involved with them. They got no scruples."

"Like the banks, you mean?"

Now we knew—and I mean we were *absolutely* certain—there was some kind of conspiracy; there was no other explanation: one bank and two separate businesses with adjoining buildings, both being squeezed? Despite fears of paranoia, there was definitely some degree of piracy involved, but how would we find out? And what could we do about it if it were confirmed? In the Little Sniffingham wealth stakes, such as they were, we owned a few bricks and a lot of crumbling mortar; we had nothing, we *were* nothing.

Sharon, bright as a pin, pointed out: "However worthless you think this place is, someone wants it, don't they? It's obvious. It reminds me of a script I read for *Eastenders*—"

"So you were in *Eastenders?*" I brightened, grateful for a diversion.

"Nah, turned it down. Vey said my accent wasn't strong enough."

And that was the point that set us on the plan. It wasn't exactly a master plan, where you get to stand in front of a room of industry professionals and write on a cheap whiteboard in circles and lines and graph thingies; no, ours wasn't written down, it was conceived out of anger, and a determination to fight off the unseen enemy. By tackling the symptoms (lack of cash to repay the bank), we might last a few weeks before going down, but we would go down fighting as we took our last breaths. In drawing a line right there and then (figuratively, you understand), we would write off everything that had gone before, and declare that everything we achieved after that time would be a bonus. Every day we managed to hang on would be another grimace at the bank. We would refuse to close until *we* were ready, and we had made ourselves such a nuisance that we would go down in memory, and maybe get them to think twice about doing to someone else whatever it was they were doing to us.

Sharon and I were laughing, our voices raised, our minds giddy, it was like we were flying invisible banners, so intoxicated were we with the excitement of the impending fight. And then we saw Greville. He was waiting close by, wearing his coat, with his new overall folded across his arm. We went silent.

He swallowed. "Do you want me to bring this back when me mum's washed it?"

Sharon rushed towards him and hugged him, telling him not to be so silly, of course he didn't need to go.

"Of course he can stay, can't he, Graham? ... Graham, what's the matter?" I was wondering how the hell we could afford him. Then something occurred to me.

"There is something we can try. It's not something I would normally consider because I don't agree with it, but these are exceptional circumstances," I said, a bit embarrassed, "but maybe we can keep him if we can get him on the YTS scheme."

Sharon laughed, more with relief, I think. "Graham, you've just said *scheme* twice."

I ignored her.

"But YTS is for school leavers, and I'm not one," Greville said, trembling.

"Good point, I said. "How long were you at Halstead's?"

"A day."

"Well, there you are, then, you're as good as a school leaver. I can't think they even got as far as writing your name down. I'll get the forms and see if we can't get some of your wage paid by the Government. But if we manage to swing it, you'll need to go to the technical college and learn some stuff, right?"

"Oh. What sort of stuff?"

"Well it certainly won't be about anything as practical as working for peanuts just to keep the bank off your back, 'cos that's what we'll be doing here from now on. Or for as long as we can last out. It'll be all book theory, but it's right here where you'll learn the grit of commercial survival. Here, where real life happens." I hesitated, marvelling at how I sounded such an expert on the subject. If only. "Here's lesson number one—the best way of sorting a mess like this is to get in the most cash while paying the least out. And so you'll become a government trainee. If they want you off the unemployment list, they'll have to pay you."

"And I'll come in full-time ..." Sharon said. I looked at her. "For what you pay me part-time—just until, you know."

"Yes, I know. Thanks for that, Sharon. And I'll tell the MD."

"Tell him what?"

"That for the foreseeable future he'll be living off his state pension. As for me, I'll manage on as little as possible."

"Graham, you been doing that all the time I've known you. This place must owe you thousands."

She was right. I preferred not to think about it. She went on:

"So it's Operation Bounceback, yeah? Only thing is we'll need some cash so we can pay for the special orders, 'cos if we stop doing them we'll give off the wrong signals. Once word gets round that we're hard up then we might as well shut up shop.

You can't get passengers onto a sinking ship. Any ideas?"

"There's that very generous consideration from the bank—one week's wages. We could use it for buying the specials."

"Brilliant! So we're sorted then? Remember, we're at war, but it's one of *stelf*, so we'll need to watch our backs," and, before he could say anything, she gave Greville a playful tap on the back of his head.

"I was only gonna say we sell brackets for them." He looked pleased with himself.

Now it was my turn. "That's *stealth,* not *shelf*, you berk!"

For some reason he flinched.

"And there's something else they won't bother telling you at tech, and that's about numbers, where the noughts go, where the decimal point goes. Have you got that?"

"Why—why won't they teach about that stuff?"

"Because I doubt they'll know themselves."


I'd like to say that Operation Bounceback began all action-like, with our tiny army of workers marching along the aisles, repelling borders against infiltration by sneaky bailiffs—okay, so we weren't at that point just yet, but we needed someone to focus on as the enforcing angel of the bank. Maybe that should be the devil. But the next day was pretty much like all those that had gone before, except that Sharon was on the premises from the moment we opened. I'd spent the previous evening at the MD's house, explaining myself and defending my allegedly reckless spending.

"You've driven that business into the ground," he kept saying, and yes, that's how it felt, and I tried to explain how we needed to expand, and that not doing so was the real reason why we were finding ourselves in this perilous state. But he was having none of it, and in desperation I called the company accountants' office before leaving for work. I'd warned Sharon when she did the wake-up call because she didn't trust accountants: she said they urinated in the same receptacles as banks, or words to that effect.

In the morning I tried to steer well clear of the office, but we ran out of four-inch oval nails and the back-up stock was kept under the desk by the MD's feet. Sharon began rinsing the coffee mugs in the sink.

"How did you get on wiv the accountant? Did she make any decent suggestions, then?"

It was one awkward question after another.

"I've arranged to see her tonight."

"*Tonight?*" Sharon turned. "Out of office hours, you mean? That's unusual. It's *decent* suggestions you want, not *indecent* ones."

"I'm not so lucky."

Sharon dried the mugs, when usually she would let them drain upside down, meaning that she was stalling for time. "Hmm, *very* unusual."

The MD tapped his pipe on the edge of the wall-mounted fire extinguisher.

"Did you just mention something about an accountant? That's another lot of leeches. So what time?"

I knew what he'd say if I told him. "Oh, it's not certain she'll turn up while we're open."

"*She?* You mean—it's a *woman?*"

"Yes?"

"For an accountant? Good god!"

"Sign of the times," I said. "They let women do anything nowadays." *This is the twentieth century.*

"Well, what's up with her, coming here? They charge extra for that, you know."

"I er, told her that we couldn't afford her hourly rate."

"A woman with an hourly rate? Whatever will they think of next? *How much is it?*" His voice raised as if in agony.

"It's like a telephone number." My voice was sounding like his.

Greville sounded incredulous. "A telephone number? Really?"

"So she said she'd call in after she's finished at the office. As a sort of favour. Because we're in a right bloody mess."

Just so long as the MD didn't offer to stay back so he could give her a hard time himself.

"They'll go bust one o' these days," he said.

Sharon and I looked at him.

"Who'll go bust?"

"Them banks."

"That's rubbish! Banks don't go bust—the likes of us go bust, not banks."

"Oh, they will. They can topple over just like anyone else. It'll happen someday, you mark my words. They're only businesses, you know, when all's said and done, just like us."

That seemed to ring a bell. "So what do you think would happen—in this futuristic world where banks are as vulnerable as the rest of us?"

A-ha! He wouldn't be able to think a way out of that one.

"Why, the buggers would get bailed out by somebody, never fear. No government could allow its banks to go under."

"But it's impossible. It simply can't happen. I mean, they're massive—like monsters."

He looked straight at me, using the stem of his pipe to emphasise his words.

"Little trunks, big boughs," and he lit the pipe and sank back into his own little world of pencil, rubber and paperclips.

## *The Apprentice*

Greville was missing. Sharon had sent him out for the sandwiches (which I said we couldn't afford, but she said it was a special occasion so she would buy them), and he'd not come back so she suggested that I go out and look for him, having told her that I had no idea where teenage lads hung out. It seems that I did; I found him lurking down the alley at the side of Maggie Newsprint's from whom he'd bought a packet of French cigarettes. He was having a right old cough, determined to finish it right down to his yellow fingertips and get his money's worth.

On the way back we watched a man and woman, obviously married and well into their seventies. He was wobbling on one of the loose paving flags outside Lloyds Bank. It seemed that every successive movement made it wobble even more, sending out little spurts of rainwater. Greville thought he was doing it for fun, so I put him straight.

"The old bloke is testing it," I said, "and asking his wife if she thinks it'll pass for a compensation claim at the Council."

"What—because it's splashing her trousers?"

"No, because they plan to walk along here and pretend to lose their balance on it. The Council's cough-up will likely pay for them a winter holiday in Spain."

Don't worry, I wasn't born a cynic.


Watching Greville serve customers was not what I'd describe as satisfying. Customers would ask him for something, he'd look startled, I would think that he already knew where that something was, and I would watch his little facial expression change from bafflement to extreme pleasure as his brain almost clicked into gear and he remembered. I wouldn't say that he had a flair for this kind of work, nor for making conversation, so I decided to give him some tuition.

"You need to be on the lookout for sales opportunities," I told him. "Just don't go making it look like you're trying to sell something."

That had him puzzled, and the startled look soon metamorphosed into a frown. I relaxed, assuming a kind of casual, matey stance, guaranteed to put the boy at ease, to make it all sound less of a lecture and more of a discussion. But it only made him nervous and he stepped away from me, so I grabbed his arm and dragged him back.

"Just stay there 'til I've finished with you," I said, trying to sound friendly, as if I were joking. "You've got to be clever—I don't mean devious, nothing like that. You see, we are here to help these people. After all, if they come in for some paint brushes so they can do some painting over the weekend, and then they get home and find they've forgotten the white spirit or sandpaper and the dust sheets, who do you think they're going to blame?"

"Well, they should've remembered—"

"Yes, yes, Greville, you and I realise that, don't we? But they'll be wanting to get their hands around *our* throats for not suggesting the ancillaries—" There was that startled look again. "I mean, *extras* to them, the other bits and pieces that enable them to complete the operation properly. It's our job to jog their minds so that the men don't get bollocked by their wives and the women don't get foul-mouthed by their husbands for getting back home with only half of the stuff to finish the job. So we're doing them a favour, do you see? Have you got that?"

He nodded. I straightened, feeling like I'd already done a morning's work.

"You want me to do this just on Fridays?"

"No! You do it all the time. They buy a hammer, do they want nails? Do they want some pincers to pull out the old ones—"

"Or the ones they bend," called Sharon.

"Or the ones they bend, because not many of them can hit nails in straight. If they buy nails, do they need a new hammer? Do they have the correct hammer for the job? There, now that's a tough one because many people think there's only one sort of hammer. But look at that selection on the wall over there."

He swallowed, and edged away, hopefully to allow what I'd been saying to sink in.

Luv Grev
x x x

*The Accountant*

It was only when I saw the Accountant standing on my doorstep, and got a whiff of the expensive perfume, that I realised the foisty smell in my hallway hadn't been banished for some years, and if it came to an all-out battle between the two smells, there was no doubt which of them would triumph.

Not even Paris's finest could battle the threat of intimidation from whatever was lurking in the nooks and crannies, or on the old lino in the cupboard beneath the stairs.

We had only ever spoken on the phone. In the half-light I caught a brief smile of sympathy, and once inside I could take in what she looked like: a dark grey business suit with skirt to just above the knees, a crimson silk blouse, the jacket perfectly fitting her upper body, and her hair, straight and reaching to her shoulder blades. If Sharon was right, she would be the double agent, reporting back to the bank every word I said. At that moment I determined to tell her nothing. She was, after all, only trying to raise her own professional fee by making a house call. I wouldn't even be civil to her; she was the enemy pretending to be nice, and over the years I'd had my fair share of such snakes.

"Can I get you a drink at all?" I asked.

"I'm fine, thanks. I don't mean to be rude, but we've a lot to get through and I haven't much time."

"So you've other clients to see."

"Hell, no. It's just that I've been at the office since seven this morning and I want to get home, kick my shoes off, pour some wine and crash out on the settee."

"Well, if you change your mind I'll get whatever you want," and I watched her as she found her own way into the living room, from where she called out to me:

"I've taken a look at your figures ..."

I swallowed, then followed.

"The bank has well and truly pulled the rug out from under you. A couple of years ago I could have got you fixed up at one of the others, when your outlook wasn't quite so gloomy. Now all that's changed."

"So you mean that you'd have helped us back then?"

"You sound surprised."

"It's just that ... well, I thought that—"

"Oh, I get it. You thought that all financial professionals would stick together, hmm?" She laughed, with a hint of cynicism. "The thing about bankers is that they are *not* professionals, they just *want* to be. Banks are simply tarted-up shops that sell money, and most times they're not very good at it. So whatever you do, don't make the mistake of tarring my profession with the same brush as those cowboys."

I found myself shaking my head, as if I would never entertain such wild notions ever again, banish the thought.

"Anyhow, what can I do to ease you away from the precipice of disaster. hmm?" She looked at some pages from her briefcase, then, "Is your staff reliable?"

I laughed, then stopped suddenly when she grimaced.

"I can rely on Sharon, but only when she's resting between parts. And I can rely on the MD to keep out of the way in the office. And I have an apprentice who on Fridays asks men if they'd like anything for the weekend. So yes, it couldn't be better."

She did that thing that only women do, that slight backward tilt of the head whilst keeping eye contact, then she pursed her lips and nodded. "O-kay. Good. I called in yesterday—"

"Where?" I said, alarmed. I didn't know why.

"To your shop. To check you out."

Did she mean me—I mean, *personally?* What a ridiculous thought.

"I didn't see you."

"I think you need to diversify, find a niche market."

I shook my head. "We don't have room for any new lines."

"So how about services?"

"Electricity and water, no gas—"

"No! I mean services that you can provide, to your customers. There must be loads of things that people need doing. Fitting window locks, door locks, new hinges on things. Last year my granny wanted someone to go and simply fit a light bulb—"

"Please, don't talk about—"

"And you're in an excellent position to maximise profit because you would get to make the full retail markup as well as the hourly rate or part thereof."

"I don't like going out to do jobs."

"Then when I see you on the street, where the bank will undoubtedly put you, I'll throw you some loose change, shall I? Think about it."

I sat down, uncertain if it was shock or plain old exhaustion. She wasn't finished yet:

"If you could take on some new lines that would help, particularly if they were unusual—not daft, like seaside tat taken on for the sake of it—and again they satisfy a niche demand."

"Have you any ideas?"

"That's for you to decide. Another thing—"

"Oh, god!"

"You see shops like yours—ones that typically hold all sorts of miscellaneous equipment for mending this, that and the other and whatever—well, all that stock represents cash outlay that, these days, is difficult to afford." She paused. "Excuse me? Mister ... look, is it okay if I call you Graham?"

Tilting her head back, she closed her eyes and massaged the back of her neck. "Excuse me?"

Where the hell had I been? "Yes, sorry."

"You need to make a list of *all* the slow lines, and considering the varied nature of your offerings I'm guessing there are plenty of them."

"You ever been in there?" I'm certain I would

75

have remembered.

"No. Anything with a stock turn of less than two needs to be got rid of. Average cost divided by number of times they've sold in a twelve month period. You got that?"

*Stock turn, eh?* My god, but she knew her stuff—well, at least it sounded that way. But it did seem a little ruthless. We had stuff in there that people expected us to keep on the shelves, just for when, and if, they needed it—I mean *really* needed it. Okay, so some of it needed to be kept for a few years, but just seeing the look on someone's face when you presented them with, say, a new wooden handle for a 5-foot pit saw was very humbling. There aren't many of them around. In fact, we were probably the only stockist in the whole country. Then I tried to remember the last time we had actually sold one. And I couldn't.

"It's up to you how you get rid of it, but I don't think a cut-price sale will work, will it? There's not enough time, and time is of the essence. I would have thought that such items were only in demand at the time people actually needed them—"

"They're called *grudge buys*—"

"Exactly, and people are unlikely to buy them just in case one day they might want a spare thingy for a mark two whatever. But however you dispose of it, and I'm not suggesting that you throw it all away—"

"Heaven forbid—"

"Precisely, but whatever it is you do with the items, just get them *off the shelves*, whether they're on view or under the counter."

*Hmm, now she was talking dirty.*

"So when we've thrown out half the shop, what do we put in its place? And more to the point, what do we use to pay for it?"

"*No*—more to the point, just how quickly can you make some dent in the outstanding balance?

Time is critical. You really do need to begin reducing the debit balance as soon as possible. I can help by preparing a repayment plan for you to show the bank."

"Maybe we can barter—we have tons of nails—"

"I'm being serious. Those people don't have a sense of humour beyond schoolboy smut. We need to get a move on. So I do you a plan and you take it to them to show your ability to repay the outstanding debt in a reasonable time. That way you're in a stronger position."

# 9

### *The Assistant*

"ROLL UP! ROLL UP! All sensible suggestions gratefully considered, " I said, clapping my hands, like some circus leader trying to stimulate the crowds. We "were clear"—that's shop talk for there being no customers on the premises—so I could engage in a little play acting. That chat with the Accountant hadn't been so bad after all, just so long as the details of the sensitive part of the conversation remained secret. "So, what can we do to bring in more cash?"

Greville was on his knees, dusting out the plastic bins where we kept black japanned T-hinges.

"How are you today, Greville? You coping okay? It's not easy work, I know. Not everyone is, well, really cut out—"

"We need more stock lines," Sharon called, "which is what I been telling you for ages."

"Precisely. Yes, we could expand the ranges—"

"Sod the bleeding ranges," Sharon said. "We need something completely different to sell. This is something for us all to think about—what can we sell that no one else in town is selling?"

Now where had I heard that before?

"So how'd you get on with that woman? Figures okay?"

"Yes, she's not bad for her age."

"And what did she have to say for herself?"

"Oh, she was in a rush to get home. So we hadn't much time."

"I see." I'm not certain that she believed me.

"She needs to analyse the books—something like that."

"So you told her about our plans, you know, to keep piddling on for as long as we can."

"Oh, yeah."

"And what she say?"

"We need to diversify."

"So she said that?" For some reason she seemed surprised. "Well, there's something in that, I suppose. If you take a good look around town you'll see what other shops are doing. All Tools is dabbling in furniture, the art shop's doing cans of pop, and Ram Raid Roger's doing computers wiv his electric guitars and violins."

"I suppose it's another string to his bow."

"In Little Sniffingham, everybody's speciality has become someone else's sideline. Just lately everyone's jumping on other folks' bandwagon—"

"Except Woolworths—"

"Except Woolworths. They've been nicking trade from other shops for years."

"Especially *our* trade. The Accountant says that other people are nicking our lines so we should fight back by doing ..."

Sharon stopped arranging the tins of Colron Wood Dyes. "Does she, indeed? Well, well, fancy

78

that. And how would you feel about losing your identity as a specialist—you know, a committed DIY shop, a hardware man good and proper?"

"Committed, did you say? To an institution, you mean? Bring back the old days," I said. "When everyone knew what and who they were. High street shops are just a free for all, now. But what could we start selling? Every time I think about it I just go blank."

"Who knows, we might end up selling knickers."

"Oh, my God! Don't even think that sort of thing."

"They don't take up too much room, easier and neater to merchandise than any of this lot. But solving one problem usually leads to another, don't it, love? Like I been saying for a long time, hardware bites. You can't fight hardware."

I nodded in agreement; you couldn't do a bloody thing with hardware apart from mend stuff: it wasn't uniform, it didn't stack neatly, it fell, toppled, rolled, and could bruise your toes when it landed on your foot. She went on:

"So where do we put all this extra, *mystery* stock? There's no room for any more. Look at this place, it's cramped as it is. There's stuff that's been here longer than me."

"Yeah, me too."

"So how about we list it, see how much we fink we can get for it, and clear it out. Get shut. It's costing you money to keep it, and it stops you keeping stuff that will sell quicker. Even losing on it is better than having it cluttering the place up."

I agreed with her, smiling to myself. Just so long as Sharon thought it was her idea, then she'd give it her full support. Yes, things were beginning to look better.

"I been thinking," she said. "How many people want us to do jobs for them?" I froze. "Because people are willing to pay for stuff getting done—"

"Sharon, I hope you're not suggesting that—"

"—and getting it done right. I don't need to spell it out in big letters, do I? So that's the recovery sorted, then. So, we get like Woolworths, we take on more lines, and we get rid of the slow-movers to make room for 'em. We cut down on wages, don't fork out much, and we maximise income." I could see it working; that wouldn't be too painful. Yes, I could live with that. "And we send you out to do jobs."

"No, I'm not doing—"

"You're a proper little handyman, you are, Graham. Stuff like that comes easy to you. Can turn your hands to anyfing. You're a natural. You'll be a success."

She smiled. She had it sussed. She was in charge, but then so was the Accountant, and the MD. So where did *I* fit into it all? Nevertheless, compared with how I felt yesterday it was like someone had lifted a 50-kilo bag of cement off my shoulders. The trouble was, it had been replaced by having to go to people's houses to do silly little jobs like hanging pictures and sticking on draught excluder whilst getting savaged by dogs and housewives.


"Greville!"

There was no answer. For some reason he didn't always answer to his name and I had to break off to do a one-man search party around the aisles and all the nooks and crannies. Hardware shops are like that: even if the building is a perfect square, the nature of the fixtures and fittings will always make you end up with daft corners and cut off areas that are wasted space and good for nothing—except, that is, for hiding in. I found him in the office making friends with the MD. He must have been born with some natural instinct for survival that told him to get well-in with the big boss. If I didn't watch out it wouldn't be him in the dole queue, but me. For the second time that day I asked him if he was alright, and now he looked at me with suspicion.

The MD was displaying some reciprocal survival instinct of his own. "Right, lad, now keep on working hard. That's how I got where I am now—and I did it all single-handed, you know. I couldn't afford staff in them days, oh no."

"We can't afford staff in *these* days," I muttered.

"Ya what did you say?"

"I said we have a lot of expensive stuff in stock. Hard to afford it all," I said, raising my voice.

"Yes, you can say that again," and he switched on his hearing aid, fine-tuning the whistles that sounded like he was searching for Radio Jupiter. "And we have a lot of expensive stock."

I had almost sneaked out of the door when he shouted at me.

"Eh—where're you going? How did you get on with yond accountant?"

"She says she'll take a look at the figures."

"Take a look at the fixtures?"

"But the upshot is that we *must* diversify."

"You must specify? What?"

"We need to do something that no one else is doing."

"Aye, like not losing money. And what's *her* out there got to say about it?"

"You mean Sharon? She suggested that I go out and do jobs for people." *Maybe I should tell her it was the Accountant's idea! Maybe then she'll agree with me.*

"Well, it's how *I* started, you know."

"Yes, but that was before you became a shopkeeper. And I do not want to be like a tradesman and going to people's houses."

"Aye, they can be difficult to find, especially in the dark."

"And I'd have no one with me to read the map."

"In my day there were no maps."

"No maps?"

"Oh, aye, just after the war. And no sign posts. All taken down."

"Really."

"They were melted down to make bullets and confuse the enemy. But you know what'll happen, don't you, sometime in the future?"

I sighed. "No, but go on." At least this sort of thing kept him happy.

He put on his mysterious voice. "There'll be gadgets that'll tell you where to go."

"We've got them already—they're called maps."

"And they'll know exactly where you are and, wait for it, if you get lost these little gadgets will be able to direct you to where you want to be."

"Sounds like a big gadget, to me. Someone in the passenger seat perhaps, with a torch?"

"These devices will have every map built in to them, and there'll be no messing about wondering what direction you're facing."

"But you'll still need to stop and look at the damned thing, won't you?"

"What? Oh, no, no ... they'll show little pictures and probably talk to you."

"*Talk to you?* What a load of rubbish!" *He's really had lost it now. I wonder if we can get him sectioned ...*

"Oh, aye, you won't have to stop and read them. No, you'll be able to keep driving. It's all down to those tiny circuits things, you know. They can do marvellous things, these days."

"Cobblers."

"They might even come with a woman's voice. But what the hell women know about reading maps, I don't know."

The only invention I was interested in was one that enabled you to print your own bank notes. But then that would be illegal, wouldn't it?

Greville was still looking at me when I asked him, politely, to join me back in the shop, where we almost collided with a rather smartly dressed woman. She didn't even think about stepping backwards, seeming to repel us with some invisible seething force field. She was holding a plastic bag. Now, even if it had been the type you can't see through I'd have still known what was inside. Got a bit of an instinct, for that sort of thing, of the finely-tuned survival variety. And it never ceased to amaze me how people—even to all intents and purposes *posh ones*—could actually handle toilet seat fittings without wearing surgical gloves, and even they were but a poor substitute for a pair of industrial Marigolds. Reaching inside she handled the bits of plastic quite fondly, explaining in her precise accent that they were broken (as if I couldn't see that already) and then—and they always do this—she held them out to me in her palm so that I could have a feel also. Now, such items of sanitary hardware usually came into the shop in the same state as when they were last used: invariably they are stained yellow and they smell. There, I've said it. And you had to be very careful because the natural thing to do when someone offers you something is to actually take it from them. Well, I'd been in this game for too long and I knew how to keep my hands away from the counter, and instead I fondled the ten-metre Stanley PowerLock tape measure that was clipped to my belt. Greville shuffled over to me and I was tempted to put him in charge of old toilet seat fittings.

"Let's hope that these new ones will last longer than those have done," she said as a kind of warning that, if they didn't, she would be back to complain.

"How old are they?" I asked, as a matter of interest.

"I don't really know. They were in the house when I moved in."

"Have you lived there long?"

"Nineteen years. I'll leave the old ones with you to dispose of."

In a flash Greville held out the medical waste bin that we kept for just such items. I thought his training was coming on nicely. Good old Sharon.

"I reckon she fancies you," he said as we watched the woman stride towards the door.

"Oh, I hope not. She's too posh for me. And," I added, "I'm too particular for her."

"I wonder how it got broke."

"Just fair wear and tear, nothing for you to get all sinister about."

And then the phone rang. It was another nicely spoken woman—in fact, her voice was so similar to the toilet seat lady that at first I thought she was calling to ask if I'd go out and fix them on for her. Okay, so she'd only just gone out, but maybe she had one of those incredibly expensive-to-run mobile telephones, you never know. Thankfully it wasn't her. This was a rather strange call from the café in the street parallel with ours. She had just taken over and could we suggest a reputable tradesman who would be able to unblock her sink? I repeated the bit about the blockage and how I did know a plumber-cum-joiner or joiner-cum-plumber. When I looked up to get Brad's phone number off the wall, Sharon was smiling and pointing—at me.

# 10

*The café*

WELL SPOKEN AND NICELY mannered, her hair was immaculate, stylish and tasteful, as was the merest hint of expertly applied make-up. But her hands were red and scratched, her apron was filthy and the toes of her shoes were badly scuffed.

"Oh, you're from the hardware store. That's absolutely great." She stood back to let me in. "I've absolutely no idea when I'll have this place ready for the big day. Been a bit of a rush. I've been scrubbing the floor—it was ... *filthy*—you wouldn't believe the things I found down there," she said, leading me through the devastation that had recently been Ethel's Steak & Chips and into the back room. "... and I emptied the pail into the sink and, well, as you can see ..."

A pond of grey water with plenty of unmentionable floating bits was what I saw. I hoped that she didn't detect my feeling of horror and disappointment.

"I'll disconnect the trap," I offered, "but I'll need a bucket for it to empty into."

"A bucket? Oh. I have a pail ..."

"A pail will be fine," I answered as I knelt down to inspect my attack on the U-bend beneath the sink. All the plastic was yellow and brown and its crannies a mass of spiders' webs. The stench was a lethal mixture of stagnant water and ancient chip fat, and my stomach felt like it would be leaving any second—or rather, the breakfast in it.

From down there—and so I could get a tight grip on the large plastic nut holding the thing together—I had to face outwards, and the lady plonked herself down on an old chair so she could, a) take a rest, and b) talk to me as it was now my turn to struggle. Entertainment value, you see.

"I'm sorry I'm unable to offer you a drink," she said. "Sad state of affairs for a café, isn't it? I'd have made one for myself but I don't like the look of the kettle. I'd guess it's been playing host to a whole lot of micro-biological thingies for some time. Can't think what the last people were thinking about serving out of *that*. It's surprising that they weren't served a food hygiene notice."

Something made me pause, it was nothing to do with what she'd said, but she gave an audible little gasp.

"Oh, they didn't, did they?"

I banged my head getting it out of the cupboard to put her mind at ease.

"Please tell me that didn't happen! It would take me decades to overcome the bad publicity."

The look on my face told her that the reputation of the establishment was okay.

She laughed with relief. "I'm Rita, by the way."

"Rita?" Perhaps it came out as more of an exclamation, but I hadn't been able to stop it, and my head moved so fast that I scraped off some hair on the raw edges of the stainless steel sink. Those bloody things can be sharp underneath. Maybe I had led such a sheltered life, brought up on a diet of *Coronation Street*, *Crossroads* and *Emmerdale Farm*, but the name just did not go with the accent and mannerisms. Don't ask me why because I don't know.

I told her mine, and she asked how long I'd been a hardware man, to which I gave her a potted biography, briefly explaining how I fell into the job due to a cruel twist of fate.

"Here we go," I said as I reached for the bucket in time to catch the evil-smelling stuff that oozed out and then exploded over my body as the trap separated.

"My word!" said Rita, crouching down next to me. "Oh, my gosh. I can see this not exactly being a low-cost job, and I don't have much money. It isn't going to be *very* expensive, is it?"

I don't think I answered her; my attention was drawn to the items that had made definite little plops into the bucket. Now don't worry, I was wearing rubber gloves—after all, I had to eat my sandwiches with those same hands. But although I could now see up into the sink, there was still something lining the pipe. I scraped it out.

"Oh, my gosh! That isn't ... don't say it—just don't say it." Rita was now on her feet, making little paces right and left. "It is, isn't it? Oh, my gosh. I can't believe this. I should have known when I first saw this place. If only he'd invested it somewhere else, then it might have ... I'm right, aren't I?"

I got out the offending item and stood up. A cupboard under a sink is no place for a man. I gave it to her straight.

"It's a condom."

"No!"

"But don't worry—it's only a local custom."

She looked shocked, this time at my reaction. My eyebrows lifted and she saw the look and relaxed. At that moment I think we bonded. Sort of.

"But that's not the worst of it," and I reached into the bucket and pulled out a little slimy grey packet. Run under a hot tap it would possibly be revealed as the missing consignment of Class A drugs that the police never found in the Malt Hovel pub when they raided it about six months ago.

Rita peered at it, complete with disdainful expression.

"Why on earth would they pop that down the sink? It was obviously an accident."

"A reasonable hiding place, I'd have thought."

"Surely not. You can dispose of these things anywhere. They'll just rot, it all comes out of the earth, after all." How very liberal she was, I thought, if not exactly legal. "It probably came out when they emptied the teapot. Just carelessness, nothing more. But the condom—ugh! I can't think what that was doing in there."

So that was it: she had led a more sheltered existence than me.

"There are more of these," I said. "And they're *not* tea bags?"

"Oh, really? Then I wonder exactly what they might be ..."

## *The Boy and the Bubble*

Greville burst into the office. The MD had been going on at me again about taking on new staff. I really thought we'd sorted the issue, but he seemed to take great pleasure in bringing up old bones of contention when he felt like a fight.

"There's a bloke out there wanting a bubble for a spirit level." Greville's breathing was heavy, he had that wild, startled look, silently screaming, *What do I do?*

The old man was on his feet so fast I almost missed it, and he grabbed the boy's arm, leading him out into the shop.

"A bubble is it?" he called to the customer from over ten yards away. I didn't know he could actually see that far.

But I could, and there was no mistaking the startled look on the customer's face. He began to shuffle, he swallowed nervously and wondered how the hell he could get out of this. Then the MD took out one of the ancient mahogany drawers (with glass knobs) from the apothecary's cabinet and put it on the counter. He turned to Greville.

"I say, are you watching this?" Then, to the customer, "This'll be what you're wanting." He held up a small glass vial with green liquid inside. And a bubble. "Right?"

By the time the man had got his lips to start mumbling, the vial was in a small paper bag on the counter in front of him, waiting to be paid for.

"Call it just a couple o' quid," said the MD.

"You what?" He gave a nervous laugh. "I only wanted a bubble."

"That's all you're paying for. You get the vial free just to keep it in."

He'd been got, and he was squirming at the thought of forking out some cash. Maybe he should come clean about wanting to take the piss out of the boy.

"But I were just ..."

"They're like gold dust, are these. You'll not find one of them anywhere else. We're likely the only shop in the country. So come on, not got all day."

The man, stunned, handed over the money, turned and left. I couldn't see Greville's face, but I knew that I was shocked and amazed. I even felt—dare I say it?—a touch of admiration for the old boy. He didn't even seem over-pleased with himself. Shuffling back to the office, he said:

"That'll larn him."


"Have you got a lot of girlfriends?"

I suppose it was my job to answer all questions posed by junior members of staff, but surely not this kind.

"No. Have you finished straightening up those bottles? You've just skittled one—watch out ..."

And he caught the bottle of boiled linseed oil, a glass bottle, not plastic, before it rolled off the shelf. That really would have made a sticky mess all over the carpet.

"What they use this stuff for?"

"Boiled linseed?" I blew out, giving me time to remember. "It's for mixing with powder mastic and, er, glazing putty, I think." It was so out of date, I wasn't certain, but we sold lots of it. But then, in Little Sniffingham, that wasn't surprising. It was likely that someone knew somewhere that had an odd bag of powder mastic (used for filling the gap around wooden door and window frames), and because word had got around now there were cells of Little Sniffingham men, meeting clandestinely in garden sheds, passing on tips about mixing ratios and, thankfully for us, information about where you could buy the correct oil so they could save money by making their own. Quite often the economies of such practises didn't stack up, here's an example: a 250 mls bottle of oil cost 99p, whereas 1 kg of ready-mixed mastic sold for £1.99. So what was the bloody point, eh? No, I don't know either.

"There's that little piece from the newsagent's."

God, he was still at it.

"Maggie *is* the newsagent."

"Why do they call her—?"

"Have you seen her fingers? They're black. Why do you think that might be?"

"Oh, 'cos she sells Spanish?"

"You mean liquorice. No. Because she sells newspapers ... yeah?" No, there was that look again. "Don't go calling her that to her face, will you? That's our name for her. It's secret."

"You'd be alright, there. Sells tobacco—"

"Which is very bad for you—"

"So you could wake up with some shag and a free copy of the *Sun*."

I looked at him and shook my head.

"How long has it taken for you to think that one up? Well, Greville, thanks very much for pointing out the advantages of procuring intimate relationships with our fellow traders."

"Well, she does fancy you."

"I don't think so."

"Fair licking her lips at you, she—"

"The point is that I do not want any physical—I mean *emotional*—entanglements with fellow traders. Or anyone even vaguely connected with this business. I need to keep business and that other thing ... forgotten what it's called, begins with P ..."

"Pleasure?"

"That's it—*pleasure!* Business and pleasure need to be kept separate. Have you got that?"

"So what about that blonde woman that knocked on the glass and waved to you? She smiled as well, looked nice. I saw her."

"I have no idea who she is." And that was the truth.


Both Greville and Sharon had been cruel about Maggie Newsprint's attraction for me. Although I preferred to think of it as *admiration*, Sharon had another word for it. But in attempting to make up for these unkind comments, one lunchtime they bought me a packet of crisps and they even put real, instead of skimmed, milk in my coffee as a special treat and sat me down in the office with the latest copy of *DIY Week* to ponder over. The best part about it was the column written by trade insiders—there was a retailer, a wholesaler, a manufacturer and a sales rep. This sort of information was invaluable; it was like rubbing shoulders with industry professionals and it made me feel as if I wasn't alone. There was always Larry, I suppose, but we didn't see enough of him for it to count.

Later that day Gwendolin, the young woman from the Sunn Joly travel agent next door, asked if she could "borrow" me to sort out the bent pin on her computer's monitor plug. Trapped between her desk and the wall in her back office, she squeezed in beside me. She wasn't a slight girl, and was much taller than me, bulked out with big bones and a fantastic figure where everything was in proportion. One day she would make someone a great wife because she'd be able to take lids off jars and shovel snow off drives. She was beautiful, but just three or four sizes wrong for me.

Despite the claustrophobic circumstances, she tossed aside her shoulder-length dark hair and nudged me playfully. I looked to see if I could introduce some distance between us, but the wall wouldn't budge.

"Hey, Chuck," she said. "Thank you."

"Oh, it's okay. Soon have it sorted."

"Not that! I mean the garlic." And when she said it, her eyes sparkled.

"Garlic?" I began to feel worried.

"Yes, Chuck. I love the smell of garlic. Not many people do, you know."

"Oh, I wonder why that is."

I expertly inserted the snipe-nosed pliers into the plug and pretended to concentrate but Gwendolin, obviously bewitched by some aspect, took my hand and whispered to me.

"It's handy having someone like you next door. I get a lot of trouble with this plug ..."

*Sound grounding*

When I returned I thanked Sharon for the lunch. But she wasn't laughing.

"But it was you who played the joke. I don't understand."

"No, you don't," she said, casting a mean look at me.

There were a few seconds of silence before she went on, unable to stop herself. "Yes, it was funny. It was the boy's idea to treat you to the garlic and herb crisps. It was to put Maggie Newsprint off demanding your personal attention. He went to a lot of trouble to find them."

"In the shop's time, you mean." I don't know why I said that.

She turned on me with her finger aimed between my eyes. "It was just a harmless joke," she said. "We didn't mean no harm by it."

"Well, I can see the funny side of it. So why aren't you laughing?"

"Enjoy your job out, didja, round the caff?" She fired, taking me by surprise.

"Not bad. You could say I've joined the unhallowed ranks of the tradesmen. It was interesting—I say, you remember that police raid on the Malt Hov—"

"Is she cheap?"

"She hasn't opened yet."

"No, that bitch accountant!"

"She was smart without being flash. I'd say she has a sound grounding in—"

"Sound grounding, eh? So you've seen her underwear."

"What?" Where was this going?

"Well, she don't have saggy bits, does she?"

"Neither do you. Isn't that a good thing?"

"How much does she want you to pay her?"

"Oh, she said I shouldn't worry about it for the time being."

"Just as I thought, the crafty little cow."

"What's wrong with that? We're trying to save money."

"I grew up with women like her in the East End. She'll set her stall so's she can have the whole street. You watch out."

"She said we need to make cuts—"

Sharon turned around. "What cuts can you possibly make? You can't cut the stock because everything we stock we sell, the stupid cow. Huh! You put a tart in a nice frock and she thinks she can take over."

I didn't think there was anyfing—sorry, *anything*—I should say to that because Sharon was quite simply on the attack, and the sooner I could get away from her the better. *Please, customers— just flood into the bloody shop so that I can be busy.*

She spotted a particularly offending speck of dust on a tin of wax polish, wiped it and smacked the tin firmly down on the shelf so that all the other tins rattled in sympathy, with some even toppling off on to the floor. When she turned, the fury had gone out of her voice, and that wasn't a good sign.

"You got anything else to tell me about this cosy little chat that lasted only a minute?"

I felt my expression drop, but I couldn't look away from her. She went on.

"You've been nice to the boy."

"I'm nice with all my staff—"

"Very caring and considerate, you been." She wiped some fluff from a screw top, then turned on me, the duster aimed and ready to fire. "You got something to tell me and I want to hear it—and I want to hear it *now!*"

I swallowed. "You won't like this." Sharon took a deep breath. "The Accountant told me there are no YTS placements."

"*No YTS?* ... I don't believe it," she laughed cynically, but it quickly died.

"She says the town has only so many and they've all been taken. At least she's looked into it for us—"

"Who's taken them all?" Her voice sounded like it belonged to someone else.

"All Tools has them—"

"*All bleeding Tools?* Shit! Sodding bleeders,

waste o' time, the lot of 'em. They don't know the difference between a tube o' plastic wood and ointment for haemorrhoids. I'll tell you this now—if you're expecting to build this place up with just you and me and Mystic Meg in there, you need your head seeing to, 'cos you and me can't do it by our two selves."

She paused, and the piles of steel wool stopped wobbling on the shelf. "So where does that leave us?" She stood, all defiant. I swear that if anyone had entered the shop right at that moment they would have been sorry. When she spoke it was with a menacing tone. Maybe she had also played one of Macbeth's three witches.

"Here's the crunch line—can the boy stay?"

"Sod the boy," I said, trying to inject a lighter tone. "Can *I* stay? Can *you* stay? Can the MD stay? The way things stand, it's wages or rates ... We can't afford to pay both."

Sharon ripped off her overall, threw it at me and left the shop.

The MD appeared from the next aisle, jiggling one of his ears, looking happy with himself.

"I'm glad to see it's all working out fine for you," he said.

I asked him to explain, but not politely.

"Two down for the price of one, eh? Now then, keep up with the good work." I was speechless. "Look, lad," he said, poking me in the shoulder, "I built up this business from nothing and I did it all by myself. I couldn't afford to employ anyone. I hadn't the luxury of someone to make me coffee and dust shelves. There was only me. I did this *all* by myself—and I'd do it again if I had to."

"Well I'm glad to hear it because I'm about to lose two members of staff and I could do with some help."

Greville walked past, but avoided eye contact with me.

"Thanks for the crisps," I called to him.

Turning, he forgot himself. "Garlic and herb, they were—guaranteed to repel any female. Proof against the likes of Maggie Newsprint, eh?"

I suggested that he return the empty packet to Woolworths for a refund.

# 11

*Two months later*

THERE WAS JUST ONE woman at the number one cashier's slot in the bank. She was emptying children's money boxes into the coin well and could be there for a while, I thought, when I saw the cashier's look of terminal boredom as he began sorting the mass of snow-drifted bronze coins into neat piles. But hey, one of the female cashiers was available so I'd be able to get seen quickly and return to the shop.

The banking hall had one of the new single queue barriers (very space age) that most other institutions had taken on years before. Okay, so the Post Office didn't have one, but that was just par for the course. I negotiated the chrome-plated railings first one way, then a hairpin turn down the other side and then another, all the time passing the usual adverts for banking services: A4 cards showing happy, smiling faces of bank staff who are there just to help us to make the most of our money—that is, the bit they leave us with when all the charges have been levied. And at last I arrived at the end. This is where you would wait to be summoned to the next available cashier by a nicely-spoken lady in a tin box saying, "Cashier number two, please". But I was in a rush, there was no one else waiting, the female cashier (who, I must mention, had never before smiled at me or been willing to pass the time of day) was motionless. They were usually fiddling around with something, like checking cheques or tidying up their elastic band collection, but not this one, not now. So I went straight to her position.

And as I approached she slapped the TILL CLOSED sign on the ledge, sounding like I'd stepped on a landmine. I caught the smirk. *Typical, no surprises there.* I was retracing my steps to the cattle run when I heard her call out to me.

"It's okay, I can serve one more."

She was smiling—okay, so it was forced, but it was a start, and I handed over the paying-in book along with a stack of ten pound notes. Her fingers whisked through them at lightning speed, almost a blur. This wouldn't have been a bad trip out, I was thinking, in fact the quickest visit to the bank in a long time, and I looked over her shoulder at the clock on the far wall. When I looked back she was holding up one single tenner; she didn't even look at it.

"This is fake," she said. The false smile was gone.

I didn't believe it; it had happened all too quickly. I mean, one second she was whisking through the notes and then, with the nano-second accuracy of a high-tech detector, she had singled out the one dud. I asked to see it, and she refused, saying it would be handed to the police. But anyone would be able to tell, she told me, stretching it in her fingers, that it wasn't "right".

From where I was standing I could see that was indeed the case, and I knew that such a specimen had *not* passed through my hands. To this day I regret not accusing her of being mistaken, and suggesting that she consider that she might have got it mixed up with a note she had taken earlier ...? When I asked for a receipt, she refused again, but I insisted and she gave in, begrudgingly handing me a bit of torn-edged paper with her till stamp and £10 written on it. She wouldn't even initial it. I'll tell you this: the loss of even a measly tenner was a big blow to us, representing the profit on a number of time-intensive sales.

I had staggered from the bank along those back streets to the shop, pausing at a familiar doorway where I could compose myself without needing to look on the ground to see what the Malt Hovel's revellers had been consuming the previous evening.

Flashback a few weeks and the lad pretending to be a manager had phoned to tell me that time was up and their legal department would be in touch. He hadn't been watching the account balance, had he? And it *had* reduced—only by a few hundred quid, mind, but it was enough to demonstrate to him that we still had a future. And a carefully-worded letter (dictated by the Accountant) had warned the bank that, in the light of us undertaking a ruthless reorganisation of our trading practices, it would not be in the interests of their shareholders to terminate our business just yet. And it worked, but we were under no illusion that we were on borrowed time. But he was, after all, only the bank's mouthpiece, and told me there was no way the business would be able to pay back what we owed.

"The bank takes no satisfaction in foreclosing on a debt—"

"So don't do it," I told him.

"But we would like to see closure on this matter, clear it off the books so that everyone, including you and your managing director, can move on."

It sounded like they were doing us a favour,

allowing us the opportunity of *closure*, that I thought was very considerate of them. That's when I told him what the Accountant had told me to say.

"The bank owes its customers a duty of care, and has been negligent in allowing this trading debt to be reached. An overdraft might, in your school books—sorry, *text books*—be an overnight loan, but we are owed reasonable notice as well as other considerations," and some more stuff. And I asked it to be converted into a repayment loan over ten years. And do you know what the little twillock did when I asked? He laughed at me, as if I were trying to pass off reality from a fairytale. The Accountant warned me he would do this. So I told him that as far as I was concerned, he was the one wearing the back-to-front ski mask and brandishing a sawn-off rifle. We settled on five years; she said that's what would happen too. The repayments were crippling, the interest rate especially calculated almost as if we were being penalised for having borrowed so much. That left us with an obsession for paying in to the bank account numerous times per week to cover the repayments. Like the bank, we too would have been forced into committing highway robbery if our takings had not been enough, for the Accountant pointed out some small print in the loan agreement that warned of foreclosure *as soon as* a repayment was not made on the due date. The beggars had even tried to scupper us by sneaking in two repayments, instead of one, in the first month.

And then the Accountant pointed out that every time we paid in we incurred another bank charge for handling. So we nobbled that unprofitable practise and just paid in once every week.

Across the street from outside the Malt Hovel I could see a stream of people walking out of the shop, and momentarily I feared that the MD had been upsetting customers again wholesale. But when I went in, the aisles were almost impossible to negotiate because there were so many people in there. The only way I could get through was to ask them what they were looking for and then get past them. From the top I could hear Sharon warning a woman about using self-adhesive pads for hanging a mirror, and I knew that I could find myself being commissioned to go out and do the job properly (with brackets plugged and screwed). They didn't half like the idea of using sticky pads to hang heavy mirrors and even cupboards on to walls. The truth was that these pads could barely take their own weight without falling off. Next, Sharon asked if the mirror was in a frame. Believe me when I say that some customers didn't know what a frame was. I didn't hear the woman's answer, only Sharon's voice:

"... so you got it from the market, did you? ... Sorry, but I don't know what they're like ... yeah, they're all different sizes, you see. Have you measured it? ... I mean do you know how big it is ..."

Then a man's raised voice : "I was only asking you to let me see your ballcocks! It's a simple enough question, Laddie ..."

Fear struck me as I realised that the boy didn't know what a ballcock was. Dashing up past the long rows of curtain rails, I sat on the garden counter and swung my legs over, and within two or three seconds I was standing there next to Greville. He was doing his stunned expression towards the customer, wondering what to do or say next.

"Is that brass or plastic?" I asked the customer. He snarled that it was plastic and it was dribbling all over the place. Then he began making unkind comments about the so-called plumber who fitted it, when all he'd really wanted was an inch or so taking off the bottom of his bathroom door, probably because they'd got a new carpet—yes, carpets in bathrooms used to be very popular in Little Sniffingham. Had Brad Hall struck again?

From somewhere over my shoulder I heard the gentle hum of the photocopier as it began churning out multiple sheets of 80g A4 paper. I could just see Lucy from Book'n'Go, the travel agent across the high street. They ran their smaller shops on a bit of a shoestring and didn't have in-house photocopiers or even fax machines, so they used our new office service (expansion, you see). And they received a lot of faxes, all of which came down our telephone line, with the machine spewing out yards of thermal paper, curling around the floor like an Andrex toilet roll that's been hijacked by a Labrador puppy.

Just then the horrific screeching of the nine-inch circular saw carved up all other sound, meaning that the MD was using his expert skills cutting plywood panels to size and it would be another hour or so before our ears stopped ringing. I set Greville on with sorting through the other customers. Super glue, sandpaper, white spirit, paint for plastic models (recent Christmas presents), sink plungers, light bulbs; as fast as the problems were fired at us, an appropriate product was dispensed. An old favourite was wire for net curtains; the people of Little Sniffingham liked to watch out at other people but didn't like people outside watching in on them, and we went through miles of the stuff. Even the concrete floor, which although it was usually bloody destructive to our feet, felt as though we were floating on air when trade was like this. Finally the door closed and we were clear. Not bad for a morning's rush.

So you see, we had been expanding our range of offerings to the public, with the fax and copier business highly profitable. The girls from the other travel agent next door, Sunn Joly, also used us, and when they came face to face with the girls from

Book'n'Go they didn't see themselves as rivals but as colleagues in one big happy travel industry, which is more than could be said for our shop and All Tools. I still couldn't get over them wangling all those training placements—speaking of which, Greville handed a wad—no, make than an envelope—to me.

"Didn't get time to give you this before you went out. Me dad says if it's not enough, to send a message."

"Send a message? What's he mean, by carrier pigeon? Why don't I just tell you?"

Squeezing it between my fingers, it felt about right so I thanked him.

"Oh, and by the way," I called to him and Sharon. "There's some fake ten pound notes in circulation, so be careful. And before we take any more round to the bank, we're going to fan them out and photocopy them. I'll explain why later."

The MD rattled his way out of the office.

"Someone's just rung. There's a job for you. They want you straightaway," and he gave me the details which he'd scrawled on the back of a supplier's invoice.

"What's the problem?"

He inserted a four inch round nail very carefully into his ear and began twisting it.

"It's this damned ear wax again."

"No—what sort of job is *this?*"

"Oh, I've no idea. That's for you to find out," and he inspected the debris on the end of the nail.


*The boat*

Raindrops began to spit on the small flagged yard of the Victorian terrace house. *Small* didn't do it justice because it was tiny, with hardly enough room for a rabbit hutch. Although this was now considered to be the posh end of the town (particularly by the estate agents), when built these particular houses would have been the homes of senior clerks and junior managers of the local textile industries. The decor of the 19th century had been darkened walls and murky-painted timber, with panelled doors and multi-spindled banister rails. In the 1960s the fashion was to flush the doors with hardboard to make them flat, box in the banisters and block up the fireplaces to accommodate the very latest electric fires—some with *real plastic coal effect*. Wow! The MD's business had been built by supplying the materials for such architectural desecration. And, just like the Victorians in their time never spared a thought for the wanton destruction of Medieval timber-framed properties, so the people of the 1960s threw out (or at the very least *concealed*, which isn't anywhere near as wicked) the ornate splendour of the Victorian era.

And standing on the doorstep I wondered exactly where my services might fit into the scenario. I mean, perhaps they needed the hardboard removing from the doors to expose the valuable panelling beneath. I could do that. At that time a whole new trade in dipping cowboys had sprung up, specialising in stripping painted and varnished doors and furniture by drowning them in large tanks of acid. And yes, it would remove most of the painted-on gunge, but it would also neutralise the adhesive holding the pieces together, and we got our fair share of extra trade selling modern wood glue, so it wasn't all bad news. Of course, when the customers didn't use it properly then they would return to the shop and slag us off for selling them rubbish. If I were about to be asked to sort out a house full of doors I would not be using the dipping merchants.

Or perhaps a banister spindle might be loose or

needed replacing with an exact match. That could be arranged 'cos I knew a woodturner. And there must be some reason why they had called me instead of one of the many tradesmen in this area. Perhaps this job required some sort of delicate touch that the others didn't possess. That was indeed possible. Or maybe, I began to fancy, it was a job far too difficult for ordinary mortals to complete with any degree of success—which meant they were now scraping the bottom of the barrel and that's where they found me. But whatever they wanted me for, they were taking their time answering my knock.

The raindrops were making definite plops on my head when the door was sharply opened and a bedraggled teenage lad pushed past me and waited expectantly at the end of the path. The door opened wider and a middle-aged woman with bleached blonde hair, an unfortunate squint and bright red lipstick took a commanding position on the doorstep. She pointed to him.

"You *will* get to school, you ungrateful little brat. After all I've done for you. If your dad was here—"

"Well he would be if you hadn't made him bugger off," came the teenager's retort.

It was only then I noticed that the woman was holding an empty milk bottle. She threw it at the boy. He ducked and it smashed onto the pavement.

"Now look what you've made me do!" she screamed, then turned to me, almost taking my head off. "What do you think *you're* looking at?"

Her expression suddenly changed. I thought she had recognised me from the shop, but then she dragged me inside, slammed the door and we were standing in the entrance hall. The sound of the rain had been replaced by an annoying gurgling of water from somewhere upstairs. She was about to prod me into the living room but I beat her to it, for in there was a boat—yes, that's right: a twelve-foot, carvel-built rowing boat. It dominated the whole room, seeming particularly high, probably because it was resting on wooden blocks. I didn't see any oars, but I did notice that it had been competently painted and bore the name *On the Rocks*.

"I want *that thing* out of here," she said.

"Right. Where do you want it putting?"

"*Out of the house!*" she shrieked, making me shiver.

"How did you get it in?"

"*He* built the damned thing in here, that's how. I just want it out. I don't care what you do with it. Just get it out of my sight."

She was still rather worked up and her breathing was noticeable and quick. I watched her looking at the item as if it were some huge monstrosity which, if you have one stuck in your front room, I suppose it is. She loathed its existence, and I could only guess why.

"So can you do it?" she asked.

By this time I was on my hands and knees, drawn to the exquisite beauty of the workmanship, inspecting the quality of the woodwork at the keel, wondering where the hell the builder had managed to find a length of wood of that particular section. It was beautifully smooth, with all the plank edges slightly rounded, and the paint surface was so good it was as if the whole thing had been moulded in glass fibre. But there was no mistaking the quality and the exquisite craftsmanship.

For the sake of something to say, I said, "Could be tricky."

"Of course it's bloody tricky—that's why I called you!" Then something occurred to her. "You are from All Tools, aren't you?"

"Er ... yes. I sometimes ... do—"

"No, you're not! I know where you're from! I wanted those All Tools people, not *you*. You'd better go."

I wasn't going to leave without that boat. Her hand was shaking. She swallowed.

"Well, you're here now, I suppose. Can't you cut it up or pull it to bits? Get it out the same way it came in?" She was talking sacrilege, now.

"What—you mean in bits? It's not just as simple as that. I mean, this is *a work of art*."

"Don't talk shit."

"But it is, it's craftsmanship. That'd be wanton destruction."

"Then I'll get someone that will smash it—and be glad of the job."

She took hold of my arm and shoved me towards the door, but at the last moment I grabbed the boat's transom and we somehow got our legs twisted and ended up in a heap on the floor. Our faces were too close for comfort. I was mesmerized by the squint. I could smell the lipstick. A quick change of subject was called for.

"Have you had a new toilet cistern fitted recently—say, in the last three years?"

"Yes. Why?"

"And now it takes about fifteen minutes to fill after being flushed?" She let go of me. "You bought it from All Tools, didn't you?"

"How did you know that?"

"It needs a new diaphragm washer."

"Right. Then I'll get—"

"And it needs putting in properly. It's a peculiar model that was never meant for the UK market. Very tricky."

"Oh. And how long would it take to get—"

"I could do it straight away for you."

The barbed wire in her voice turned to soft grass. "You mean ... now? You've got one with—"

Her eyes softened, and she closed the one that didn't line up properly. I must have been too close, making her feel uncomfortable with both of them open. I remembered seeing that very look in the eyes of teenage girls when I told them I had a car—when I was also a teenager, that is, although none of them had an alignment issue. She swivelled around on her knees then rested on her haunches, her skirt riding pretty much all the way up her thighs—and she wasn't bothered. I stood up quickly to distance myself. What was it with these women? Later it would occur to me that maybe, subconsciously perhaps, they considered me to be some kind of house doctor, thereby trusting me with ... things. Anyhow, she followed and shuffled to her feet and put her hand on my arm and tried to smile. I could tell she wasn't used to it. I needed to be firm.

"No, really—you don't need to do that."

"But I don't have a man, you see—"

She tightened her grip. Have you ever heard of vice grips or mole-grips? They're like big pliers that lock closed. Well that's exactly what her fingers were like on my arm. I couldn't help thinking that we kept spare springs for such equipment, as I tried to prise her away.

"Really, it's okay. It'll take me about ten minutes and then I'll make a start on the boat." I had been nodding like some toy dog in a car's rear window (a relic of the 1960s).

She backed off, hesitantly smiled, rubbing the red marks she'd imprinted on my arm. Then she looked down and went into the kitchen. After a few minutes upstairs with her toilet cistern, I set to work measuring up the dimensions across the widest part of the boat's beam and the depth of the bow (the highest part of the boat). Then, when I heard her filling the kettle, I measured the window frame and, with a feeling of excitement, determined exactly where it was fastened into the wall.

# 12

"SO WHAT HAPPENED?" SHARON always liked some involvement in the various activities. It made her feel less isolated.

"The old dear had poured a pint of straight thirty down the cooling vents."

*Straight 30* is a type of engine oil used for petrol lawnmowers.

"Isn't that the right grade for a mower?" she asked.

"Not for an electric one."

The MD opened the office door and waved us in. He took out a stick of tar-like tobacco and began motioning with it.

"It seems to me that you want to see how much money you need to take to keep on going and still get them buggers at the bank off your back."

I nodded.

He sighed. That was suspicious. "We might need to make some changes—"

"But not to the staff," said Sharon.

"Well, we'd have to see about that." Using the pipe as a thinking prop, he went on. "No, I think the best way is to work out how much we've got going out and how much we need coming in to pay for it all, and then make some adjustments."

Oh, it sounded so simple. I mean, why hadn't Sharon and I thought of that? He would ignore my expression tinged with sarcasm. And he hadn't yet finished.

"You'll need to up the stakes a fair bit, like chucking out some useless lines," He meant low profit margin power tools. "And have a bit of a sale—not much of one, mind. We can't do with giving owt away. And maybe even increase the opening hours. Little sacrifices, that's what we need. Everyone'll have to chip in and work a bit more for a bit less."

We told him that's exactly what we would do, making him feel like he was the first to suggest it. He began to refill his pipe with the plug of liquorice-coloured crap he had just cut with a knife. I think the tobacco connoisseurs called it "twist".

"And there's no time to lose," he said.

"Right then," I said to Sharon. It looked as if we might get some extra time out of him. Little sacrifices and all that. "That should certainly help with Saturdays, shouldn't it?"

"If you think I'm coming down here on Saturdays, you've another think coming," he said.

Sharon and I looked at each other.

"Maybe we can discuss this another time," I said.

"Just so long as it's not tomorrow, because I won't be in."

"Oh. Right." He was usually in. Maybe he had an appointment. "The day after, then."

"I'm going on part-time from today."

Sharon and I looked at each other, speechless.

"I'll be doing just two days a week from now on. And that doesn't include Saturdays."

I knew it had all been going too well, and I felt my shoulders sink.

"Why not? I mean, it's not as if you've got children that you want to spend quality time with, or that you need to pick up from school."

"Saturdays is out. That's when the missus wants to go shopping. Saturday is shopping day. Monday is washing day. Wednesday is mashed potatoes, processed peas and pork chops. And Saturday is definitely shopping day."

"Shopping day," I said, but I didn't sound too convincing.

"Aye, that's what I said. It's a big tradition in our family."

"But if you go part-time you can take her shopping some other day of the week, when the shops will be quieter. Much better for her."

And he stuck the pipe in his mouth, turned down his hearing aid and said no more.


"Have you got any legs?" was a common enquiry. Sharon was always tempted to ask the customer what the hell they thought was holding her up. Another one was, "Do you have much in the way of legs?", to which we would have loved to reply, "Well, I think they're okay." But you had to be careful because some people didn't have a sense of humour, and if they had it was only on their own terms, when they thought fit to joke, usually not at their own expense. So she kept quiet.

Yes, we stocked a large range of legs for coffee tables. These tables were mainly slabs of compressed sawdust with a picture glued on top, popular in Great Britain from the 1960s, and still the height of fashion in Little Sniffingham thirty years later. We also kept a small selection of other legs in the hope that someone more discerning might fancy doing a weekend repair job with barley twist or Queen Anne—see what I mean? What do you think goes through a teenager's mind when someone marches into a shop and wants to look at your Queen Annes, or says "Can I have a look at your legs?"

Greville had already fallen foul of the confusing terminology: nipples, male end, female screw (not that there's any such thing, but confusion was rife in Little Sniffingham). On many an occasion men had asked Sharon, "Can I see what knockers you've got?" I kid you not—and the really sad thing is that few of them realised what they had actually said.

Greville was upset when someone asked him for a ball pein (an engineer's hammer), but without actually saying the word "hammer". "I want to see your strippers" was another old favourite. When someone told Greville, "I want some thinners," he was proper flummoxed. He kept asking the customer, "Thin as what?"

Oh, and the number of men asking for Vaseline (petroleum jelly). We sold a lot of it for screw-on plumbing fittings; I personally swore by it because the lubrication meant they could be eased that little bit tighter, thus forming a better seal against water pressure, without damaging the threads. We went through loads of the stuff. At least, I assume that's what they were using it for.

In our own way we needed to be linguists, translating vague descriptions, wildly-incorrect terminology, malapropisms and old wives' tales into sales. And mind-reading was a very necessary skill. Okay, so we are all talking in English, but we certainly were not speaking the same language.

I'd just come down from upstairs and went to the till. Sharon had a customer.

"Now then, love, what are your legs like at the top?"

See what I mean? Roughly translated, it means: "How do your table legs attach to the top?" She sold him a set of nine-inch legs and plates (for easy fitting).

"We nearly sent a search party to look for you," said Sharon. It wasn't like her to comment on the length of time someone had been in the toilet.

"There's something not quite right up there," I muttered.

"Oh. It's probably nothing. I've been sorting the sandpaper out. All mixed up they were. People never put things back where they found 'em."

"No, there's a smell." But I had other things on my mind, so the stink could wait until another day. "It's a sort of *farmyard* smell."

"The MD will have something on the shelves for that," she laughed, nervously looking for some other distraction. It wasn't like her not to exercise her forensic obsession for the elimination of unpleasant smells.

"It's like animals." That would be my parting shot on the matter. For today.

"Oh—it's these old buildings, you know. My great grandma had a—"

Sharon stopped when she saw I was counting the notes in the till.

"Is everything all right?"

"Just checking," I said, quickly trapping the notes under the retaining spring and closing the drawer.

"Is there anything I can do to help?"

"What? No—nothing, thanks. Everything's okay." I began to walk away, but she hadn't finished with me.

"Graham, I'm not blind and I'm not stupid."

"It's okay, I'm just monitoring the situation—just so I know what's happening. Got to keep tabs."

I didn't tell her that I hadn't been paid for five weeks—well, it was no longer a wage exactly, more like the absolute minimum that I needed to pay my electricity bill and rates. And other luxuries like a loaf of bread and a tin of SPAM. Margarine had become something of a luxury. I was aware that we had all entered into what later would become known as a policy of financial transparency, whereby we were open about the money, or lack thereof, but at the same time I felt I needed to put a cap on the severity of the situation, for making available that degree of information to even a modest workforce could amount to professional suicide—you know. where everyone jumps ship before depression takes hold. I had made up my mind to never tell her just how desperate things were, and I was determined to stick with it, no matter how much pressure she applied to make me spill the beans (or should that be nails?).

"Right then, so I take it you're hard up—personally, I mean."

"Yes, I am."

"Hmm. How hard up is that?"

"Pretty hard."

"Compressed fibre board hard?"

"What? That's not hard. You can poke your finger through it."

"Okay. Three to one mortar, then?"

I screwed up my face and wiggled my fingers towards her.

"Surely not as hard as concrete?" she said.

"Perhaps, but only a mix of three-two-one with *small* aggregate." It was still concrete, though, and you wouldn't ever want to bang your head against it.

She blew out. "Well, that's not good, Graham, that's not good at all."

"Could be much worse," I said, wanting to get away and have a minute or two alone in the glory hole.

"So will you be able to manage?"

"Oh, yes. No problem, no problem at all."

But she knew that I knew that she knew that I was lying.

## *Drilling a-loan*

Sharon placed the coffee on the MD's desk—we'll it was his desk when he decided to turn up, and I have to say that I missed him being on the premises six days a week. I was looking through the latest power tools catalogue; that's the sort of thing hardware men do. Sad, I know. Even sadder was that we didn't have the wherewithal to buy any.

Sharon's perfume wafted my way, not just as bold as the Accountant's, but I knew that she had stepped it up in recent weeks. There must have been some sort of power contest going on.

"I can't think why it is that some men's mouths water when they look at electric drills. They're like kids in a sweet shop," she said.

"But it's not just drills—"

"When all they really want is *holes*." One look at my face would tell her I was in no mood for philosophical discussion. She sighed. "You seen the post, have you?"

Oh, the post. I had begun to delay looking at it straightaway because it tended to be statements from suppliers and I would need to set aside some time to carefully balance the money between paying them and the bank; a real knife-edge decision. On top of that were the bank charges that we were desperately trying to reduce. Like I've said, the bank charged us every time we paid in. In fact it was a system of multiple charges so if we paid in cash, cheques and credit card vouchers, then we were charged four times and all for one credit slip. They certainly knew how to rack up their profit, but it was sod everyone else. To reduce them we had taken to paying cash to the wholesalers' reps. But it was something of a juggling act. Squeezing blood out of a stone is one age-old cliché that describes how it felt.

I ignored the pile of envelopes, but Sharon pointed to a fat one on top of the pile. It looked rather like an end of the month statement from Bird & Sons, but this wasn't the month end and it could only mean that they had learnt of our difficulties and decided to close our account before they ended up with a whopping great loss. That sort of thing happened; Larry had told me, and Bird's didn't offer second chances if it meant they might lose even more money by trying to be helpful and flexible. "We trade in hardware, not sentiment," old man Bird had once told the MD about fifty years before. I remember the feeling in my gut that morning. Ninety per cent of our stock came from them, and finding a replacement for that huge range, as well as someone else who would deliver twice a week to a tiny place like Little Sniffingham, would be damn near impossible. Squashing the small envelope between my fingers, I began to feel angry—I mean, who the hell had said anything to Bird's about the pickle we were in? Who had blabbed? Or had the bank bounced one of our cheques? Yes, that was more like it. News in the trade of unpaid cheques could have disastrous consequences and usually meant premature business closure.

I dug the old paperknife into the brown packet and its contents dumped on to the desk top. Then I sat down, involuntarily, and tentatively reached out for the wad of fifty pound notes. A bundle of bank notes in the post should have been accompanied by a fanfare of trumpets, but since the bother with the bank had begun (no alliteration intended), suspicion had begun to taint almost everything, and we had been warned that there were a number of forgeries in circulation. But despite that, there was something about the smell of these notes that told me they were real. My hands were shaking as I counted; there were fifty of them.

"Wotcha got there, Graham? Ooh, looks like someone's paying a bill in cash."

I shook my head. "But no one owes us this much."

"Where's the note? There has to be one."

"There's fifty of 'em. That's two and a half grand."

I remember her sharp intake of breath. Even she was stumped for a comment. I shook out the envelope and a small, insignificant piece of lined paper wafted out of it. so light it evaded my fingertips as it spiralled towards the desk. It was typed and all it said was "a loan".

Greville burst in.

"What is it?" we both shouted at him.

"There's a woman out there wanting baguettes."

"And?"

"I sent her to the Co-op Food Fair."

"You did what?"

"Well, she wants 'em for her barbeque. She says she got them from here last time." He spoke as if he had the edge on me, as if I was hard of hearing, or maybe just daft.

Sharon stepped in to help. "Down by the charcoal and lighting fuel, my love, you'll find the briquettes."

He straightened a little, with an indignant expression. "That's not what she asked for."

"But it's what she wants," I told him, getting up to deal with the customer. There was something about the unexpected cash that frightened me; as if it had no right to be there, on the desk—or even on the premises at all, and I wanted to put some distance between me and it, just until I got used to the idea of it being, well, *available*, if only temporarily. Greville's eyes homed in on it and I caught a glance of him pulling a face at Sharon. Just as I went out I heard him say to her,

"Does that mean them upstairs can stay a bit longer?"

He must have thought I was out of earshot. The pieces fell into place; I heard it quite distinctly because it happened right inside my head, and when I'd sold a bag of compressed charcoal, I shot upstairs to the redundant attic. The way through had been blocked with large pieces torn from cardboard boxes, stretching untidily, and quite dangerously, across the stairway like some sort of barricade, and I fought with them as I pushed through to where, in the centre of the floor, was a clumsily-cobbled together six-foot square melamine pen containing seven rabbits: four white, three grey. Rushing back down the stairs, I bawled out Greville's name but the shop doorbell clanged as the perpetrator got clean away.

"There's a woman out there," said Greville, seeming somewhat flummoxed.

"That's good."

"And she's really taking the piss. What do I say? Can *you* come and sort her out?"

"What has she said?"

He laughed. "She's wanting steel wool."

"So?"

He hesitated, trying to gauge if I was joking. "Steel wool? I mean ... no. She's having me on ... *Isn't she?*"

"How do you think they knit chain mail for jousting knights?"

I had to go out and show him where we stocked the steel wool (it was a big selection, with all the different weights and grades), and I wondered just how many hundreds of times he'd walked past the stand and never given it a moment's thought. Then I was interrupted by a voice from across the shop.

"I hear you've got a boat for sale."

It was Rodney, the town's *character*, an example of "care in the community" or deinstitutionalization. Let's just say he was exceptionally eccentric and always managed to detect someone's sore spot and wallop it with unerring accuracy. He never bought anything from us, but had certain shops in the town that he liked to frequent just for, I suspected, socialising

117

purposes. As a child I remembered that he had once made a parachute jump, and he had fascinated the MD with his description of giving himself to the air and trusting his life to harness and fabric. The problem was that he was still able to make *me* jump whenever he sprang out from behind a shelf unit, like now, grinning rather cruelly.

"How daft can you get?" he wobbled at me, his eyes spinning almost like targets through his milk bottle-bottomed glasses.

"Indeed," I said. I had to look away because making eye contact with him made me go dizzy.

"There's no sea round here! It's miles away! Hasn't nobody ever told you?" It really did sound as if he was telling me off.

"There's a canal," I fired back and, just as he was about to open his mouth, I went on. "And a river." *So there! Try getting round that.*

"Ah, but there's big boulders in that river. You didn't know that, did you? But you see I know about these things, and the keel of yond boat you've got will catch on 'em, wreck it to bits."

I couldn't help but frown. "It's not got boulders."

"It has! You'll get your bum wet."

When he put his head to one side and made his eyes go bigger, then you really were in trouble, and he knew it and pressed home his advantage. "And don't think you can go sailing it on the canal 'cos that's not allowed."

It was easier not to argue any further, and he backed off, grinning.

"Right, I'll be off. Got other people to see. I do hope you've enjoyed our little chat as much as I have," and he reached out to shake my hand .

"Yes, Rodney, I have. Thank you for calling in."

Shaking hands with him always lasted an uncomfortable few seconds longer than necessary, but today it was as if we were stuck together with cyanoacrylate adhesive—and that's strong stuff. Drawing me closer to him, he said in a lowered, intimate tone, "You'll be alright now, won't you?"

I had no idea what he meant (I never did), and just wanted him to let go of my hand, so I nodded, and as soon as he let go he was on his way to mess up someone else's day.

But what did he mean by *You'll be alright now ...?*


"Have we seen anything of Adrian from the chip shop lately?" I asked Sharon, after the MD had settled himself at the desk to have another go at completing the PAYE return.

"I see his lad up and down, but that's all."

"Can't think how he's managing to hang on all this time. I mean, when does he actually sleep? How long has it been?"

"Maybe he's also had a little brown envelope, like you."

"I'm not at all happy about that."

"I hope you've used it to pay something off the loan."

"You mean I've used one loan to pay something off another one?"

"There's no point in having it stand idle. Someone's done you a big turn there. Not good to throw it back in their face."

"I wish I could put a face to the mystery benefactor. I can't think of any Magwitch-types round these parts, can you?"

"I played Estella in *Great Expectations* once. In Hackney it was. That was a while since. They'd probably give me Miss Havisham, now. We need to be very careful. It's in our interests for Adrian to keep trading, 'cos if *he* goes then the bank only needs to turn the screws here."

"And we've got something on the shelves for

that," I said, impersonating the old man.

"Then we'll be the prime target." She shivered, which was as infectious as a yawn. "And, whoever or whatever's behind it all, then they win."

"At least then we'd find out what it's all been in aid of."

# 13

*28 weeks later*

"HAVE YOU MANAGED TO pick that Yale cylinder lock, yet?"

I'd been teaching Greville a few of the more basic lock-smithing techniques.

"No. I can do the Chinese one, but not the Yale."

The Chinese imports had been manufactured from the tooling that had been sold off cheaply by the British manufacturers because there were no longer any spare parts for them. I have no idea what they thought the foreign buyers were going to do with it all. Melt it down, perhaps? I'll tell you what they did: they set up their own tooling industry to make the required spare parts and then moved into manufacturing traditional British-looking locks at imported prices. And who do we blame for that? Having explained what happened, though, there were some differences in quality: the brass was soft stuff from India, and the intricate workings didn't quite come up to our old traditional standards which was why it was easier to pick a lock from the Far East. Greville was working with the genuine lock cylinder held in a vice, with two picks inserted, but kept sighing.

"Quality, you see," I told him. "British craftsmanship. Best there is." *Or was*, I thought.

"So what about Japanese electronics? They're the best."

"Well, yes, but—"

"And Swiss watches?"

The MD, who was unusually late (maybe he'd had a hospital appointment; I never asked) shuffled in with his briefcase, but stopped off at the counter on his way to the inner sanctum.

"I thought you'd better know summat. Yond chippie mate o' yours round the back ..."

I felt my shoulders sag. Of course, he could have been about to say that he'd been talking with Adrian.

"Well, there's a couple of big vans out there loading up all his stuff—tables, chairs, even them big frying ranges. And the shifters are going on, cursing at the tops of their voices because there's no electric."

He waited a few seconds for the news to sink in, then nodded and went on his way.


"Do you mind sending your lad to sort out that plug—it's gone faulty again and I'm getting sick of it."

And that was it; the man from the Pru was gone. This wasn't the first time he had requested— no, make that *demanded*—that we do a house call to sort out his problem. By *plug* he meant *socket* (the thing you stick the plug into), but they were always getting them mixed up, except when it came to sex. As for *Pru,* that's *Prudential*, an insurance company whose reputation was founded on boot leather men that called on housewives in post-war years and collected premiums in instalments—a shilling a week, that sort of thing, a custom that lasted about forty years, beginning in the days when very few working class people had bank accounts. And the faulty plug? The failure rate for telephone plugs—I mean *sockets*—in that house was high, very high. In fact it was more like an epidemic.

Greville was now six months into his apprenticeship and had taken a liking to installing telephone extensions, so much so that I encouraged him to work out in his own time for extra money, even allowing him to make the profit on the parts. No doubt, reading this, traders will be shocked and wanting to burn effigies of me for being so bad at maintaining the them and us policy when it came to staff perks, and people from the other side of the counter will (or might, at least) hail me as a saint. But we should remember that for the past six months it was his father, a baker as it turned out, who was ... how can I put this? ... *easing* the facility by which we managed to keep Greville in training (or "off the streets" as I termed it). After all, I said to Sharon, he could afford it because he had plenty of dough. But back to this particular client who was proving a great source of butt-ache.

The lad returned from an errand. I knew he'd been out for a crafty drag with one of the girls from the travel agent's (I never found out which one—agent or girl).

"The good news is that you've a phone job, tonight," I said to him.

"But I can't—"

"And the bad news is—what do you mean, you *can't?*"

"Baby sitting."

"You? Baby sitting? Whatever next?—Hey, I hope it's not your own ..."

He began to look frightened. Or was it surprised? I interrupted when it turned to pride.

"Well it's tough. A customer has asked for your personal attention."

"Ooh, not that pair at the Lodge. The buses are one an hour. That's no good. Well, they can't have me."

"He realises you're the best we have."

"I'm already booked. And he'll claim that we sold him a duff socket. There'll be no money in it."

"What time are you babysitting?"

I explained how he could make just a slight detour, do the phone job and be on his way and arrive with the infant in good time. He argued back that it was impossible to get out of the Lodge in good time and that every paying job he'd ever done there had needed to be undercharged on labour.

"I'm not going," he shouted. "Just the thought of those people keeps me awake. They're horrible."

"I don't care if you lose sleep."

"You go—then you'll see what I mean. I don't ever want to set foot in that dog piss-ridden hole again."

"That's not very nice. Our customers deserve respect. You're going."

"I'm not. It stinks."

"You are."

"No way." Greville was adamant.

So was I.

## *The Curious Incident of the Dog in the Evening*

The doorbell burst into a cheesy Hong Kong medley of 1960s' British top ten hits, every one of them well and truly murdered. That set the dog barking—a high-pitched tin can sort of a sound that jarred one's eardrums. The suit opened the door. It was the same one that had summoned us (—that's a royal "we") here.

"Oh," he said, looking round behind me. "So where is he?"

"He had a previous booking," I said, and with

some degree of telepathic grunting he let me in. The first thing I noticed was the pincer-like teeth clamped around my ankle. It was a whitish West Highland Terrier and it wasn't for letting go of me. It bothers me to this day just how it could sink its teeth into my leg and bark at the same time. That bloody *Yap! Yap! Yap! Yap! Yap! Yap! Yap!*

The woman came into the room and told it to be quiet, but it didn't hear.

"He's just excited," she said, moving towards me and leaning down for the dog, with her cleavage about to empty onto the floor. She had to pull whatever-his-name-was away from me and almost took my leg and threw that into the bedroom along with the dog. It was all fuss and excuses for the mini-mutt and telling me about his pedigree and how his father almost sired all the pups in one county. I can't remember what it was that stopped him. Her husband pointed to a telephone extension socket on the skirting board and I plonked down the toolbox and knelt beside it. That was when the stench hit me, I hadn't realised I had hairs inside my nose until just then when they started to burn.

"Dead, is it?" I asked, but they didn't hear. I plugged in a line-tester; there were no little red lights, so right enough there was no dial tone. I removed the socket cover—which was extremely sticky. In those days disposable latex work gloves had only just made their way into hospitals so there was no way we could have them. But what I wouldn't have paid right then for just one pair.

It was as I thought: the terminals inside the socket were corroded. Unfortunately they were made from steel so they weren't the best material to use as proof against dog urine—and that was why the sockets kept on failing.

I looked around, trying to get some eye contact, but the couple was discussing some papers as if I was not there. Tradesman, you see; to them I was a mere underling.

"I've found the problem," I called. The suit raised his voice to drown me out and I was ignored. There was no way I was going to leave them with a brand new socket free of charge, so I packed up my stuff as loudly as possible, throwing the tools into the box and giving them a good rattle and I made for the door. That got the suit's attention.

"Have you fixed it, then? Oh, good. How long do you think this one will last?"

I turned to face him. "It wasn't a faulty socket. It's been drenched with ... some liquid." I don't know why, but I didn't like to say.

"Don't talk bloody stupid!"

"Harry, let the man finish."

"Dog urine." I put it nicely.

"Don't piss me about."

"I'm serious. I've left it down there on the carpet. I'm not picking it up and I must charge you for the replacement if I fit one. Which I haven't."

Harry the suit looked at me with the look of someone who wished he dare thump me. But it was the cleavage that spoke.

"Erm, what are you trying to say? That we've had some sort of ... animal in here?" She was very good, I'll give her that. Her expression was faultless: I could almost believe her.

"He's trying to make out that someone's been pissing against that wall."

"Yes," I said. "Most probably a dog."

"Oh, no," she said, sounding quite frightening. "No dogs, ooh no, there are no dogs here, pet."

Now *I* was the one looking incredulous. I must have been.

"So ... you don't have a dog, then." It wasn't a question. After all, I knew the answer, didn't I?

"Well no, we don't." This time her voice had suddenly changed back to being caring, with a hint of puzzlement.

Nodding, vaguely, I said, "Right."

The cleavage moved right up to me, pressing its foundation underwear into my chest, making me breathe out involuntarily. "I'm very sorry but it must have been a faulty part your boy used last time he was here. Maybe it had been involved in some sort of accident somewhere else."

The suit poked me in the shoulder. "That's more likely, isn't it? It's second hand—it was a used socket, something he'd taken out somewhere else. Selling old parts as new is illegal. We could have you for that."

This felt like I wasn't really there, as if I were watching this on television.

"Well, the proof is down there on the carpet. It couldn't have been like that when my boy—I mean the *apprentice*—"

"*Apprentice?* What do you mean by *apprentice?* Have you been sending bloody trainees?"

"I mean, *my assistant*—er, colleague. It wouldn't have worked at all if it had been in that state when he fitted it. It's common sense—"

He grabbed my lapel. "Just you watch what you're saying! Trying to make out that we're—"

"Logical, I mean it's logical, if you just think about it."

The cleavage was up for trying every trick in the book. "But it's never really worked, you see, has it, Harry?"

"But he fitted it on the 19th January—that's nearly four months ago."

"Yes? So?"

"So why have you taken this long to claim there's a fault?"

Harry the suit piped up. "There is a fault—and it's not just with the crap you're selling."

At that moment we plunged into darkness. And I so wanted to get out of there. Could I get away without being seen—I mean *detected*,

126

discovered, found out or just plain old persecuted?

"Oh!" said the cleavage, grabbing my thigh. She was so close I could feel her breath on my face. "It's gone again." I could tell that it wasn't a surprise to her.

"Yes, and the bloody torch battery's done. I told you we needed another one."

"Perhaps this man can lend us a torch."

"I've no fuse wire with me," I said. It must have sounded as though I didn't give a damn.

"Oh! Well, what on earth can we do, Harry?"

"I can give you the number for an electrician—or, better still, a joiner who thinks he's one."

"Can you?"

"But you won't be able to call him—"

"Why ever not?" said Harry the suit.

"—seeing that your phone line's dead."

Harry's voice sounded a little less severe. "Oh, I see. Come on, surely there's something you can do for us? We've been good customers in your shop for donkey's years."

I wasn't so certain of that claim, nor was I convinced that he was ready to owning up to having a dog on the premises, even though its teeth marks were still imprinted on my leg.

The cleavage's voice took me by surprise, right next to my ear, having stealthily got extra close to me in the darkness.

"Please," she said. "Come on, pet."

"Well ..." I began—but only because it might be the quickest way to get out of there.

"It's not for a man like you to be stuck, is it? I mean, well, men that are good with their hands are very useful, aren't they, Harry? What have I always said."

"Salt of the earth, they are," Harry said. "Salt of the earth, people like you. This country can't do without 'em. Should be given medals, the lot of you."

"So what can you do for us, darling?" she asked.

The consumer unit was in some kind of closet that was smaller than the usual telephone box, so it was a squeeze, especially with the cleavage pressing tightly against me whilst shining my torch in all the wrong places. She was finding cobwebs and telling me how they must have come overnight because only the day before she had been in there cleaning.

"Yes, it's the fuse wire that's gone."

At least it was simple: inconvenient, perhaps, but simple to sort—if you have spare fuse wire. And the fuse next door seemed to have been replaced at some point with a hairpin, of all things. I could smell Mrs Harry's liberal sprinklings of talcum powder and I didn't like it.

"And I have none with me," I said.

There was a second or two of silence, and then Harry had a brainwave.

"But I bet you have a nail with you, eh? I mean, you sell nails so you must have."

"A nail?" I was only too aware of the insanity he had in mind.

"Aye. You can always use a nail. Much better than fuse wire. Much stronger. They don't blow."

"No, but for a reason," I said, almost shrieking.

"My father swore by them."

"Did he die of electrocution, by any chance?"

Harry used his lighter to find my pen torch to find a nail in my tool box. I felt somehow distant and remote as, having first of all turned off the power switch, I squeezed out of the closet past the cleavage, and Harry replaced the fuse wire ... with a bloody thick nail.

Packing up my tools as fast as I could, I felt it was my duty to warn them. They must sort the fuse with wire of the proper amperage or, better still, replace the whole holder with a mini RCB; they cost more, but could be reset with the flick of a switch so no more messing with wire. Or hairpins and nails.

I got out of there as quickly as possible; there was nothing else I could do. *All Tools* could have these people from now on. Greville would be pleased too, and it might even put an end to his nightmares.

A week later we learned that the dog had been electrocuted. He had, apparently, felt unable to continue putting his mark on the telephone point so instead had chosen a nearby electrical socket. I was guilt-ridden for some time after that. It was Sharon who explained that the fuse would have blown as soon as the dog came into contact with the socket, and the reason it hadn't been afforded that simple safeguard was because Harry the suit had used a nail. Yes, I said, but it was *my* nail that had killed their dog. Then she put the matter so succinctly into perspective when she said,

"What dog? Don't you remember? They told you they 'aven't got a dog."

# 14

## *The Joy of Flex*

THIS WAS THE 1990s and we were still getting this kind of thing:

"Is your boss in?" he asked Sharon, casting a quick glance to see if he could scan her cleavage.

"No. Can *I* help you?"

Watching Sharon single-handedly deal with this patronising sexism was better from a distance, otherwise I'd become involved and Sharon would be denied the satisfaction of sorting it herself.

"I'm wanting some cable."

"What you want it for?"

"It's your boss I want. Just get him for me."

She didn't breathe in, like you would when preparing yourself for battle.

"If you just tell me what you want to do with it, I'll sort you out the right one."

You have to ask so that you sell them the *right* sort of cable. We independents wanted our customers to stay alive, and not just so they could come back and buy more stuff. When I was caught out one time on a job, and it was quicker for me to get some cable from one of the multiples, I was shocked (no pun intended) that I could have simply self-served and ended up killing myself.

"I know what I'm looking for," said the customer as he peered around Sharon to get a look at the bank of cable reels hanging on the far wall, but also getting a good look at her backside on the way. "How much is that one, three down, two on."

She could see me watching from behind a gondola shelf unit, and she pointed to a reel, counting from left to right, then bottom to top. That's what we were taught at school when doing graphs. The customer shouted at her.

"Not that one! Three down, two on—*two on*, no—that's five."

So she pointed to the one he meant, from the right, biting her lip and giving the outward appearance of extreme calm.

"Let me have a feel of that one."

She pulled the end from the reel and walked it to the counter.

"That'll do," he said.

She told him the price and he made some grumbling noises. He would have done the same if it had been free. Then she asked him what it was for.

"I'm putting a socket in my garage."

"But this is lamp flex," she said. "This is the one you want—two point five twin and earth—"

"I've used it before. Just give me what I want. I know what I'm doing," he glared at her.

"So do I, and if you use lamp flex it's likely to cause a fire. Or maybe even kill you," and she pulled out the correct grey cable so he could inspect it for himself. But he was having none of it.

"Hey, what is this? They don't ask nosy questions in Woolworths. I could go there and get what I want with no bother."

"You got any kids?"

"What's that got to do with you?" He was smirking.

"I'm concerned about them. I don't want to be a party to your negligence."

She began reeling up the lamp flex. His face turned a shade of crimson and he pointed at her.

"You thick slapper! You're all tits and no brain. I'll tell you what I'm going to do—I'm going to give Woolworths my business—all of it from now on."

Sharon said nothing, but her expression told him "fair enough". And before he stormed out he delivered a final volley:

"And I'll tell you something else—I'll buy an even thinner wire!"

The bell jangled, and Sharon caught me recovering from my cringe.

"There's only sodding bell wire left," I said. "And that'll certainly fry his fingertips."

I shot out into the street, hoping that the silly bugger was on his way straight to Woolworths, which liked to think it was the town's biggest store, when that dubious pleasure actually belonged to the Co-op, where they were almost as bad.

He must have run all the way there because by the time I had snaked my way down to the DIY department the girl was about to cut through the wire with the tiniest pair of nail-clippers. See what I mean? And do you know what? Thinking I was a fellow customer, he took my word for it that using such a small cable might burn down his home and, worse still, blister the paintwork on his brand new second-hand Ford Mondeo. That particular day I knew exactly which buttons to press. As far as he was concerned, I was just another punter passing through, and he thanked me for taking the care to stop and advise him.

That was one of the guiding principles in selling hardware: saving people from themselves, even if it meant allowing the likes of Woolworths to get an extra sale; at least I had a free conscience.

## *Strippers, grippers*

Talking to various reps had shown that many hardware shops were broadening their ranges of goods and services even to the point of becoming the pirates I had taken great pleasure in denigrating so many times in the past. Never one to miss a trick, during February Sharon suggested that we plant a display of boxed silk roses on the counter.

"But what's it to do with hardware?" we asked.

The thing about Sharon was that she knew how to sell, largely because she'd worked on many East End street markets in between bit parts on television (and I suspected she was better at selling than acting). Over the years I'd watched her and I was in no doubt that she could sell ice to the Alaskan Eskimos, sand to the Arabs and poverty to the poor.

"You watch," she said.

Sure enough, men saw the roses whilst asking for, say, a packet of tap washers, and by 14th February they'd all gone, with other customers coming in for more. One man wanted four of them, leaving us speculating about his rather hectic social life. You can see how desperate we were for excitement.

But, like with most of the lines that we sold, which were low-ticket items, the profit could be good but at the end of the day fifty per cent of not much is still only half of bugger-all. All three of us knew that we needed to sell stuff with good margins and which, at the very least, would sell for a few quid. One of us suggested work wear—overalls, shop uniforms, fluorescent builders' coats, hard hats, that sort of thing. Okay, so Arthur around the corner at the man's shop might end up feeling the pinch, but then he liked that sort of thing. During the following week we received a trade show invitation from a supplier of industrial work wear and somehow—and to this day I have no idea how this happened—we ended up with tickets to the Harrogate Lingerie and Swimwear Exhibition. Well, at the very least it was all to do with stuff that covered flesh, I suppose—or, I was to learn, *partly* cover it. Sharon was most insistent that we attend. But what had this to do with hardware? we asked.

"You'll see," was the reply. She obviously had something up her sleeve—if not a great deal as we found when we got there and actually inspected the stock ...

The show was held in three huge adjacent exhibition halls floored with white carpet—*white* carpet. You just do not get white carpet in hardware. Hell, you don't even get invited into anyone's house if they've a white carpet. The first thing we noticed were the young women wandering around wearing jeans and bras and nothing else, handing out flyers to anyone willing to grab them (the leaflets). The first stand on the left was the large ladies' specialist and the model, who we later discovered was on a break, was sitting on a stool wearing a see-thru robe whilst drinking from a paper cup and reading a magazine. To all intents and purposes she looked like she was in a shop window in Amsterdam waiting to make a sale. Although she was displaying a huge cleavage, the rest of her underwear was enormous, and doing a very good job of holding everything in place.

She was not a small lady and was in stark contrast to the many others who were wandering around wearing only the briefest of lingerie.

"Is he okay?" Sharon asked me.

"Is who okay?"

"The *boy*," she hissed in my ear.

"Sod the boy! Am I okay?" I joked. "Ask him yourself."

But her attention was torn away by the stock.

"Now, that's what I call walking stock," I said, amusing myself.

Some of the models would seek eye contact and tell us that this bra or that was available with extra under-wiring and would we like her to demonstrate how it affected the appearance. And any of the models were willing to change to show us a different range. Some wandered around the smallest of stands, expertly compensating for the lack of floor space. Other stands were bigger and had two models where one would change behind a curtain whilst the other would show and tell on her own. Each stand was administered by either men or women, immaculately dressed, to take care of buyers and answer queries. Sharon had us stop at *every* stall to admire the underwear being exhibited on real ladies who were quite happily standing there as if fully clothed. There wasn't a dummy in sight. We ploughed through the well-behaved crowds. There were another two halls to explore after this one.

"Is the boy okay?" called Sharon in the loudest

whisper I've ever heard. I nodded my head fervently. That's all I could do. Greville was still standing upright and hadn't keeled over with the excitement. Not yet, anyway.

It was certainly an eye-opening experience to see the quality and amount of care and attention that had gone into the displays. Some stands had catwalk fashion shows and such was the professionalism that the models were akin to those in the opening titles of a Bond film. Their movements were expertly coordinated and in sync with the music. Not all of them were tall and thin with the ridiculous American size zero—in fact, very few were. Most of the young women (I say *young* but their ages ranged from late teens into the late twenties if not early thirties) were less than five feet eight and had perfectly ordinary figures. And why wouldn't they? The world is made up of perfectly ordinary people, and these realistic models were what I would describe as *practical*.

Then Sharon looked at Greville. I could tell she wanted to feel his brow to see how he was handling all this excess.

"You don't fink he's getting too hot, do you?" she asked me.

I told her I'd make discrete enquiries. Standing next to him watching the *Blewgurl* show, I asked him if he was okay.

"Yeah?" he answered suspiciously. "Why?"

"What do you think—about the show?"

He glanced around. Everywhere was awash with busts, briefs and bra straps.

"It's getting a bit warm in here," he grunted and dragged me off for a brief rest to a spring water drinks dispenser to quench his thirst. There the lower noise levels effectively placed the exhibition proceedings in another room and we could hear each other speak.

"That's better. Bloody hot in here." Greville

savoured the iced water in his mouth.

"Can't do with freezing the models, can they?" I said.

"But what is she playing at?"

"Sharon? She's got our interests at heart. It's a question of survival," I said, although I wasn't certain if I sounded convincing. I mean, I understood the theory, but could I embrace it wholeheartedly?

Greville frowned. "Ours is the sort of shop that deals with burley chaps, not *Berlei* bras," he said. I wasn't sure if he was merely trying to hide his embarrassment. "You know what I mean—knickers, in *our shop*?

"Oh, we get plenty of them on the premises—but they keep them covered."

"But it's stuff that women wear."

"Yes, I believe so."

"I suppose we could sell some to the girl at the butcher's. Hers must be worn out by now," I smiled.

"But lingerie—in a man's shop?"

"Er, hang on a minute, Grev. That sounds like we should serve just men. Or nudists."

"And the blokes we get in ... well, none of them would like us flogging this kind of stuff. No way." So now the apprentice had turned self-appointed sales tactician.

"Are you suggesting that we're only supposed to be serving men? That's what's kept us going, you know—particularly in the sixties and seventies when times were hard. The fact that women could feel ... *comfortable* in our shop, unlike in All bleeding Tools where they're made to feel insecure and unwelcome, is what kept the MD in business."

He shrugged and took another drink from the cone-shaped paper cup. "Suppose."

"You know, we really want women to feel okay in Little Sniffingham Hardware and DIY. We can't do with being seen as purely a man's domain. There needs to be something for women as well as getting a handful of nails for their old man."

We watched some of the models walk past going on their break wearing designer bathrobes.

Greville nodded after them. "Bruno Borlonni," he said.

"That's a daft name for a girl."

"No, it's a brand. Three-dimensional fabrics. Very nice," he nodded, knowingly.

"Oh, right." I stood corrected.

"I'm still not convinced about this," he said. "Perhaps she wants to flog this stuff from a barrow in the street outside the shop," he added with a touch of bitterness.

Although he'd made a couple of good points, I told him that I recognised the look on Sharon's face and that when she was ready she'd reveal all. His face lit up, for a brief instant, and as we set off back he threw away the last of his drink.

"Nice cups," he chuckled and we rejoined the crowds.

"Is our Greville okay, ven?" asked Sharon.

"Yeah. He just got something in a twist."

She took my arm and led me to a stand with a lovely young woman modelling for some kind of sheer lingerie with built-in swirly-type patterns.

"*Claudette de Parièle*," she said with what I was convinced was the correct pronunciation. "Paris," she added, knowingly. I nodded. "Now, I don't want you to fink this is what I've got in mind. Don't get me wrong, it's lovely. Just feel this fabric," and she invited me to run my fingers over what bit of material formed the front part of some knickers on a stand. I looked around nervously, almost expecting Gerry from All Tools to tap me on the shoulder, "How's it going then, pal? Eh— don't go clicking them knickers with your rough fingers ..."

"See what I mean?" Sharon motioned to one of

the models who came over to us with a smile.

"Can we just see what vis feels like?"

"Yes, sure," the girl said.

And Sharon took my hand and ran my fingers under the bra cup.

"See what I mean. That's beautiful, init? Yeah, lovely. Not like the usual crap you get up and down."

The girl almost laughed at my shocked expression. Sharon hadn't yet finished with her.

"And them down there. Go on, have a feel ... Vat alright wiv you, my love?" she said to the girl. "*No, like this, use your fingertips* ... How's that feel?"

"A bit awkward," I muttered.

"Aren't they superb? You just can't buy that sort of quality in our town. It's a pity, but it would be wasted. Until maybe later."

She looked up and scanned for something a bit more expensive than the beaten track but within buying tolerances of the Little Sniffingham consumers. The look on Sharon's face told me she had sensed something, and within a couple of minutes we were inspecting a range made by *Mooie Pasturette*. I saw the stallholder motion the model to approach us.

"Hi," she said, smiling. "Welcome to Pasturette. The brand was developed in 1958. It is Dutch and means beautiful. Would you be looking for wholesale or retail terms?"

Sharon dealt with this exceptionally well, coming away with brochures, a price list and having got the model to show us a range of strapless bras for what they call "off-the-shoulder" wear. I found myself, unintentionally, you understand, rather fascinated by this because for as long as I could remember the women in our town had been content to wear strapless clothes with plenty of other straps from all different directions and in full view, reminding me of multiple guy ropes fastening down a circus marquee. Greville had agreed with me and called them "strap happy" women. Maybe they were like that, not through choice, but because there was no outlet offering a range of suitably-designed undergarments. We had a lingerie shop in town, run by the beehive-haired Joan, a relic of the 1960s. So what the hell was she selling in her shop, I wondered?

Both women introduced me to an amazing variety of different bras—I mean, I'd had no idea that there were so many types, including underwired, plunge, three-quarter, balcony—*balcony?* (now that was more for a hardware store, don't you think?)—full, smooth, sports ... there were almost as many different types as there were kinds of industrial fastenings. And Sharon didn't need any of this explaining to her and, with the model, I seemed to be plunged into an in-depth training session that—and you won't believe this—included teaching me how to accurately measure for a bra. Not a lot of people know how to do that. Of course, you shouldn't use a Stanley PowerLock tape measure, but then how many times have I said that there's a special tool for every job?

And then the Accountant's advice began to bounce up and down in my mind.

We walked away, having paid particular attention to lingerie sets (available with or without suspender) and actually rather excited about the prospect of taking on a new line. Actually, it would be a whole new department. I was seeing our shop fitted out with a white, or tastefully cream, carpet. There would be custom-made racks, each one made to measure and professionally installed and not squeezed in any old how with a couple of M5 set screws and a steel corner brace. We would have a measuring area at the top where the keyhole is now. Measuring and hardware go hand in hand.

Measuring women couldn't be difficult, could it? Naturally, I wouldn't be doing this myself, but I would share the technique with my staff. Remember—you get the band size by measuring around the rib cage; add five inches to odd numbers, four inches to even. The difference between the full bust measurement and the band size gives the cup size ...

"Have you got a piece of wood this big?" men occasionally asked, holding out their hands, expecting us to make precise guesses of the actual measurements—and get it right. It used to make us laugh. That could almost become "Have you got a black bra for a woman this big ...?" And of course they would expect us to know who she was and her vital statistics.

The ceiling would be lowered and fitted with high quality refractive lighting to spread an even illumination across the whole store, eliminating any dark corners where (heaven forbid) old timber offcuts might still be stacked. An over-door heater would gently blast a shroud of warm air on customers as they entered, and we'd have purchased the licenses to legally play suitable background music. Dummies with realistic faces and poses would model the various bra-wearing options. They would show how bras are supposed to be worn, with a range of styles, types, single shoulder, both shoulders, evening dress, smooth, seamless, T-shirt, whatever.

We'd pay extra for realism, if we had to, and—better still—we could hire some of these real models for special exhibition days, perhaps to launch new ranges, and put on a show that people would be willing to attend from miles around. As for Joan ... well, after her takings had plunged we could take her on as a specialist to deal with the mature figure; there were plenty of those in Little Sniffingham. And yes, we'd offer those ladies the very best in foundation wear that would make men turn their heads from across the street, and not turn away as they usually did, I'm sorry to say. Our town would have the best in mature figures, and *we* would have dressed them.

We might perhaps convert the rooms upstairs into specialist swimwear departments and employ a couple of the girls I'd noticed working in the Co-op. I'd often thought they'd look very nice in bikinis. I don't know why. We could offer special rates to the customers of Sunn Joly next door in return for reduced-price holidays for our staff (of which there would be a growing number as our sales went through the roof). We would be the lingerie specialist—not only for our little town, but for the whole Cottondale area, supplying the wants of one large town and its five satellites. Just like Marks & Spencer after the war, we would be supplying the underwear for the majority—if not *all*—of the women for miles around. Yes, every one of them would be wearing a label that said—not St Michael, but—*Bottoms Up! of Little Sniffingham*. I could see the logo now: a silhouette of a young woman elegantly stepping into a pair of our finest.

I felt thoroughly uplifted. No more the smell of creosote, sawdust, sweeping brushes and beeswax. We would be one hundred per cent lingerie. Naturally, we would need to be aware of hardware sneaking in; that's what hardware does, as Sharon had always said: the bloody stuff gets everywhere. I could see just how awkward it would be to totally get rid of all the bits and pieces that made up our business. It's just so difficult to let go. I mean, discarding a spare float for a central heating header tank can be like taking a stray puppy to the RSPCA; the guilt ... well, it can be overwhelming. But the idea of those smart and clinically-clean shop premises I had in my mind right then was the stuff of dreams, and no longer did I care for selling rubber door stops and sinks chains.

And then it suddenly occurred to me: I would be selling ladies' underwear.

The image of the smart shop faded and I was in a crowd of professional lingerie buyers, experts in this field. I knew as much about midi and maxi control as they did about Yorkshire plumbing fittings— so far my only experience in working with nipples.

We watched another live display with three models doing a routine to *The Avengers* music. It was superb and the more I admired the absolute professionalism, the more I began to laugh at the idea of men coming into the shop and asking for a couple of M12 Rawlbolts and a Playtex 36B. At that point I decided that we shouldn't be there; this gear was more soft-wear than hardware. I should not be looking at the pattern on the bra cups to see how it might show through the fabric of a woman's top, or whether her knickers were seamless.

We fought for a table in the café area. I say *fought* because I had to get firm with the effeminate foreign chef who accused us of spoiling his layout plan just by our sitting down. That was where Sharon explained the purpose of our visit. Men had bought the Valentine's day roses in our shop on impulse because it was more comfortable than purposely going to a florist. And whilst we didn't usually sell flowers, we did have men who wanted them. There was a demand and we provided the supply. Simple.

"And at Christmas," she went on, "they might buy coordinated sets of underwear for their wives, girlfriends, whatever, because it will be preferable to them than going into a lingerie shop and feeling a bit awkward. See?"

"Or having to face Joan," chipped in Greville.

"There's nowhere else in town, only Brenda with her nineteen sixties bouffant hairdo. And because it's a line we don't rely on, not yet, anyhow, we can take it steady to begin with and see how it goes."

"I agree," piped Greville. "There'd be no point in going bust."

Sharon smiled. "I have to say that at one point back there—'ere, you won't laugh, will you?—but I almost imagined us kicking hardware out and having a shop full of this stuff. Great long rows of neat racked lingerie, a nice light carpet, tasteful lighting and special display days with some o' these gels to model for us."

"Models?" Greville's face lit up.

"And dummies—loads of 'em parked all over the place. Fitting room, bikinis, measuring service ... Ha! Can you imagine?" She laughed, shaking her head at such a ridiculous notion.

"Yeah, what a daft idea," I said.

Finest lingerie from Paris
and a huge range of
industrial fastenings

**Bottoms Up!**

of
Little
Sniffingham

Tel. 048

# 15

*Hard graft*

THE CUSTOMER GRIMACED AS he asked for a packet of Stanley blades.

"You don't look happy," I said. "These are genuine. The imported ones are cheaper."

"Yeah, but they're not as good," and he held up his heavily-bandaged finger.

I pulled a face. Greville was serving a few feet away and stopped to stare at my customer. His was still talking to him, but her voice trailed off.

"I hope it wasn't bad," I said, feeling like it was a stupid remark if the size of the dressing was anything to go by.

"It was my own fault, not watching what I was doing. The cut itself wasn't so bad—it was having the skin graft that was the most painful ..."

I heard a bump as Greville hit the floor.

*Taming of the Screw*

The doorbell jangled.

"Roll up! Roll up! Stand by your beds! I want ten two-inch twelves steel countersunk ... half a dozen quarter-inch number noughts ... a quarter pound of two-inch oval nails ..."

"What the hell is he doing with all these screws?" I muttered.

Greville was already whipping open the boxes and trying to count out, as well as remember, what Sergeant Major Jim was ordering. I rested my hand on his arm and motioned for him to stop. The orders were still being barked out, so I got half a dozen paper bags and emptied a full box of one-inch number eights into them. By the time he arrived at the top they were ready: six open bags, their contents exposed, but eleven orders had been called.

He handed me a fiver. "Hey, where's the Queen of the Aisle today? She's well, I hope."

"Fine, thanks. Got your stuff out. Do you want to check it?"

He gave the packets a cursory glance, and saw that each held screws of the same size. I could almost hear a faint sigh.

"Did we get everything you wanted?" I was trying to disguise my tone, and failing. He was a little over six feet tall, stockily built, and even at his age would be capable of making a mess of another human being.

"Yes. I think so, yes. I'm sure it'll be fine." His voice was missing its "joy to be alive" spark. In fact, it had a definite tone of resignation.

"Now, Jim, see that bag you've got there? It's a grand 'un, isn't it?"

"Yes. It's er, a good little bag, this. Had it some while."

"I'll bet you can fit a lot o' stuff in there, can't you?"

He swallowed, said nothing.

"You've been coming in here for years, haven't you? So you know what I'm going to say to you now, don't you?"

He looked straight at me, and his mouth began to tremble. "Do you think we can er, go somewhere else to do this?"

He can't have missed the look on my face, and he placed the bag on the counter. I motioned for Greville to unzip it and look inside. He didn't want to, so I trod on his toes. I almost passed out when I saw the stuff he had in there—I really did feel a little faint, for a second or so. Tins of wood varnish, electrical sockets, switches, a high-amperage shower switch, a replacement switch for an automatic Russell Hobbs kettle (would you believe?), an assortment of packets of curtain rail fittings, tins of paint, cans of tile adhesive, a thirty-eight piece socket set in hardened steel for air-impact tools, an Estwing claw hammer with leather handle grip (very expensive—for a hammer, that was) ... there was easily over two hundred quid's worth of stock at cost prices. I felt gutted. It was just so bloody disappointing. And then he had the barefaced cheek to start crying. I was looking at the stock filling the whole of the counter and he began making little squeaking noises, punctuated with odd, unintelligible words designed to illicit sympathy. That made me even more disappointed in him. A rogue was one thing; a bloody thief without even the moral (bad word) of his own convictions was another.

"I can't believe this. Oi, be quiet a minute! All these years, sometimes twice a week, you've been coming in here, barking out orders to distract us and nicking stuff. What you been doing with it? Opening your own shop somewhere?"

"Please, just let me go, forgive me—I'll bring it all back, I will ..."

"What? *All* of it?"

"Well, some of it."

"So what's happened to it, then? You've been doing more screwing than Casanova."

"I've been doing a car boot sale—not *every* week, mind. And it's all because ..." (I missed the next bit) "... died and I was heartbroken. And I loved that man, I really did, and it were his shears you once said couldn't be mended and I thought, because I didn't believe what you were telling me, you see—you see now, don't you?"

"Let me get this straight. We condemned his

shears and so you thought, I'm gonna get my own back? I've heard every bloody thing now—I say, do you mind not doing that, you're wetting the counter. We've to serve honest people over that."

When I told Sharon, she was as surprised as I was, and launched into her recollections of similar case histories from her days on the markets in London., which prompted me to wonder why, if she was so streetwise, she hadn't realised what was happening here in the provincial sticks. Greville couldn't believe how I had rumbled Jim, and suspected that I was psychic and regarded me in a new light, but it didn't last. And we never saw the sergeant again, despite his promises. I suppose I felt that I should accept some responsibility for not fully addressing in-store security. It had been easier to believe that most people were honest.

## *Magic Carpet*

Sliding past Sharon, I was getting impaled by the pegboard hooks sticking out of the wall, when I noticed a small roll of carpet that a woman customer had put on the counter. She was explaining something in hushed tones. I needed to check that Greville was up to some good, but as I squeezed through I couldn't help but consider the range of scenarios: maybe she wanted to nail it down, or to join it, or maybe to remove a nasty stain of something unmentionable that had been spilled on it (ether is very good, but not at all easy to get hold of). We sold a lot of double-sided carpet tape for sticking stuff down, though it was better to explain just how to remove the paper backing from the first edge because it could be damned tricky. I preferred slicing down with a Stanley blade, but Sharon had warned me it was so dangerous and we shouldn't be encouraging people to use that method. I was just doing a mental cringe at the thought when she grabbed my arm and pulled me into the confidential exchange.

"Got a little job for you," she said. I groaned, silently. "This lady here wants you to make a box to fit inside her camper van."

"Oh, a Volkswagen?" I asked. Well, they were iconic, a great talking point.

"No," she said. "Ours is a lot bigger than one of them."

"Sorry." I hoped that she hadn't detected my disappointment.

"It's her husband," nudged Sharon, as if that slight gesture would be enough to give me the full picture.

"Oh, I see," and I tried to show my most understanding expression.

The woman seemed a little embarrassed. "We've got this camper van, see, and when we're away there's me and him and our three little children—Owen who's nine, and then Branwen, she's seven, very clever at school, she is, and Thomas who's four. I was just explaining to your wife that at home everything is fine, no trouble at all, there's just perfect. No, it's when we're away in the camper and my husband Emrys ... well, it's with me and the children, see, just outside the cardboard walls. That's what he calls it. He can't go, you see. No, just can't do it, and we have to hurry back from our holidays just so he can."

I nodded, giving the impression that I knew what she was talking about. But I didn't.

"So I was wondering if a kindly man like you would make a little box for him."

Some unwanted picture was beginning to form in my mind, and I didn't want it to. I heard myself mumbling, "A box?"

"That's right, a little box to fit snug in the toilet."

There, my worst fears were realised. I didn't like toilet jobs. In fact, I didn't like toilets at all—not other people's, anyway. She must have seen my expression of horror and smiled to calm me.

"No, it's for his feet, see. This here is the same carpet in our bathroom at home and if he can take off his socks and feel this under his feet then he'll be able to go in peace, nice as ever, not a care in the world."

## *A little gem*

Sharon thought that Greville was coming on a treat, as she called it, and liked to think of him as a fully-fledged member of our little staff, quick to learn and polite. And despite *little* being the operative word, thanks (I suppose) to the advice of the two women who seemed to be running the place (although I believed they met secretly to fight it out), the shop's takings had increased to the point where the contribution from Greville's father had been reduced. Of course, we were nowhere near out of the woods yet, but we managed to keep up the payments to the bank, and every so often we spotted some officious-looking git snooping around and I assumed that he could see that we were doing okay. He didn't look "bank", and he only grunted when Sharon picked on him to see what he wanted, leaving us without saying a word.

On the quiet, as she described it, Sharon ran a steady line of bras and certain other items that flew out the door, merchandised from a neat display behind the rodent poisons' stand. That's where we would find 15- and 16-year-olds lurking after school, but we didn't shoo 'em off. Instead it was her little speciality to get them to buy the merchandise.

"Straight up," she said, "I ask the girls if they

like the sort of gear we have and how they think it might make them feel with it on. And I ask the lads if they fancy buying some of it for their girlfriends. Believe me, the whole lower sixth form at the local high school have most of its girls wearing some really posh stuff under their school uniforms, and most of it's been bought by the lads. It's great! Yeah, we got a lot of happy customers whether we've fixed them up with nails or knickers."

So the Accountant hadn't done a bad job in encouraging our expansion, then? Sharon would baulk at such an appraisal, but it seemed to be all good fun, trading on a knife-edge, on the cusp of bankruptcy and the ever-so-fast descent into trading oblivion.

It didn't go down at all well that the Accountant, who she called "that woman", was having a positive effect on the business.

"Got her feet well and truly under his table, she has," I heard her telling Greville when I was in the glory hole one day. "He don't need me no more." She must have seen his little eyebrows raise because she rushed on with, "Don't worry, nothing like that. It was *me* getting him up every morning and now it's *her*—yes, and every bloody night, too, I shouldn't wonder, except when she's off working away doing one of her ord-its, or whatever they're called. Then he has the cheek to ask *me* to ring him. 'Oh, so you want me back now, do you?' I say. 'Well, I'll have to see if I can manage to break off from what I'm doing and help you out.' Still, though, she's good at doing his socks—least I think that's what he said."

Anyway, with business on the sort of up, we found ourselves rather pushed on Saturdays because that's when most people went out shopping. The MD and his missus would be out there, somewhere, because he certainly wasn't *here* with us where we needed him. One day the phone rang. I can't tell you word for word what the Far Eastern woman said because someone will accuse me of some form of prejudice. She sounded to be a long way away, and when I paused she became very impatient.

"... you not want Thai bride, you not waste my time," and she'd gone. That must be where it started, with phone calls from across the world becoming much cheaper to call the United Kingdom to flog us cheap merchandise.

"It's a long way to go for a Saturday girl," I said, recovering from the verbal onslaught.

That was when it dawned on us: instead of going on about the MD not pulling his weight, what we really needed was some proper Saturday help, something like a Saturday girl. I liked the idea of taking a girl off the streets where she might otherwise have to sell her honour or illegally deal in pruning knives so as to maintain her dependency on modern music and mobile phone calls. In those days, incidentally, we were allowed to specify gender when advertising a staff vacancy. We'd had Saturday boys, but the last one had begun his own sideline wiring up computers using telephone plugs that he was nicking from us. Girls were more dependable and better with the customers.

The notice advertising the job had been in the shop window for less than a minute when in walked Sapphire. She was about the right age, although it was difficult to tell with all the muck on her face, and she had bright red hair that wasn't natural—confirmed by Sharon. "Believe me, I know about these things." She was wearing a boob tube that was like an old sock and pushed her chest in all sorts of conflicting directions. I didn't think that was natural, either. Her belly was wrapped around her middle like a stray limb from the Michelin man. That *was* natural. And she sported a ring through her navel.

"I was just on me way to the tattoo parlour," she grinned, "when I saw your sign."

"At least it shows you can read," I said to her. That was one box ticked.

"She looks like she's on crack," whispered Greville.

I hadn't seen the MD lurking behind us. "We've got something on the shelves for that." We looked around at him. "Polyfilla," he said.

"I wonder if she's got pierced nipples," Greville said.

"She's certainly got something else tucked in there," the Accountant told him.

"Greville—look busy!"

"But I *am* looking busy."

"We live in modern times," said the MD, grinning to himself (this was one of his "days in").

"And aren't you glad of it," I said, seeing the hint of a twinkle in his eye. I was betting he hadn't had one of those in a few decades.

They all seemed to be looking at me, willing me to commence the formal interview. I could swear they were almost nodding, willing me to set her on. There was no way I thought we could ever give this girl a job—I mean, to me she didn't look right at all.

"Just step this way into my office," I said to her, leading her out into the yard—it was seen as a joke, by the way, that the saw-cutting bench was where I did my paperwork when the MD was in-house. I took the girl's details and said we'd be in touch. And I *would* get in touch because I always felt it was the right thing to tell someone they hadn't been successful.

A couple of weeks went by and we'd had no other offers. We couldn't believe that there wasn't one teenager in Little Sniffingham that didn't need a few extra quid. None of the sixth form girls even wanted to sell lingerie. All the time Greville was constantly reminding us of Sapphire's attributes. One afternoon after school she called in to ask him if he knew anything yet, and I overheard her telling him that if he put a good word in for her, and she got the job, then she would show him where else she just happened to be pierced. I remember cringing at the thought.

Despite the MD being the biggest stick-in-the-mud since the *Mary Rose*, he was willing to give Sapphire a try. That gave her a fan club of two. I sided with Sharon and the Accountant: we were determined that our standards should not be allowed to fall below the likes of the more traditional hardware retailers such as can be found in old places like York and Hadleigh in Suffolk.

"I feel awkward about it, Graham, but that girl is more suited for work in a record shop. I know because I done that. There's no way I can see that girl is going to get a job here."

Sapphire began work the following week.

# 16

IT WAS THE DAY that Greville dropped not one box of woodscrews on the floor, but three, and of similar sizes, meaning that they'd need to be sorted carefully. And it happened at a rush time, with the sharp little buggers scattered all over the most-used customer aisle. At the very least they would stick into people's shoes, at the worst they would send them rolling across the floor, causing personal injury, not to mention damage to merchandise. He froze, wondering what to do. I could feel him tensing, he was going stiff as a board. If we'd not been so busy I would have made him kneel right there on the floor and sort them into their respective boxes. And to make a point I would have surrounded him with some traffic cones for ridiculing purposes. But instead I went and got a massive magnet belonging to the MD, one that he'd salvaged from an old WW2 loudspeaker. I gave it to Greville, told him to get all the bloody screws scraped off into a bucket and he could sort them out before he went home. And I pointed out that he was getting off lightly. Then I remembered the countless boxes of screws, nuts, washers and all manner of industrial fastenings that I had sprinkled on that same floor over the years. Still though, the trainees had to learn.

A customer was asking Sapphire for timber in feet and inches. In fact, he called the metric system *new money*, which brought back memories of my childhood, I can tell you, when decimalisation was chucked at us and for ages shop prices were labelled in both old and new money. I stepped in to help, smoothing out this customer's obvious dislike of our new punk-look. If this were to be the norm, and customers gave her the big thumb's down, then I could envisage her leaving us of her own accord.

On the first Saturday she had turned up with an electro-brassed chain linking the third ring in her right ear to the second ring in the left. We didn't like to tell her it was lopsided and that if she'd bought the chain from this shop it would have been genuine brass. This one was shedding gold flakes like glitter all over her black top. Over the years I'd seen much worse which is why I said nothing. But I planned to, after she'd settled in.

At that time, with all the changes we were making, we didn't have time to encourage her to improve—no, that's wrong, make that *change*—her appearance, making it more suitable for the job she was doing. Of course, what she wore away from the shop was her business, but here there could be safety implications. Or maybe not if she didn't hang around that long, which seemed the more likely. The girl seemed pleasant enough and willing to please (more about that later), and seemed to be known by many of the customers—particularly the older ones, strangely enough. This faction seemed to accept her as if piercings were the norm. I lost count of the number of old ladies who reached over the counter to hold Sapphire's hand or touch her arm and ask how her mum or her grandma or any of her umpteen sisters were doing health-wise or bingo-wise or blue-rinse-wise.

"If this girl is so damned well-known," I said to Greville, "how come we've never heard of her before?"

"You don't mix in the right circles," he said, as if *he* did. "Do you know something? A lot of older women are pierced in some very surprising places."

"Like where?" I asked.

Sharon whispered, "If you're so green, maybe you should be running a garden centre."

Greville explained to me exactly where the these little gold rings could be found, just in case I came across one or two of them and wondered what the hell they were. I didn't think there was any chance of me finding any. Not where *he* said, anyhow.

"It's fortunate that we can't see them," I said.

Sapphire smiled a lot. She smiled at everyone and it seemed most disarming, apart from with the dye-hard awkward sods. We got plenty of them.

"If a customer comes in without a smile," she said, "I just give them one of mine."

If I'd been any more of a cynic, my stomach might have turned over there and then, but there was something rather sincere and unquestioning about her, so I left it. Even so, I still had my doubts about the girl who didn't just sell hardware; she actually wore it. She was, however, beginning to win over the Accountant. As for Sharon, she said she was used to working with all types from all different walks of life and if she had any misgivings about Sapphire she hid them so as not to encourage the others to be negative about her. The MD (who began to pop in on a Saturday while his wife was "doing the market") would watch her moving about the shop whilst chuckling to himself. A lot.

One day something happened that made us all realise that appearances can be deceptive. A customer accused Sapphire of giving her the wrong change. I'd seen this happen so many times, particularly on the run up to Christmas when shops and staff are so bloody busy and it's very easy to rush and make mistakes. This was when the petty con merchants crawled out from under their stones and targeted the young and inexperienced. Men baddies could be particularly nasty; women baddies were far worse, and would stoop to using any mucky trick to hand.

I was at the other end of the shop at the time, but I heard the woman's words as plain as day:

"This isn't right—you're trying to *do* me," she said with raised voice, enunciating perfectly.

Putting on my best smile, I dropped what I was doing to take charge. Sapphire remained calm, despite the constant, unremitting attack on her honesty.

The woman was in her mid-30s and unusually smartly dressed. That put me right on my guard. She turned to me almost as soon as I got there and told me what had happened. She didn't repeat herself, and played the aggrieved victim to perfection. Sharon told me she couldn't have played the part better herself.

"This stupid girl has short-changed me. I gave her a twenty and she tried to fob me off with change for a five."

I remember when the con was done with a ten

bob note for a pound; that's inflation for you. Sharon was standing a few feet behind her, waiting for her to look around and check, but that would have put a chink in her performance. Oh, but this woman was good. She stared at me and then pulled the trigger again.

"It's quite obvious that she's fiddled my fifteen pounds for herself. It wouldn't surprise me if you didn't discover she was an addict of some sort."

Sapphire was sound, but I did detect signs of her quickened breathing. Apart from that she stood her ground and looked calm.

"I've been shopping here for many years, now, and I have to say that I might have to change that if you don't pay me the difference. After all, it's my money she's taken."

Well, I couldn't say that I recognised her and, looking across to Sharon, neither did she. I didn't want to argue; experience had taught the both of us that it's best to let the victim blow themselves out before trying to sort it.

"So what do you intend to do about it? I know a lot of people—"

"Sapphire?" I said.

The girl looked at me. She didn't smile—not even a smirk. Christ, but she was cool.

"It was a five pound note," she said, looking at the woman.

The woman raised her arms. She'd done this before.

"You can't be serious. If she's stealing from me then she's also stealing from *you*."

"Okay, just to be on the safe side—"

"I want the manager!"

"That's me."

"What? You?" She didn't sound at all impressed, but then that was her intention.

"Yes, sorry. I'm going to go and check the video."

"Oh, that old one! Videos are useless. You can't see a thing. Any proper manager wouldn't need to check—he'd take the word of a valued customer over a little trollop he had working for him."

I looked at Sapphire. "Will you be okay?"

She smiled back. She would be okay.

Anyhow, Sharon would watch over the girl and step in if needed. Of course, there were other customers waiting at the counter to be served or pay for stuff, and this incident had to be gauged just right or they might all leave in disgust—with us. It was a real tightrope, getting the tone just right, not letting it be known that we were a walkover for such tricks, whilst also seeming to be the victims. But whilst I was gone the woman tried staring at Sapphire, with a glowering intensity, and after a minute or so was forced to look away and fold her arms. *That* was when she dropped her performance. Sapphire just stood with her arms by her side. She was so cool, I nearly shivered.

When I got back, the woman turned on me for employing cheap, incompetent Saturday girls.

"Particularly ones that look like *that*, the little slut," she hissed with so much venom she had to wipe her lip dry.

Yes, she was losing it; it was all going wrong. Had she been better experienced in the con game, she would have known that it's better to keep a possible ally (such as me) on her side until all other avenues were done.

"It's on camera. I'm sorry to tell you—"

"Sorry? You? You're not sorry—"

"But I am. If you'd been right, I'd be only too willing to make everything okay for you. But I've checked the tape and the camera has picked up the colour of the note you passed over. It was a blue one. The transaction was sound."

"I don't believe you. You can't get that sort of detail on a camera—and where is it, anyway?" She looked around. "Come on—show me. You're just a con-man just like the girl."

That was when I pointed to a small, unobtrusive white box between two pegboard hooks. It looked straight down at the till.

"If you come this way, I'll play it back to you."

There was a moment of realisation on her face, followed by a half-hearted attempt to exhaust her repertoire of derogatory adjectives. Then she left, mid-insult.

# 17

*Night of the Demon*

THE BLONDE LADY (JANE, was it?) tapped on the window and tried to deliver some sort of cryptic message using her forefinger and wristwatch. At the time I was trying to explain to a customer why she (or her husband) needed some barrier cream as well as Swarfega so that his skin wouldn't go dry, so all I had time to do was smile and wave back. She tried again, then she was gone.

Forty minutes later the three of us were outside pulling down the steel door shutter when a woman called out from the bottom of the street. This usually meant that someone wanted us to open the shop again for something as trivial as a picture hook, and our instincts told us to clear off, but our hearts said we should keep customers happy because today's 35p sale could mean a £350 sale tomorrow. Hmm, so were we considerate or just plain old mercenary? No, it was definitely the former. Anyhow, it was actually the Accountant tearing up the street, laden with a couple of bags, and she was out of breath, having run down from the railway station with something important that she insisted we needed to see.

Back inside, the temperature had dropped alarmingly and we made our way along the darkened aisles towards the office. No one said anything. I flicked the switch and the couple of fluorescent lights flickered on, accompanied by their little pings and pops and clicks, and the four of us stood blinking as they hummed and rattled.

Looking around, the Accountant shivered. "I've spent all afternoon looking through fifteen months' worth of accounts in a shoebox—that's me in the shoebox, by the way. There's more room in a straight jacket. And now I'm standing in a fridge. You'll have to excuse me if I don't sound too happy, especially with what I'm about to tell you."

She took out a wad of pages and we peered forwards as she held up the first one. Then teasingly (I imagined, but I think I was wrong) she lowered it out of sight.

"First of all, you have to promise me that you won't breathe a word of this to anyone—that means *anyone*. Got that?"

I swallowed. My god—what the hell was this about?

She went on, letting us see the page again. "I'm not supposed to have this. It was shown to me in confidence. In my job we sign the Official Secrets Act—"

"Really?" Greville perked up.

"No. But we must not divulge confidential information. It's simply not done. Hanging offence."

Greville's jaw dropped, so she stepped in to allay his concerns.

"Out to dry, I mean."

Sharon made me jump. "So why you doing it, then? Why you implicating all of us in your sordid secret? We risk getting into bother too—I don't fink

I should be here."

I placed my hand on Sharon's arm and squeezed gently. Her breathing had quickened and her expression spelled trouble for the Accountant if she didn't gauge this, whatever *it* was, just right.

"It's okay. In all the years I've been dealing with people's affairs, I have never divulged information to a third party. Never before, that is. And, if truth be told, I'm not really doing that now. It's just that ..." she sighed, "certain documents have passed through my hands from someone I can't name, and I've been thinking about this all bloody day, it's been bothering me, and so I've rushed here because ... well, I—I think you all have a right to see this.

"These are just the important bits—you don't need to see all of it, we'd be here all night, but this is a photocopy of a receipt from Cottondale Metropolitan Council for outline planning permission."

We shrugged our shoulders; it meant nothing to us, but I was amazed at the figure.

"Crikey! Is that how much the mean buggers charge? Bloody councils!"

"Make a note of the company's name," the Accountant said in a menacing tone, "... and the address for the proposed erection," she enunciated. I rather liked her when she did that with her lips.

Peering closely, it wasn't easy to read because the receipt was a copy of one those shiny thermal printed slips, like fax paper, no doubt bought in by the Council to save them buying printer ink. She briskly changed the exhibit.

"Did you get that—where this erection is supposed to be?"

"That can't be right," I said. "There's nowhere down here for anyone to build a multi-storey car park. Just not enough room. And why would they bother—I mean, we have free parking in this town.

There'd be no point. In fact, free parking is the one thing that's kept this town going, our one advantage—"

"Just pay attention," she said. "There's more. *This* receipt is for consultation services for such a building on such a site in the town centre. Four storeys, in fact. You can fit a lot of cars in something that size."

"I don't see how," I said, thinking someone had made a whopping mistake. Then it hit me and I straightened, knowing what type of revelation was about to come next. Something about me went numb. Was it my brain? I'm sure that wasn't the case because it lived in that state permanently and it didn't feel any different now.

"... so I went to the Council offices at lunchtime, making me late for my afternoon appointment in Harrogate, by the way ..."

We mumbled some thanks and apologies, whatever.

"... and I was shown these. They charged me a fortune for the photocopy, the robbing bastards," and she unfolded the large sheet of paper, with grey fading around the edges. It showed the recognisable parts of Little Sniffingham town centre, but with the very middle of it blitzed, and labelled in neat draughtsman's handwriting, PROPOSED SITE OF DEVELOPMENT. It stretched between our street, right the way back to the road running parallel with ours.

"Now you can see where all that space is coming from ..."

Sharon, Greville, me—we all swallowed. She went on,

"Your friend on the other side of this wall—the fish and chip restaurant. Knock this down, knock his down and that's a pretty big piece of land, worth a small fortune—" We gasped, but then, "—just so long as you own it outright, that no other interest has a charge on the property ... like a bank does when they've loaned you money."

Now we knew that the intimidation wasn't by chance or whim. It had been so much easier to believe that maybe various circumstances had come together at that time and almost caused our demise: the backlash of the 1980s' recession, an unsound overdraft made by an over-friendly bank manager, changes in banking policy, some over-zealousness by the bank's young blood seeking the thrill of control and power. Yes, I had almost accepted that there was no one single entity responsible, that simply we were the victims of an unfortunate set of bad strands, a threat that we had managed to fiddle or fudge our way out of. But now it seemed like it would be possible to put actual faces to this demon or demons.

The Accountant was jiggling a photocopy in front of my nose. Sharon and Greville were sounding worried.

"What's wong wiv him? Graham? You alright there, my love?"

Blinking, I took the paper from the Accountant, noticing her long, blue fingernails. That has nothing to do with the story; I'm just saying, you know.

"This is a paid cheque, a copy," she said.

"It's got ink all over it."

"That's the crossing stamp that the account holder's branch uses when the cheque's cleared."

I tried to see the name of the payee, but the Accountant tapped her painted fingernail just below the amount box. "That's what you're supposed to be looking at—the account holder." Then she snatched it away.

I looked up at her. Had I missed something?

"You saw who's made it out, yes? And which bank is it? ... That's right. And which *branch* of that bank is it drawn on?"

Sharon patted my shoulder, as if easing the

lumpy thoughts through the strainer.

"Now the account, that I'm not prepared to name aloud—"

"X Y Z Development—oh, *sorry!*" Greville slapped his hand over his mouth.

She sighed. "... never mind," and she began gathering together the papers and stuffing them back in her case. "I'll be shredding these as soon as I get home. I've said quite enough, already—more than enough."

"I didn't know you had one o' them shredders, Graham." Sharon couldn't disguise the bitchy tone.

"But what's the point?" I said. "Why here? Why this town when we've already got free parking?"

The Accountant closed her eyes for a second and shook her head. "It doesn't get any easier," she muttered before stealing herself. "Look, this is yet another example of ... No, I'm sorry, but I can't do it. Look, I know I can trust you—all of you—to be discreet. We're all, to a greater or lesser extent, in this together." She blew out. "But if I say anything more, and someone makes just *one* tiny slip, no matter how innocuous, then it could be traced back to me. Any blind illiterate fox can follow a paper trail these days." She turned to me. "I'll see you at home."

"Where are you going now?"

She closed her eyes, her shoulders sagged, and she turned back.

"Sorry, yes, I know. I don't think I'm cut out for all this espionage. I'll come with you, yes."

Sharon gave Greville a sly, disapproving nudge, and he grinned at me as if to say it would be my lucky night.


For what she called "professional reasons", the Accountant wouldn't say anymore about what she had already divulged to us. I told her it was too late and, if caught, she might as well be hung for a sheep as a lamb, but that night she was determined to keep things to herself, in more ways than one, so Greville was wrong. At last we could put a name to the monster in the mist which, after all, had failed because we were still in business, weren't we? We were still trading and we had made savings and done some ruthless and, if I say so myself, well-overdue pruning that made us what we were today: lean, efficient, progressive. And charging for parking in Little Sniffingham would be a non-starter, end of story. Yes, the efforts, the wheeling and dealing, the greasing of back pockets and the exchanges of favours of the old pals' network of big businesses and mates at the bank had backfired on them.

# 18

*From beyond*

SHARON THOUGHT THAT MAGGIE Newsprint was becoming a nuisance. Whenever the phone rang I was dreading it was her—well, either her or someone desperate to deliver me a bride from overseas.

"It's Maggie, love. I don't suppose you could bring me another bottle, could you, darling?"

I tried my best to explain that I was pushed for time and could she possibly hang on until her boyfriend, Steve, joined her after he finished work about four-ish? But she always seemed to give a barely-audible grunt whenever I mentioned his name.

"Well, we shouldn't rubbish her," I told Sharon.

"After all, she has been keeping this shop fully heated for the past couple of years. In fact, she has been almost as instrumental in battling the bank as any of the other strategies. She was worth her weight in gold when we were really hard up."

So one day I sat her down in her tiny back room and explained that, in the first instance, she should really make certain that all the gas in the bottle was used up before buying another one. The MD was present when I told Sharon what I'd said and he said that I needed certifying.

"You'll never make any money in this trade," he admonished.

Of course, in order to get Maggie to take any notice I had to accept a drink of her awful coffee. And I pointed out to her that she wouldn't have to wait for me to deliver the gas if she got Steve to collect it. She was reluctant to go along with that— and no, I didn't want to know the details of their sex life (or rather lack of it). So I told her we could always get Greville to deliver it. He could even have a crafty drag on the way, I said, which might go some way to keeping him happy, although I would never let him know that I was building his frequent unofficial smoking breaks into our shop routine. Maggie didn't like that idea, saying that she preferred the personal service. From me; someone she felt she could trust.

"Greville *is* personal," I offered.

But it didn't work and, reminding me that she was my personal customer, and that to an old-fashioned girl like her the old ways were always the best, I lost the battle. Maggie grabbed my arm as I was leaving.

"Promise me, Graham, that you won't send your boy with me gas."

"You're probably right. I think young lads are losing their strength. Our Greville won't be able to manage the weight. They don't build teenagers like they used to."

At least from that point onwards Maggie began to actually run down the gas bottles until they were empty, which was a step in the right direction. Maybe the Chancellor's tax increase on cigarettes had forced her to consider my money-saving proposal—I mean *suggestion*.

One Saturday afternoon in December, leaving Sapphire looking after the shop, Sharon and I were about to go out in the back yard to mark out some timber. I would need her to hold the long lengths still.

"Trade must be pretty quiet," she said. "The butcher's girl is still at it out in the lav."

That explained why Greville kept popping out, presumably to check on her progress.

"She's not as noisy as she used to be," she whispered. "Just going through the motions, now. I know, I can tell vese fings."

"Noisy enough," said Greville. "She's either having sex or training a seal."

And then it started—an awful scraping noise like a low guttural screeching. The words banshee and wailing came to mind. The notes being made went up and down enough in pitch to make multiple spine-shudders.

"Crikey, what's she doing, now?" Greville asked.

Sharon looked sharply at him. "It's stopped—the slapping sound in the lav."

"What—what do you think it is?" he gasped.

By this time, it was so close to us that the noise was beginning to echo across the high street.

"Bleeding hell," she said. "It's like something nasty's being dragged out of the bowels of the earth." She used her best *Jackanory* voice.

We listened.

"It's getting closer." Greville grabbed my arm, and without any embarrassment.

"Greville!"

"Sorry." He slackened his grip.

There was a knocking on the yard door, making us jump. It was Sapphire. She froze when she saw Sharon's face, white and expressionless—not a good thing for an actress, unless you're in a Hammer horror film.

"I've heard vat sound before," she said.

"What was it?" asked Greville, his lips barely moving.

"It was when I was with a company doing a play in an old theatre in Glasgow. It's not there any longer. They pulled it down—they had to. It started off like it was a long, long way away. Then it got gradually closer. And closer—just like this is doing. It's like ... like the end of the world is nigh."

"So what was it—did you ever find out?"

"I know that sound, all right. And it's going to get about as close as it can. And then ..."

"What?" we gasped.

"It'll stop."

"Where will it stop?" Now Greville was white.

"It'll stop right outside our door."

"Why?" His voice barely made a sound. He swallowed noisily.

We listened as it scraped and it bumped and it hesitated and it clattered and screeched some more. Then its wailing changed as it turned the corner where the old slippery flags hadn't yet been replaced by 20th century tarmac. Now, just on the other side of Sunn Joly, the noise was louder and more intense as it echoed across the narrow street.

We retreated inside. We all knew there was no escape, no back door, no way out of the yard. At least inside we could hide.

After one cruel, agonising moan ... there was silence. Greville said nothing. I looked at Sharon, not knowing whether to be suspicious of her or just plain scared. Then it happened—it was the sound we had been dreading: the shop bell sounded, hollow and searching, and Sapphire let out a sharp cry. Even *I* froze and then some object kicked open the door further. Greville jumped. Standing at the top of the shop we could see down to where Sapphire was making her way slowly towards the street.

"Don't do it, Saph! I—I love you ..." No one was more surprised by that than Greville himself.

I thought that if a Saturday Girl thought it okay to venture down there, then it should be okay for the rest of us. We found Maggie's Steve. He and a gas bottle were wedged in the doorway.

"Hi ya—d'ya mind giving us a hand with this," he squeaked. "God, it's bloody heavy."

Sapphire grabbed the bottle, slinging it against her front, giving it a bear-hug, she carried it, almost without effort, to the top of the shop.

Greville turned to me, trying to disguise his relief.

"So why did they have to shut the old Glasgow theatre down?" he asked Sharon.

"Like I said, it had no heating."

## *A Fight at the Opera*

That night there was a council "do" on at the little town centre theatre, where the local operatic society liked to put on *La traviata* and particularly *Carmen* (where the audience could happily sing along with the *Toreodor's Song*). In fact there was a buzz amongst the shopkeepers that made me feel a bit of an outsider because not one of them would say exactly what the meeting was about, just that everyone needed to attend, almost as if it was a matter of life or death—or, which seemed more important (to a shopkeeper, that is), a matter of livelihood or destitution.

It was a last minute thing, but I persuaded Sharon to come with me because Greville was off seeing to a woman's bathroom floor tiles. I expected there to be usherettes and uniformed officials to direct us up the grand Victorian staircase. But it didn't seem as if the local council actually wanted us there—or anyone, really. The place seemed dead; no one passing could have guessed that there was a function on and anyone who'd heard about it would have thought it had been cancelled because the door had been kept closed, the lights in the foyer dimmed. The poster box outside showed only an out of date banner for some rock 'n' roll concert two years ago.

Sharon and I were the first to arrive and although the doors *were* unlocked, inside the foyer seemed abandoned. Eventually I found the light switches and flicked on a selection until the place at least looked as if there was something going off that night—even if it was a public hanging. A tiny A5 poster in a corner said:

**COTTONDALE METROPOLITAN BOROUGH COUNCIL**

PUBLIC MEETING TONIGHT
PARKING CHARGES:
THE FUTURE & MUNICIPAL BENEFITS
NO PROSTITUTES, ACTORS OR
UNCLEAN TRADESMEN MAY ATTEND

"Bleeding cheek, no actors," said Sharon.

"Ot unclean tradesmen! That's out of the ark, isn't it?" Then I saw the part about parking charges. "Am I reading it correctly? Does that say ...? It's no wonder they don't want anyone here."

"Yeah, but anyway, look—we've got the doors open and the lights on. Word will get around. You just see if this place ain't a full house. They'll never get away with whatever they're trying to sneak through."

The actual theatre was in an upstairs room above the shops of extortionate-rent on the street below, and it was empty. The meeting wasn't due to begin until 6.30 and, if the Council had its way, most people would not have found it. It didn't seem like they wanted to tell anyone where the meeting would be held. Confusion, that's what they wanted. But when it came to matters of town centre trade, the Little Sniffingham shopkeepers had a finely-developed nose for anything that affected their livelihoods and phone messages had been buzzing around all day between the shops, advising of last-minute changes in the time and the venue. And now we were here, on council premises. Legally, they had to hold a public meeting at some location even if, for whatever reason, it was a no-show by the public. One thing the theatre staff had done was to pull on the blackout curtains. That way the long narrow windows would not be seen from around the town, another attempt to divert attention from what was happening; the fewer people who would turn up, the better. I wasted no time in pulling them back. I mean, who was there to tick me off?

The curtains were the right ones for the job, heavy lined velvet, but they dragged on the rails and they shouldn't have done. The drapes must have been at least fifteen feet long and should have been hanging on a specially made steel pole. Peering upwards I tried to see what sort of track had been used—that's the sort of thing that hardware men look at. Sad, I know. My pocket torch sent a searchlight beam to the offending area.

"Bloody Woolworths," I said.

Sharon gazed up with me. She couldn't believe it.

There was another voice: "You're wrong there,

Pal, that's not one of Woolworths'."

When I turned, Gerry was there, the smug git, casting his expert gaze upwards.

"No, it's a Swish," he said and began to walk off.

I hadn't done with him. "You still in this trade, or what?"

Gerry grabbed the torch, clicked it off and jammed it in my breast pocket with his *I know everything* look. "There are training courses for this stuff, you know."

"That rail has never seen *Swish*."

He set off. "Yeah, yeah, yeah, I've heard it all before. I get customers telling me crap all day long." Then he turned and called, "Don't suppose you've still got that boat for sale, have you, Pal?"

I was disappointed to hear my tone soften. "Yes. Still, still got it."

"I hear it's a grand 'un."

"The craftsmanship is quite beautiful." I was rapidly reassessing my unkindness towards my fellow hardware retailer.

"Good," he nodded, like someone who was able to appreciate such excellent workmanship.

"Don't suppose you know anyone who ... might be interested?"

"Of course not." Gerry grinned as if I'd asked him to model a mini skirt and he walked off sniggering.

"You're shaking, Graham," Sharon rubbed my forearm. "Don't mind about him. He's just a sleazy shit. If he drives his car into a tree then he'll find out how well his Mercedes bends."

I missed the joke. "Do you know what's annoying? Remember a couple of years ago when Cottondale Metropolitan bleeding Council asked us to tender for supplying," and I quoted in an official tone, " 'suitable and appropriate curtain fixtures as befitting a commercial application'? We spent hours on the phone hunting down a specialist supplier that that did big poles for big halls like this one."

"Yeah, I remember. We never heard anything back from them. It's funny, though, isn't it? I mean, look what the toss-heads have gone and done."

Before long the hall was packed, with standing room only. Some sort of minder popped his head in, presumably checking for weapons and cameras, then nodded to someone outside on the staircase. The double doors were flung back and a troop of council officials entered, three men and one woman. I got the measure of the woman just by looking at her: she was above, we were below. When I was a kid there were certain junior school teachers like that, and later they or their sisters seemed to have retired to become pub landladies.

"Here, boyo—I don't suppose you've brought any garlic, have you?" Ram Raid Roger had not mastered the art of speaking in whispers and a number of heads turned and smiled.

I thought I saw one woman cross herself, but it was Myrtle, who suffered from congenital fidgititis. You could tell by the way the group walked that they weren't mere mortals like the rest of us. The woman was particularly scathing in the way she demanded to be let through the people standing in the aisle, without actually touching anyone. I guessed she'd be pissed off that their attempts to ensure a poor turnout hadn't worked. The group sat at a table on stage, the woman taking particular care to arrange her long skirt securely before sitting down. That was the only way she could prevent attack by rats. One of the men savagely brandished a gavel with as much ferocity as a lumberjack with an axe. During the few seconds it took to quieten everyone I caught Maggie Newsprint waving to me.

One of the men introduced the woman as the councillor who was the brain behind the proposal to implement town centre parking charges. I think we were expected to give her a round of applause, but instead there were one or two disgruntled comments from the crowd. She outlined a list of advantages for the town as a result of charging our customers through the nose for the privilege of shopping here. No one seemed impressed. Then it was time for questions from the floor—and we were warned that "inappropriate comments" would not be tolerated.

"What will they do," asked Gerry, "slap our arses?"

At this point things became animated. One irate shopkeeper called out: "*You*—the council—have bent over backwards to help the damned supermarkets, at the expense of independent shops, the true lifeblood of this town!"

The councillor pointed him out to one of her henchmen, who stood up and warned:

"Irrelevant point. Who's next? *You there*—speak up!"

"It's not irrelevant! The supermarkets have taken trade away from the small shops and all we've got left is free parking—that's the only advantage we have in this town—and now you want to take it away!"

The henchman looked across the room for some council bouncer. That was when I spotted him, and he made his way towards the shopkeeper who had done such a good job of expressing what the rest of us were feeling. Within a few seconds the crowd moved around the intended victim like some sort of swirling mass and he went out of sight, leaving the bouncer desperately picking through the crowd as if he was rummaging through a box of rags.

Then it was time for the vote. The councillor's tone was as hard as concrete and now she spoke with a sarcastic edge that could have cut through a marble kitchen worktop.

"All those against these excellent and far-reaching proposals that will provide a future and prosperity for this town—a show of hands." She'd almost whispered that last bit.

To say the response was unanimous would be an understatement. We couldn't hear what she said to the other two, but she didn't look pleased.

"And all those in favour—a show of hands!" Now, that was a lot louder. She could have been cheering on England in the World Cup.

I did not expect anyone to be so small-minded, but there was one man, quite happy to stand there, holding his hand high, standing his ground.

"There's always one, isn't there," Sharon said. "His life wouldn't be worth living if this was down in London. You're not as hard on arseholes as they are down there."

"I know him. He works for the Council. He was the clerk when we applied for planning permission for a new shop sign."

"Oh, so he's a bleeding plant, is he?"

I expected the crowd to jeer him, but there were just plenty of disgruntled murmurs and some mucky looks. The councillor made some comments about our lack of judgement, saying that in any event it would have no bearing on the inevitable outcome. Someone in the crowd knew more about public meetings than the rest of us and made a point of order, reminding her that this had indeed been properly declared and that the overwhelming vote against the introduction of parking charges must, in law, stand. The stage stooges got up and marched out of the hall, determinedly looking straight ahead.

The crowd gave a cheer. Ha! There would be no parking charges in this town. We had won, our future as town centre traders was as secure as it could be.

# 19

*Christmas is coming*

"IS THIS CHAP GIVING away money or summat?"

Despite being up to our necks in a crowd like a scene from *Ben Hur*, on the quiet I think we were all pleased with the customer's remark. It was Christmas—by that I mean we were well into December, which was rather late by Woolworths' standards where they had been selling Christmas trees since July. Our shelves were full and the shop was packed with customers and that was just how it should be. If only every day could be like this. It was a classic scene for the festive season and we were ecstatic. In fact, the countdown to Christmas had started earlier than usual for those recessionary times. All strippers were out on hire (wallpaper steam strippers, that is) so that people could redecorate in time for the house parties, and sales of curtain fittings were at their highest for four years.

"This level of excitement illustrates a definite improvement in consumer attitude," I said, sounding like some classic Pathé News voiceover announcer. All I knew was that trade was almost (dare I say it?) *exciting* due to some complicated cocktail that had come about quite by chance. We rode with it, keeping our heads and the shop's bank balance well above the waterline, knowing full well that if there was another recession we'd be clueless in putting the mystery ingredients together and hoping for another recovery.

It was a Saturday teatime and I heard Greville lock the door after the last customer. This was twenty minutes after the official closing time and it was my policy never to throw customers out—unlike one of the famous high street multiple retailers, which would dim the store lights to dispel the shoppers. I shan't mention the name; let's just say that this shop should have stopped selling medicine long ago—particularly as it leaks out of the lace holes.

In the office the staff seemed reluctant to get their coats on and were willing—unusually—to hang around and chat. It seemed as though they needed to continue getting their fix of adrenaline-rich dope. Sharon told me she had seen that sort of thing in her theatre days and could now almost feel herself tingling with the buzz. Greville was very animated.

"So come on then," he said to me. "What do you think we're doing right?"

"Well, it could always be better."

"Bleedin' spoil sport," muttered Sharon.

My comment seemed to provoke much jeering and someone threw a till roll middle at me. I think it was Sharon.

"Alright, alright. I think you've *all* done well."

"How well?" she asked.

"Marks out of ten," said Greville.

"Okay, then—how about *very well* or even ..." There were gasps of expectation. "Very well *indeed*?"

Satisfied grunts all round.

Sapphire said, "My friend and me really enjoyed dressing up as Santa Claus. Did we look all right?"

"What? Not half," said Greville.

"Sapphire," I said, "the pair of you looked absolutely fantastic. You were beautiful."

I'd told Sharon that I wasn't too sure about all the thigh they had been displaying, but couldn't deny they had attracted a number of appreciative comments and grunts throughout the day and shoppers from around the town had followed them into the store.

"And," I added, "the improved appearance of the shop might have made a difference."

"He means the new paint job," Greville explained to Sapphire.

"And the lack of charity shops down this street," I said. It was a valid point.

"And higher than usual stock levels," Greville added. He was learning, you see.

"Don't tell the Accountant," I said. "She doesn't like all that cash being tied up."

"Not forgetting the Christmas lights," Sharon said.

"That *I* put up," said Greville.

"Yes, you did too," she added.

"When you know I don't like heights."

Sapphire kissed him on the cheek. "I think you're brave. Oh, and it was me who put up the mistletoe!" she said.

"Been taking the *kiss* again, Greville?" They groaned at my sad joke.

"The pensioners seem to like it, though. All those old ladies, eh, hanging around expectantly?"

"There's not many places you can go to see expectant pensioners," Sharon grinned. "Anyhow, I like all that kissing—reminds me of my time in rep. Lots of kissing went on there." Her eyebrows raised at the memories.

"And remember, we have documentary proof that people actually like us," and I pointed to the wall of Christmas cards. "Look at that lot—from our adoring public."

I could swear one or two of them twinkled at that very moment, just to prove the point.

"So are we going to celebrate?" That was Sapphire.

It went a bit quiet then. All eyes were on me.

We weren't used to celebrating.

"That sort of thing usually means spending money in a pub or," *Heaven forbid*, I thought, "a restaurant."

Sharon knew I didn't feel comfortable suggesting such frivolities, probably because of my ruthless training over the years by the MD, who at that moment was packing up his various sandwich boxes into his briefcase. Yes, he'd actually worked a Saturday, somehow excited by the much-increased sales.

"I'm not certain that we're doing *that* well," I said.

Sapphire immediately read the signs. She's a bright girl. "All Tools is treating *all its staff* to a Christmas meal at The White Swan." That certainly plonked in a pregnant pause. "I know because a lad I know is a Saturday boy there."

I saw Greville gave her an awkward look. I shuffled uncomfortably and looked at Sharon, who nodded ever so slightly.

"Don't know about The White Swan." It wasn't in our town, which meant it would be well out of our price bracket.

"There's always Rita," Sapphire said.

Now it really did go quiet. No one liked to say anything, but Sharon thought it would be better to fill the awkward silence.

"That's maybe not a good idea, love."

"Why not?"

Now, when a young woman fixes you with eye contact and demands a response, that usually means trouble.

"Rita—bless her—ain't got the best reputation for food."

"She can't be all *that* bad—there's always someone in there."

"You mean besides the health inspectors," I said, laughing.

"As far as I can tell," she said, expertly easing the situation, "Rita's caff is spotless. At least she doesn't have wipe-down seats."

"But have you ever noticed her clientele? No?" I got blank looks. "None of them are under seventy. They're like a bunch of extras from *Last of the Summer Wine*."

"Yeah," said Greville, "they're all stuck there suffering from reclining health and doting on her buns."

"Not to mention Rita's prune nibbles."

"Now, hold on," said the MD, shuffling from behind the desk. "What was that about Rita's prune nipples?"

"Good for the older residents," I explained.

"So what? Don't you like old people?" Sharon asked.

"*No*, I didn't mean that. It's just that somehow Rita has cornered the market for senior citizens."

Sapphire said, "Maybe they like Rita's low prices."

"Maybe they can't taste much," I said.

"Well, I wouldn't mind giving it a try." Sapphire was determined to get in there, somewhere, *anywhere*.

"Whatever you do, don't order one of her decapitated coffees—ugh!" choked Greville.

"Well, there's nothing wrong with my taste buds," said Sapphire.

*Not yet, there isn't, Sapphire,* I thought. *Not yet.*


## *The Wind in the Pillows*

It was the night of the party.

"Where is that bloody lad?" I was not best pleased because it seemed amazing just how, these days, whenever I wanted him he was nowhere to be seen. And the Saturday girl could be equally elusive. I suspected that he was training her in evasion. I was chasing about the shop looking in the most unlikely places: under the stairs, under the desk, in the storage area under the bottom window. Sharon told me the boy was most likely running an errand for me that I'd forgotten about. That was possible, bearing in mind the backlog.

"Have you checked the lavatory?" she asked me. "That's usually the first place to look."

"No, and do you want to know why? Because it's at the top of the bloody building."

"It's on the middle floor."

"Oh, all right—but it's up two flights of bloody stairs."

"He might be checking on his rabbits—yeah, that'll be it."

And so, in full-flap mode (as Sharon called it), I charged off upstairs. But I soon wished that I hadn't. Barely five minutes later I was frogmarching both Greville and Sapphire down the stairs. The girl was scarlet in the face—I'd seen Sharon use less-intense lipstick—and the boy had a look of indignation about him. When we got to the bottom they stood side by side, and Greville thought to pull up his zip. Before they went off in different directions, heads bowed, Sharon gave them both a nod to remind them to be careful, she later told me, and said it hadn't occurred to her that the boy wasn't the only one missing.

It was half past six and all we could see out of the shop windows was the Halifax Building Society sign reflecting on the wet pavement. We had decided to leave on the window lights to attract any town centre stragglers to window-shop whilst we were out celebrating. The five of us had changed into our best togs and even Sapphire had turned out looking a bit on the conservative side. We filed down the stairs to find a woman tapping on the shop door. Shop policy said we must never turn a customer away—whatever the time—so Greville unlocked it.

"Ooh, are you open?" we heard her say.

Sharon groaned, "I mean, it's pitch dark outside, none of the other shops is open, and here we all are dressed up and looking like we're on our way to a party. *Are we open?* Do we look like we is bleeding open?"

I told her we were never closed to customers, though I hardly believed it myself. I could hear Sharon sort of mumbling between tight lips, "No, don't do it, don't let her in," but the woman squeezed past me—all five feet two inches of her, slim with blue-rinsed hair (very popular at that time for the over-60s). Then she told us the story of the enormous gale blowing through her bedroom door. It was a common problem (for all house doors, that is) and there were many products and sort-outs for it, but as a hardware man I would choose to offer a solution that was appropriate to my assessment of the customer's abilities. So I started asking her questions and going through the rigmarole of matching a solution to the problem, even though I could sense the seething going on in the little crowd.

"You know what he's gonna do ... " I heard Sharon in the background. "He's gonna get out the little display door frame and go through *all* the options. I'd give her the first that come to hand and say, 'Here, take it, it's on the house,' just to get her out of the shop. But no. He gets more and more like the old man every day."

Right enough, I was torn between doing a proper job and trying to get away for the first ever Christmas party we'd had. But some of the draught excluders were over five quid. My professionalism was taking over.

"Oh, I don't think I want that one," the woman said, having in an instant turned into a discerning expert. "My next door neighbour says that stick-on stuff is rubbish and doesn't work. Haven't you anything else?"

"That'll be because your neighbour has stuck it in the wrong place. It's what people do, which is why we've got this model, to show you how to do it right ..."

Sharon was giving a running commentary. "It wouldn't be a bad result if he flogged her one of them at five quid, but no, she wants the ninety-nine pee one. He should've offered that one first, instead it's took over ten bleeding minutes to get there."

We were already twenty minutes late for the outing. Rita had been surprisingly (we had thought) booked up but had offered to squeeze us in between other bookings. And if the previous party hadn't yet left the premises, she had said we could wait in her kitchen and drink her mulled wine. I wasn't the only one looking forward to it, and the later we arrived the less were our chances of being treated to a traditional beverage.

The MD shuffled around. "What's the flaming hold-up? Is someone ill or summat?"

"No, but I'm nearly starving to death," Sharon told him. "I haven't eaten today."

"Ya what did you say—you haven't seen *who* today?"

"I said I haven't *eaten* today."

"You haven't eaten? Well, it's a good job the firm's buying you a good meal, then, isn't it?"

"That's why ... oh, sod it!" I saw her look at her watch.

"You're looking very nice, my darling," the woman said to me.

That was guaranteed to knock any bloke off his stride, and I realised what she was playing at. I heard Sapphire ask Sharon what was the matter.

"She's getting round to asking him to put it on for her," Sharon pretended to whisper.

"Would you be a dear and come out and put it on for me?" The woman placed her hand on my arm, imploring, with a hint of naughtiness.

Greville seemed impressed. "My God, the boss is on a promise, the randy git."

"Watch out," Sharon said. "She's old enough to be his mother."

"Well, I've heard that older women—"

"You're a lovely looking young man, I have to say," the woman said. "Very handsome. My husband was, too, so I know what I'm talking about."

Greville groaned. "Oh god, she's desperate."

"She's not the type to pay in hard cash," Sharon said out the corner of her mouth, but if I could hear her, then why didn't the woman? Selective hearing.

I thanked her, searching desperately for some get-out clause.

"If you come up to my house and put it on for me, I'll make it worth your while—oh, don't worry, I'll not insult you by offering money." My hopes sank.

"Well, there's a surprise," Sharon said. Little Sniffingham—all deep pockets and short arms."

"Oh, come on. If you do it tomorrow—come up during the day, mind, before my son comes home, and I'll look after you. I know how to look after a man."

Of course, in this town that could just mean that she would make me a drink of tea and, on a good day, mind, it might come with a biscuit—a plain one, of course.

I heard Sharon say something to Greville and Sapphire that if she has a son then why ...?

Then I felt a hand on my belly.

"I don't like men that've gone fat in middle age," she said. "You'll do for me just as you are.

Shall we say about two o'clock? That'll give us enough time."

# 20

WALKING PAST THE SILENT shop frontages was eerie. Greville nudged me.

"Ha! Looks like the Accountant's got competition. Where is she tonight?" he asked me.

"It's her office do."

Sharon squirmed a little. "Well it's not as if she's staff," she said and marched off in front.

"There's nothing like a bit of Christmas romance, is there? You can still pull the old ladies, can't you?"

"You should know all about pulling," I said. "Just tell me this—what was with the chimney sweep's brush?"

He pulled a face and grabbed Sapphire's arm. They strode off ahead. Tonight was certainly the night for thick pullovers and waxed coats—not shirts, ties and jackets as if we were going to a summer's ball. We were definitely underdressed.

Down the street and round to the left in the market courtyard, Rita's Edwardian frontage stood out like a beacon of hope, its welcoming Christmas lights deliriously sending a message of good cheer. We stumbled in the dark across the wilderness of cracked and wobbly concrete flagstones.

"I've heard," Greville began, "that Rita does a good joint." He sniggered and Sharon smacked the back of his head.

As we drew closer, the sounds of laughing, party-poppers going off like spatters of gunfire, some singing and general good-natured rowdiness permeated the bleak setting.

"Sounds like we're in for a good time," I said.

"Hey—hey! The previous lot's still in there," said Greville, rubbing his hands together. "Can you hear them?"

We arrived at the door, checked ourselves in the freezing stillness and went inside.

Rita's café was empty.

The door closed behind us, shutting out the cold air. And the party noise. Only Rita was there. She was wearing her chef's white top and stylishly-fitted check trousers.

"Hi," she smiled. "I'm so glad you could make it."

"Of course we've made it," I said, smiling. "We booked it, didn't we?"

She looked as if she'd been crying. The MD put in his two-pen'orth: "I hear you've been very busy. You've managed to get the previous lot cleared away nicely."

Sharon and I gave him a savage look. It went quiet for a few seconds.

"Oh, does that mean there'll be no Cliff Richard," said Greville.

"Cliff *who*?" asked Sapphire.

"That's *Mistletoe and Wine*, you twerp," I said.

More silence, during which we smiled abstractedly at no one in particular. Sharon attempted a kick-start.

"Well, Rita, we've all been looking forward to this, so what've you got for us, then?"

Rita looked stunned, if only for a second or two, then suddenly brightening:

"You'll see," and she went into the kitchen.

No one was licking their lips. Not even Sharon.

"Oh, my God!" I said. "I was afraid this would happen. We'll be lucky if we get tea-bag soup."

"Or cremated salmon," said Greville.

"Deflated *what*?" asked the MD.

Sapphire looked around at the empty tables. "Where do you think we should sit?"

"Take your pick," I told her.

"But aren't all these tables booked? I'll go and ask."

"This one here's a five-seater," Sharon said. "Just plonk your arses down."

"How does she earn a living," asked Greville. "She can't cook."

"Shush!"

"She probably lives off family money," Sharon suggested.

"She'll have a man tucked away somewhere," I said, knowingly.

"There's no bloke," Sharon said. "Believe me, I can tell."


*For Your Pies Only*

We sat in silence and unfolded the tissue-thin party hats, stretching them around our foreheads. There must have been a paper shortage that year.

"Nay, I don't know ... What on earth made us come here?" asked the MD.

"It was cheap," I told him.

"Oh, very good. Right then, we'll come here again. But surely they should have a Christmas tree."

"There's one over there." I pointed to a small spruce branch wedged somehow on top of a builder's bucket that I must have left behind on one of my plumbing trips. It looked like it might fall in if it wilted any further.

"Call that a tree? Now *that's* a tree that they get in London every year. That's what I call ..."

"Okay, keep your voice down." I was looking nervously towards the kitchen door.

"That thing looks like it could do with a good

feed. Got something on the shelves for that. I hope *we* won't be looking so under nourished when we leave." His voice was getting louder and echoed throughout the emptiness. Now Sharon was trying to shut him up.

"I've got bigger bristles on my chin ..."
"Shush, please!"
"Well, it's nobbut a twig." It seemed like he'd finished, then, "Looks like it could do with a splint."

At that moment, Rita came out, expertly carrying five plates on her arms that she set down for us. No one really wanted to look, and then Sapphire said:

"Hmm, that looks nice."

So we risked it and—sure enough—it was what seemed to be a professionally-presented prawn cocktail. Okay, so the seafood sauce may have come out of a jar, but it looked and tasted absolutely fine. This was confirmed by the agreeable noises from my fellow diners. So far so good.

"Well, let's just hope that the main course is just as nourishing," said Sharon. "After all, our colleague, there," and she pointed to me, "will need all his strength tomorrow—woncha?"

I thanked her for reminding me. Thankfully, the MD had been out of earshot whilst I'd been negotiating with the customer, so I didn't expect any lectures or other splinters of earache from him. Then he grabbed my arm.

"Eh—now don't forget to charge her. The full rate, mind—I don't care how many pillows she offers to put in your coffee."

There was more of this. They even joked about fixing me up with another woman of dubious domestic arrangements, Mrs Lipstick. Whenever she came in, she would look around shiftily and turn her back on all other members of staff except me. If they pushed her for an explanation of her requirements, she'd say, "Is the man in? I want to talk to him, no one else."

Now don't get me wrong, she didn't fancy me; I don't think she'd fancied anyone, ever, although she did have that one son: the spotty teenager of about 16 who never said a word, but accepted his mother's sniped orders: "Just move to one side. Keep that shopping bag straight. Don't look like that. Watch where you're walking. Don't ask questions."

"... it could even be Mrs Lipstick's older sister," laughed Greville. "Fresh out of the pantomime. Hey, boss—you could get more than you bargained for, tomorrow." He turned to Sharon. "Three in a bed, though—not bad, especially for an aging hardware man—"

"There's every chance there's an attractive woman under all that lipstick," said Sharon.

"It's not as if she's got it all over her face. But what does she want with *the boss*?" he asked her.

"Usually toilet stuff," I said. "She won't talk toilet to anyone else. It's like a patient discussing delicate issues with her doctor."

Rita served the main course: turkey and roast potatoes. Delicious. To say there were only five of us, by this time we were making quite a lot of noise, with the party-blower things going off all over the place, little popping bang things and the dreadful jokes courtesy of the budget crackers. And for a moment I seemed to detach from the little group, and watched myself and the others laughing, talking, joking. I think they called it "having fun", and it occurred to me, maybe for the first time, that having fun wasn't something you retired into, when and if you lived long enough, but something to enjoy whenever you could, and as often as you can. And for the first time I realised that, compared with Gerry's lavish party at The White Swan, it didn't matter that this was very much a budget occasion, and that the most important ingredient of the whole evening was *the company*. Then I was back with them in the present just as Sapphire was saying,

"That was lovely. I think people have been very negative about Rita and that's wrong. The first two courses have been fantastic."

"Just as well they have," said Greville. "Because I didn't bring my metal detector."

"And it looks like we got vee whole place to ourselves ... I wonder why that is." That was a conversation stopper. "Well, they have no idea what they've missed," said Sharon, mopping up the gravy with the last potato. "I had a sneaking suspicion that Rita's cooking just might be all right if we gave her a chance."

"But what about all the horror stories we hear about this place?" Greville whispered.

"It's quite simple. She hasn't a clue about baking. She has some cute romantic idea about having a little caff selling coffee and buns, but she don't know how to bake. Can cook, can't bake. That's how she makes scones you could use as aggregate in concrete mix."

"That's all you'd want for Christmas," said Greville. "A gift voucher to spend on buns like bullets at Rita's."

We asked him to keep his voice down, and we talked a bit about the seasonal gifts that the suppliers presented to us every year. These days they were beginning to get a little thin on the ground, as if they were hard up too.

"At least we can rely on Bird's for the MD's sherry," I said. Traditionally, every year he got the Harvey's Bristol Cream.

"Bit much for a part-timer, don't you fink? Do they do part-bottles?" said Sharon.

*Ooh,* I thought and changed the subject. "Greville, what is Father Christmas bringing you this year?"

He seemed quite proud, sitting up straight and raising his shoulders. "A Sony Playstation."

"Ha!" said the MD. "We were happy with a tangerine and a few nuts in a sock."

There was a unanimous cheer as Rita appeared to announce the impending arrival of the dessert.

"What is a dessert?" asked Greville.

"That's pudding to you," said Sharon. "What you got for us, ven?" she asked Rita.

"This is the part I've been waiting for all evening," said Greville. "Hey—hey!"

Sapphire smiled demurely.

"Has she said owt about the pudding, yet?" asked the MD.

Rita smiled and waited and then, having built up the excitement and expectation, she clasped her hands together and said:

"For the dessert—Yuletide scones!"

"*Scones?*" Greville said that with a fairly hefty dose of incredulity.

"What did she say—*stones?*" asked the MD.

"She might as well have done," said Greville.

"Does she mean mince pies?" asked Sapphire.

"With genuine Devon clotted cream," Rita added with a half-baked smile. "However, there *has been* a bit of an accident in the fridge ... so the sherry trifle is *off.*"

Greville was most concerned. "So the trifle's gone bad? Do you mean it's *mouldy?*"

"Oh, no." Rita paused momentarily, cooking up some appropriate explanation without giving away the precise ingredients. She whispered, "There was an incident concerning a glass trifle bowl." She'd have winked at us, but I doubt that she knew how. As she trotted off into the kitchen, Greville asked:

"So what's happened to the trifle, then?"

The first two courses had led us to expect a fitting end to the meal—in fact, we were expecting

192

it.

"I know what'll have happened." Sharon was no longer speaking quietly. "She'll have sprinkled hundreds and thousands all over," she said, nodding. "But what of? That's what I'd like to know."

We sort of went into a daze, imagining the multitude of decorations on top of the whipped cream. Then Rita appeared, smiling—to all intents and purposes the professional hostess. But this time she had just the one plate on her arm from which she plonked two pieces of scone on the table before each of us. They had already been jammed and creamed, quite neatly as it happened. We thanked her; our expressions were mixed. No one wanted to be the first to take a bite. It was Greville who said what everyone else was thinking:

"Should this cream really be looking like this?"

Sapphire said: "It has green bits in it. Ugh! I think it's gone off."

Greville was already performing a post mortem with a terminal screwdriver that he had taken to carrying with him at all times (he was learning fast). "Oh, yes—it's off, alright. I'm not having any of that."

Sharon sniffed the cream, then she dabbed in the tip of her finger just like Poirot or Inspector Morse would have done, and touched it against her tongue, then expertly licked her lips. We waited for the answer. Cyanide, arsenic, strychnine or just plain old penicillin?

"Cheese and chive," she said.

"What?"

"It's cheese and chive dip. It looks like clotted cream, but really the sprinkles of chives should've given it away. So vat's the good news—it won't kill yer."

"What's the bad news?" asked Greville.

"It don't go too well wiv strawberry jam."

"I think it's grand," said the MD as he put the last piece in his mouth. "Aye, it's champion. I'll have to get the missus to get some of that. Does anybody know what it is?"

"So what do we do, now?" Sapphire, like the rest of us, looked quite outdone.

Sharon was most definite. "We say nothing, d'ya hear? We don't want to upset her. The woman's got feelings just like the rest of us."

"I wonder if she's also suffering belly rot," muttered Greville.

I inspected a piece. "We could probably scrape it off. And just imagine the cream."

"I'd rather not imagine the cream," said Greville. "Not after this."

Sharon was inserting a knife. "If you do it like this and ... wait a bit ... there—no, damn it! I was trying to scrape it off without interfering with the jam."

"We don't want to interfere with any jam," said Greville.

She had another go, then impatiently scraped away the whole pinkish gunge and ate the scone. We watched her intently; there was something wrong. Eventually, she forced down the obstruction and, patting her chest—the gunge still hanging on to the knife—she delivered her evaluation.

"Bleeding hard. Christ! Go on, everybody—scrape it and gobble it down before she comes back."

"What do we do with the slime?" asked Sapphire.

Sharon looked around furtively, then removed her party hat and scraped the knife in it. She passed it to me.

When we'd consumed the bullet scones, we were left with the evidence in the form of a dollop that was a cross between *papier maché* and a rancid dish cloth. We were urged by Sharon to search our pockets for a polythene bag, but it wasn't the kind of thing you might find in your best gear.

"What the hell's gone wrong with the scones?" I asked.

Just then Rita appeared at the door.

"Anyone for seconds?"

Silence. Then Sharon asked for a doggy bag. We filled in with declarations of being full up. Rita looked uneasy, and I realised we'd blown it.

"I didn't mean to eavesdrop, but I couldn't help but overhear what you were saying. The thing is ... oh my gosh, I'm so sorry ... you see there *was* a little problem with the scone mix. Yes, I er ... might *not* have included the butter."

"Vat would explain it, then, Rita. It's an easy mistake to—"

"It was quite silly of me, I know—"

"Don't worry about it," I said.

"At the time I *knew* I was supposed to put *something* in there ... But I couldn't for the life in me remember what it was. And I was getting so flustered with all the bookings and the excitement of showing everyone how well I could do and how much I'd learnt."

"So instead you put in three parts sand and one of cement," said Greville, laughing.

Rita closed her eyes. There was a distinct whiff of sherry about her. I thought she was about to faint. Sharon motioned Sapphire to get her a chair—there were plenty spares—and we sat her down.

"Oh—and how was the cream?" she asked.

Now was the time, I thought. "Ah, the cream—"

"It was just fine," Sharon got in at lightning speed.

"Oh, really?"

"Yes, it was lovely."

"Right—because, you see, I wasn't absolutely

certain about it—"

"No, it was beautiful, Rita, it really was."

"Oh, I *am* relieved. There had been an incident—"

"Oh?"

"Yes, at the back of the fridge. The cream had become rather frozen ... So I'm glad you enjoyed it."

Rita took a sip of my sherry. I wanted to know more, so I asked her what exactly had happened with the frozen cream. She looked blank for a second, then:

"I ... found some more in a little plastic carton. Didn't realise I had it. At least, I think that's what happened." She hiccupped.

Sapphire sipped her sherry then looked at the glass and downed the whole lot. Another satisfied customer. The MD was tapping his fingers impatiently and humming abstractedly. I had no idea what he was waiting for; I don't suppose he knew himself.

"It hasn't been a good year." Rita spoke softly, the confidence gone. The MD, unaware that anyone was speaking, went on tapping. "Do you know, you're the only people that had the downright decency to turn up."

Sharon played stupid: "Really. Do you mean there were other parties due tonight?"

"Five. Forty-three covers in total."

Greville thought that amusing. "Covers? It's a caff—" But Sharon jerked under the table and Greville went, "Ow!"

"You were the only people to honour the arrangement." Rita's head wobbled a little. "You people are my true friends. All of you. I never found it easy to make friends—not *true friends* like you are. Although I have to say that since I was allowed to mix, I've found it easier to get on with people. Some are very decent, but none of them has been as decent as each of you. You are my *true*, true friends."

I didn't want us to have to mop Rita off her own floor. A change of subject was called for. Sharon must have been thinking on the same lines.

"So are you ready for Christmas, Rita, at home, like?"

"All of this might be laid at my father's door, you know. He bought this for me—oh, yes, even the freehold. I think he was somehow ... ashamed of me, maybe even a little embarrassed. Well, not *of* me, but ashamed of how or *why* I'm here. Does that make sense?"

We shook our heads, dreading what she might be about to tell us, and wondering whether we would get home to our beds that night.

"He was a very important man—*still is*, but I can't be a part of any of that."

Sharon asked the question on all our lips: "Who was your mother?"

"My mother? She was the housekeeper—or rather, she dealt with the administrative duties such as paying the house bills, buying in the food, paying the house staff." She tried to smile but her face was not working properly and she began to cry again. "I am a love child," she said, brightening momentarily.

"So you mean you were illegible?" I couldn't think what had got into Greville that night. It seemed that we couldn't take him anywhere. Further snippets of Rita's tale began to filter through the silence.

"One day the house was sold and my father was somehow able to marry my mother." She'd smiled, but it was exaggerated. "And I acquired his name, at long last."

She had asked if any of us wanted more sherry, but we declined, politely. When Rita eventually came out of the kitchen she ripped at one of Greville's ring-pulls, lined up all the sherry glasses and filled each with lager. We thought she was going to offer them around. Instead she drank them all one by one. I didn't think that Greville was too pleased.

"So what *is* your name, then?" he demanded.

Rita put a finger to her lips and ran the last drop of lager onto her tongue, her arms making wide, exaggerated movements like some dying ballerina swan.

We were walking back to the shop, every one of us quite a lot the worse for sherry—except, that is, for Greville, who'd been on cans of lager. It was freezing and the night was still. Only total idiots would be out burgling tonight.

We let ourselves into the shop, with its familiar smells of wax polish, creosote, softwood and coco brooms. It was sort of welcoming, but wasn't right for that time of night.

"Do you fink she'll be okay—Rita?"

I thought she was probably well-practised in looking after herself, and said so.

"I wonder what her name is—hey, she could be a royal! I was right about there being no bloke." Sharon said.

Greville preened himself for the imparting of sensitive knowledge. "I know what she's called. Do you want to know what it is? It's a mouthful." He didn't need much urging. "Are you ready? Her name is Saint John Choll-mond-elly. And she's got her own little dash between the bits."

"Christ, that is a lot, innit?"

"I saw it on her food hygiene certificate."

"Oh, so she managed to get one, then," I said.

Sapphire tried the words, but had forgotten them partway through. It was the MD who piped up next:

"Oh, you mean Sin-jun Chumley. Aye, the Sinjun-Chumleys. Course, they don't spell it like that. They had a big house over t' other side o'

Leeds. I knew it just after t' war, when I were a joiner. I used to do loads of jobs for them, mainly sticking sash windows, mouse-retrieval—"

"Mouse-retrieval?" Greville was still learning, you see.

I butted in: "You've sold plenty of waxed sash cord. What did you think it was for?" He looked as if I were about to insult him, so I carried on. "They use it to hang mice."

Sapphire winced.

"No, not like that—that's what they call the old lead weights that help the windows move up and down, yes ...?"

The MD was shaking his head. "Oh dear, oh dear. Heaven protect us." He sighed and started again. "These lead mice are hidden away in the wooden linings either side of the windows. Well, they used to drop off or the cords rotted, and I used to sort 'em out and make it all look like new again. It was always windows at that place—well, it was mostly the bloody mice."

Sharon stopped swaying about. "So what was he like, the owner?"

"Oh, I never met him. But his housekeeper was always ready with the tea. Now there was a nice woman."

"Yeah, sounds like it," I said.

"And by heck but she could make a grand scone, she could that."

"Pity she didn't pass on the recipe," I said.

Greville's brain was clicking away. "Perhaps she did," he said. "I mean the MD even likes those things of Rita's."

199

# 21

*A Winter's Tail*

HALF-PAST TWO THE next morning and the telephone rang. The easiest thing was to turn over and wait for it to stop. Eventually, it became part of my dream where I was an unqualified doctor beating the hell out of someone's heart whilst customers—make that patients—were banging on my door and the telephone was ringing non-stop. Sometime later, a woman nudged me with the new cordless telephone.

"It sounds like one of your Christmas party pranks gone wrong," she said.

I listened. At first it sounded like someone impersonating me, something about there being intruders on the shop premises. Then I realised and I got to my feet so fast it made me dizzy. The Accountant asked what I thought I was playing at.

"I'm on call," I grunted and hurriedly dressed.

When we got to the shop the street door was securely locked just as we'd left it only a couple of hours before, and there were no signs of a break-in. The alarm siren was cutting through the cold night with a horrible relentlessness and there would usually be a police presence, but that particular night they were having their Christmas bash. Of course, the burglars may have got in at the back— something I wouldn't discover until I was inside and it was too late and I'd been nobbled. It could be very dangerous going into raided premises, so I took the Accountant in there with me, just in case, you understand, and for the second time that night I was on the premises out of hours—which somehow never felt right; it was almost as if something was telling me that I had no right to be there. The only sounds in the unnerving stillness were our breathing, our careful footsteps and the occasional shake of the torch and associated cursing when the bulb dimmed. Creeping slowly along the aisles with the pathetic little light, one by one the gondola shelves and display units sank into the darkness as if taking a breath and steadying themselves before making their move on us once we'd passed.

We found the clues in the garden section: chewed pre-pack header cards and part-devoured packets of bird food scattered over the floor.

"You need some mouse traps," whispered the Accountant, still in her dressing gown. "They sell them at Woollies."

"We sell them here and I have no intention of using such barbaric items."

"Why ever not?"

"They're living creatures, that's why not."

"It's past three in the morning and we're here in our slippers wandering around a town centre shop in the dark. *I'm* not properly dressed."

"I won't tell anyone."

"And we could get arrested."

"Because you're not wearing any—"

"Because we're creeping around with a torch."

"It's bloody strange, this is."

"You're telling me."

"No, there hasn't been a rodent on these premises for over twenty-five years. The MD blocked up all the holes so no more rats. Oh, I tell a lie—we had a VAT inspection a couple of years back."

"They need catching."

"Wooden mousetraps are bloody cruel. If I thought they actually worked, I wouldn't sell them. We must have some small gaps somewhere."

"How small do they need to be?"

"Mice have floating skeletons, and this cold winter will be forcing them indoors to find shelter. It's either squeeze or freeze."

"So what do we do?"

"We leave and don't set the alarm. And we don't tell the MD."

"You probably could set it 'cause whatever it was it will have gone by now."

We listened carefully and, sure enough, it was the night before Christmas and not a creature was stirring.


*Snowbound*

It was a cold mid-January and I stepped out of the office, shivered and listened. The only sound came from amongst the aisles. I recognised it as the discernible noise that Sharon made when she was *almost* satisfied with whatever it was she had been doing. It usually meant that further improvement was not possible, but that never stopped her trying. I stretched before setting off to find her.

She stepped back to admire the new display of scissors.

"You'll not improve on that," I told her. And she knew that was the case. I'd had no idea there were so many varieties. I knew about kitchen scissors, household scissors, haircutting scissors, wallpaper scissors ... but this new lot filled every conceivable use.

"You know what? I think they've invented some new uses just so they can fill the display stand."

Sharon leaned forward and flicked away a trespass of dust.

"Feels like I've been at it all afternoon," she said. "How'd you get on wiv vat safe key? Got it to fit, now?"

"Yes, managed a clear run at it, with no interruptions." As soon as I'd said that, a niggling doubt tapped me on the shoulder. "Don't you think it's a bit too quiet? How strange," I said, walking towards the window.

"Yeah, as if the four-minute warning's gone off and they never told us."

It was dark outside, and unusually still. Even the silence was muffled. I opened the shop door to look out and eighteen inches of snow tumbled on to my feet. There was no movement in the street, just an unfamiliar wasteland of white that was picked out by stray neon shafts from the shop signs. Ice slithered down my sock when I stepped out on to where the pavement used to be. Where the main street crossed ours three cars had been abandoned and were now igloos. A solitary figure clumsily made his way, blowing short erratic bursts of vapour as he stumbled and slipped. Then he was gone. There was only me standing stranded in the shadow of the building opposite, the blackness of its walls going forever upwards.

"Bleeding 'ell. When did all this come down?"

When indeed. "The town's deserted. There's just you and me. When it began snowing dustbin lids everyone must have cleared off bloody smartish. Can you blame them?"

"I don't think your lady admirer will be tapping on the window tonight," she said, making me wonder how the poor woman was likely to get home in these conditions.

We shuffled inside, forcing the door closed with our joint weight and bolting it. We shivered in unison. It was four-thirty. We realised we'd not had a customer since three-ish and she'd not mentioned it was snowing. Sharon and I looked at each other.

"There'll be no buses. I'd better ring for a taxi."

"Forget the taxi," I said. "It's over two feet deep

out there."

"So how do I get home wivart an helicopter?"

I pulled a face. "You don't. We'll have to stay here."

Just then the phone rang. We looked at each other like Adam and Eve must have done when the Kleeneze lady left them a catalogue. We raced to it but Sharon got there first.

"Hello, Little Sniffingham Hardware and DIY. Can I help you?" A pause, then she handed it to me.

I listened to the woman at the other end of the earth and said, "Yes! I'll take one, but only if she comes with her own helicopter."

Pause. Then she turned impatient and angry with me. Maybe it was my fault for using the word *helicopter* and something was lost in translation. However, she did assure me that her girls could do kinky, but I thought it best to put down the phone. Sharon was amused, but not for long.

"It's showing no signs of melting," she said. "I don't fancy spending the night here wiv you."

*Thanks a bunch,* I thought.

"No, I didn't mean it like that. It's just so bleeding cold. Ugh!" and she paced up and down, rubbing her arms. Then, suddenly coming to terms with our predicament, she said, "Right then, come on—where do we do it?"

That was a good point. I had a brainwave. "The rest room!" I was about to run up to the attic to make preparations, but she grabbed my arm.

"No, don't bovver going up there."

"Why not? Greville's still got his rabbits, hasn't he?"

"There's plenty of hay, but the settee's gone."

"So that's you on the floor, then," I joked. Actually, both of us would be on the floor. I looked at my watch. It was a quarter to five—*a quarter to five!* "It's going to be a long, long evening."

"Yeah, and an even longer night. Look, I don't

want to be spending it up there."

"Why ever not? At least we have heat, electricity and a phone line, for all the use that is."

There was something spooking her. I didn't think it was a good idea to press it, so we began tearing up cardboard boxes that would provide some form of insulation between us and the floor. This was an old trick from Sharon's days working on the East End street markets where the stallholders used old packaging underfoot to prevent the cold striking up—through their feet, I mean. I'm not trying to make out that they laid down on the job.

Then I heard the unmistakable click of the phone line relay. It made that same noise whenever we switched it off. I checked the line. Nothing. So we couldn't even order a Thai bride if we had room for one.

"Better get an 'ot drink while we've still got the electric," said Sharon, and checked the grub cupboard.

There were just a couple of chocolate digestives that Greville had left, bless him. Better than nothing. It seemed the best idea was to put on our coats and retreat with the gas heater and cardboard upstairs to the middle floor because any heat produced in the shop during the day would have risen up there. We arranged the cardboard on the floor up to what would be the warmest wall, the one that adjoined Sunn Joly, hoping to get some residual heat from them, seeing as they had plenty of money. It could be quite cosy. Or there again, perhaps not. As we cleared away old display stands from the alcove I began to explain how there was once a doorway through into what was now Sunn Joly's staff room. It was blocked up many years ago when the property was re-allocated. Sharon was already jittery.

"You don't expect me to lay against *that*, do you?" she asked.

"Do *you* know something I don't?"

"It's just that my grandma once told me about a door that was itself a ghost. True story. Makes me shudder to think of it."

I said nothing but a tingle chose that very moment to scuttle down my spine and I looked up at the light bulb, willing it to keep working until morning.

"What time's it got to, then?"

It was twenty to six going on half past eleven. And neither of us felt like going to sleep. We settled down with our drinks, a biscuit each and the makeshift bedding. At ten past eight the light went off—that is, *all* of the lights went off. I'd just looked at my watch, that's how I know. And we sighed into the darkness.


The Southwold promenade was ridiculously quiet for such a lovely summer's day, and the tide was out. But the beach was empty. There should have been people, lots of them. Even the endless row of brightly-painted beach huts was deserted, every one of them boarded and locked as if it were winter. I looked around to see if any of the promenade cafés were open and told the person by my side to stop shaking my forearm. But they persisted and as I grew more anxious about the lack of people so the shaking became more determined.

"Wake up, wake up," whispered Sharon. *What the hell is **she** doing in my bedroom?* Her tone of voice told me something was very wrong.

"What is it?" I whispered back, already shaking.

A sharp intake of breath. She froze. I listened. There was a knocking. And it wasn't a vibration or any sound caused by an inanimate object. This had purpose behind it. Sharon moved away from the wall but still gripped my arm.

"It's the door—it's the bleeding door! I knew we shouldn't be up here!"

I tried to listen harder, but Sharon's heavy breathing was getting in the way. The knocking seemed to have stopped. She held her breath.

"It's okay," I said.

"No, we're not! There's something else here with us ... in this very room."

Then it began again: *tap tap tappety-tap.* Pause. *Tap tap tappety-tap.*

"Oh my God! Oh Christ! Please tell it to go away. I'll do anything ..."

"Just listen!" I said, and placed my ear against the wall.

"Don't do that," she hissed. "Come away from there!"

After a few seconds I knocked the same rhythm on our side. There was a pause, and then a succession of bold knocks.

"You were right, Sharon. We're not alone."

Out on the street, with my legs rapidly sinking in a three-foot snowdrift, Gwendolin—the tall girl that she was—called out to me through the fanlight of the travel agent's toilet window.

"By heck, Chuck, am I glad to see you."

"So what's it like in there," I called up to her.

"Well, Chuck, it's lovely, really lovely, would you believe. We've got all the comforts of home. It's fair paradise. Except that we're effing freezing and we've no idea how to bypass the air conditioning timer."

"Right." I was playing it cool. I mean, conditions were probably better on our side of the wall.

I could see the canny lass weighing things up in her mind. "So what've you got your side?"

"We've got some cardboard boxes. To lay on."

"Well, Chuck, just so long as you're all right," and she began to shut the window.

"Oh yes, and a gas heater."

She stopped. The window opened just a fraction.

"We've got reclining chairs—enough for all four of us. And you could always cuddle with me, like I once learned on an Outward Bound course."

That got me thinking about how I could get the reclining chair but without the reclining maiden? It was risky, and compromises may come into play before the night was out. It would take some careful consideration.

"So do we have a deal, Chuck?"

"Deal."

I wasn't quite certain exactly what the arrangement entailed, but I assumed—nay, *hoped*—that it was comfortable chairs for heat. But then the opportunity to exchange body heat also entered the equation. I just hoped that Gwendolin had a sense of humour. She met me at the staff entrance and took her fair share of the weight of the heater, mentioning in passing as we struggled up the steps in the pitch darkness that she couldn't wait to remove her tights as they were now sopping wet. Indeed, I would need to be careful.

Within twenty minutes of hearing knocking from the other side, we were watching the intense orange of the gas burning in the pots and savouring the comfort of the mild hissing sound with its occasional pops. It was one of the most beautiful sounds we had ever heard. The extra run of adrenaline had made us all wide awake and we joked about Gwendolin and Julie, Sunn Joly's latest trainee, having heard my snoring and believing at first they were hearing noises from the past. Julie didn't say much but seemed to be taking everything in, watching us with her big eyes, making me wonder what they might have witnessed in previous incarnations. I noticed her watching Sharon, weighing her up. Perhaps she recognised her from being on television. I asked Julie how long she'd been working there.

"Five weeks and three days," she said without hesitation.

"Sounds as if you're really liking it."

"No." There was nothing more.

It was the wrong time of day, but by now my mind was racing and ready to go—not that there were many options, so I broke the silence. It was more of a desire to find out more about the quiet one.

"So you thought it might be snoring from the past, did you?"

"It could well have been from the past." She was quite indignant. "I know about these things. My gran told me." And that was it; a medium-height girl who spoke in small paragraphs. When she finished speaking you knew instinctively that was it, and this was confirmed in the way she gave a final disdainful sideways glance at you.

*But I'm not yet ready to go to sleep*, I thought. "Your gran sounds like a mystical woman."

"She knows things."

"O-kay. Go on then, tell us a ghost story."

I caught her expression of surprise in the reflected orange glow.

"No!"

"No? What do you mean, *no*? It's gonna be a long night. Might as well tire ourselves silly."

She sighed heavily. "Well, my gran knew a woman lived down her street and every Tuesday at four o'clock she heard a child's footsteps running up the stairs and it left the bedroom window open. But she hadn't opened it."

Gwendolin whispered, "Oh."

Sharon shivered. Julie had everyone's attention. It sounded like this one was going to be a cracker of a tale. She had stopped again.

"Yes? Go on."

"Anyway, it all turned out that many years before, this little boy had run up there and out on to the balcony but he'd forgotten that the balcony had been taken away."

And we were left listening to the hiss of the gas fire.

"And that's it?" I asked, feeling incredibly cheated. "You mean that's all there is?"

Julie merely pulled a face as if, what else could there possibly be? It was done, finished. End of story.

"So it starts off okay, a bit lacking in detail, perhaps—and then fizzles into nothing? Great. Thanks."

"What more did you want?"

"Well," I began, "as hard as it is to believe, I could tell you a story that's actually shorter than that one."

I waited for some encouragement, but only Gwendolin smiled at me.

"Right. Next door in our shop, whenever we're in the office, we'll sometimes hear a footstep right outside the office door. Greville will say, 'Crikey, there's someone in the shop,' but when we go out there's no one there. That's it. The end." I looked at Julie. "Beat that for the world's shortest ghost story," I said.

"My gran's been in your shop and she told me there's an entity in there."

"What does that mean—*an entity?*"

"Something's moving around, wandering the aisles, searching—"

"And does this entity move fast or slow?"

"Ooh, very slow—"

"Uncertain where things are, trying to recognise things that weren't there in its own time?"

"Yes!" she said, a spark of life at last. "How did you know?"

"That's only the MD."

She grimaced. For a while no one said anything. We sat there, the heat burning our foreheads, but the overall temperature not warm enough to even think about removing our coats.

"I've got a story." said Sharon.

All heads turned to her.

"Not a *ghost* story, though." She paused as if waiting for permission to carry on.

I'd have used my hand to motion for her to continue but it was firmly clasped beneath Gwendolin's in my coat pocket. I was glad I hadn't put it in my trousers pocket.

"It was when I was at the BBC back in the early eighties. *Doctor Who*. I played an alien. No one could tell who I was because of all the rubber and sticky latex that they brushed over me. It was horrid. All I had on underneath was this sort of thin nylon leotard that they hoped no one would be able to see. It took hours to put the make-up on. It was bad enough not being able to go to the loo, but when it came to doing me face ... well—"

"Hang on—you were in *Doctor Who*?" That was Julie. There was hope for her yet.

Sharon continued. "The other problem was not being able to see where I was going. This thing didn't have eyes, see, so they gave me a tiny earpiece and this girl directed me from the gallery."

"So who was the doctor, then?" Julie again. She was turning into a right little chatterbox, wasn't she?

"It was Peter Davison at that time. Oh, he was lovely. Good fun. But the BBC were a right set in those days. Very mean. They were going through some crisis or other, I don't know. And that's what the problem was, see? This particular day we was running late. Couldn't begin recording 'til after five. By half nine we was nowhere near finished and at that time the BBC had this rule that come ten o'clock all the power to the studios would be pulled.

"And yet they knew we was working like bleeding hell to get finished. They had post-production people expecting our stuff to be ready for them to work on the next morning. So we carried on. Me, I had no idea even what time it was. Couldn't ask because me mouth was gummed up. All I had was this little squeaky voice telling me when and where to move. I hadn't had a thing to eat since seven that morning and I couldn't remember the last time I'd had a pee. And I was bursting, I can tell you."

By now the three of us were leaning forwards to this excellent storyteller. She did the atmosphere, the voice, and all the hand gestures. We were hooked.

"So there I was, standing there like a ... like a clapped-out dog chew waiting for a bus. There was always a lot of waiting in filming so it was normal. You just waited 'cos someone would always come and get you. The minutes could seem like hours but then the hours could seem like minutes so you see you never knew where you was. So I waited. And I waited some more. I thought about chewing away the latex around me mouth so I could call out but if I ended up ruining a take there'd be the extra time and work in making me up again. They wouldn't be pleased, so I kept quiet.

"Couldn't hear a bleeding thing. Noffing. I got to thinking, after what seemed like hours—but like I said it might not have been—that either the earpiece was bust—they was always on the blink—or, worse still, they'd all gone on a break and they'd had to leave me 'cos of me make-up. Then it occurred to me that if they was resting surely they'd have told me, wouldn't they? And there wasn't time for a break, unless we'd been given an extension, which wasn't bleedin' likely."

"Latex?" said Gwendolin. "That must have felt

horrible."

"It was very warm, pulling at your skin. And under them lights it's sweaty and very, very hot. Trouble is, there was nowhere for the sweat to go so it was like being in a plastic bag. The thing is, I began to feel cold."

Julie's mouth had actually dropped open.

"So I decided that I'd count to a number and then I'd jiggle about and attract their attention. That way I wouldn't be spoiling anything much."

"What did you count to?" asked Julie, almost whispering.

"At first I thought about a thousand."

"A *thousand?*"

"But I reached three hundred and thirty-seven and then I felt that I just had to get out and I jiggled and I wriggled and struggled and fell over and couldn't get my arms free. I was desperate to get my arms and my face uncovered at the same time and I just couldn't."

Sharon was almost in tears. Then I saw an orange droplet glistening down her cheek.

"What the bleeding hell was I supposed to do? What was I supposed to do to get all that shit off of me? And no one—not one person in that bloody place—came to me."

"Steady on, Chuck, steady on. You're with us now. You're not stuck in a sausage skin any more," soothed Gwendolin, splitting herself between Sharon's shoulder and my hand.

"But we are stuck," said Julie, her voice rising an octave. "We're stuck here and we might never get out!"

"Shut up!" snapped Gwendolin before turning back to Sharon. "Don't think about it. It's all in the past, you're okay now. You're with us, aren't you? We're here with you. You're not alone."

Sharon produced a tissue from somewhere and wiped her cheeks.

"So what happened next?" demanded Gwendolin.

"I rolled along the floor until I got to a piece of set. I think it was the Tardis's console, but not sure, and I rubbed against it 'til I got an arm free. But I couldn't reach my face. And I couldn't breathe. I really felt like I was suffocating, I really did."

Each of us was seeing this woman so cruelly encapsulated in rubber, rolling about in Doctor Who's Tardis, gasping for breath, desperately trying to rub through to her skin on the plywood set. It was far more horrific than anything that had ever been on that damned programme in the eighties.

"I don't quite know how I managed, but I supposed I was panicking and whenever I moved my elbow the elastic slapped it back against my side, and I kept trying and trying, again and again ... until finally I got it out and I was able to rip away that godawful stuff from my face." Dramatic pause. "And then I saw it."

"My God, what was it?" shrieked Julie.

"Blackness. Pure blackness, it was. Thought I'd gone blind. Nothing. Nothing and no one. No lights. Everyone had gone. I realised what had happened and I ripped that crap off me and I didn't bother about it as I stood there in that huge place as good as naked 'cos the leotard was in shreds, shivering and alone."

"My God, that must have been awful, Chuck."

"I staggered through the sets falling over things, bumping into wooden walls, scraping the skin off my legs on raw edges and supporting props, desperately trying to remember the layout so I could find the exit. It's as big as an aircraft hangar and to this day I don't know how I got out of there."

Each of us was living the experience with her.

"But you did get out okay," said Julie.

There was a pause, then, "Yeah. I mean I'm here now, aren't I?"

"But you're not ... *affected* in any way."

"Nah. Right as rain. Never looked back—not 'til now, thinking about me eyes glued over and me arms stuck by me sides waiting for a silly bitch with a dodgy accent to tell me to inch forward a bit, right a touch, left a millimetre, back a little more—the stupid cow."

We agreed that the Daleks had nothing on that little real-life horror story and we settled down, relieved for Sharon as well as for ourselves because, after all—although right now we might *feel* imprisoned—captivity is relative. Come the morning everything would be getting back to normal. The snow should be melting, the buses and cars would be able to move and shoppers would fill the town just as they always did. The gas fire hissed and popped and baked our faces and our eyelids began to close.


It was the sound of the snowplough that woke me up at just passed six. All three women had turned over and were sleeping on their sides. Gwendolin had somehow managed to retrieve her hand that was now clenched beneath her chin. I got up, curious to inspect the quality of the plumbing in the staff toilets and see what sort of cowboys a big company like this had employed, like you do when you're a hardware man. As it flushed on the third attempt (and not through any fault of mine) I heard the sound of a vacuum cleaner downstairs. So at least the power was back on.

At first I thought maybe Gwendolin or Julie had gone downstairs to tidy up the shop, so I went down to chat with them.

"Hello, love." The rounded and rather middle-aged woman with obviously dyed black-hair was pushing an ancient 1960s' Hoover Senior vacuum cleaner. There were still quite a few of them around because they were built like tanks and infinitely repairable. She switched it off and began winding up the flex. Strangely, it had an old 15-amp round-pin plug on the end. You get to notice these things.

"Hello, don't I know you?" I asked.

"Of course you do, love—or you should."

"That's right, you used to clean here when it was Timothy Whites chemist."

"Aye, love, I did that."

"Crikey, that's going back a bit." She must have looked far older back then than she really was. "And you're still here."

"Still going strong, still going strong. It'll be a bad day when they make me give up. And tell me, my love, how's your boss these days?"

"Er, he's doing okay, thanks. Still puts in a few hours every week, you know." I tried very hard not to mention the exact days he was there. I had my reason.

"Ah, I'm so glad he's all right. He was a lovely man. Very kind and gentle."

Was she getting confused in her old age? I mean, did that sound like the MD?

"I can't get over you still being here. We'd no idea. You must come with the premises," I joked.

"It'll take a lot to get rid of me, love. By, but I've seen some changes. Stuff's always changing. They can't leave owt alone, can they? Well, I need to be away. Got lots to be getting on with. Give my love to the gentleman, won't you?" she said, winking at me, and she wheeled the vac into the rear office.

Back upstairs the ladies were straightening themselves, jostling for the one and only mirror. I switched on the kettle and prepared the mugs.

"The power's not on yet, Chuck," Gwendolin yawned.

"Well, it's on downstairs. Hey—you'll never guess what," I began. There wasn't much interest but I was determined to tell them anyway. "Listen, when I was a kid this place was a chemist's. Anyway, the cleaner fancied the MD and she used to get his attention by talking to his dog out in the yard. He was a bit of a nasty brute—the dog, I mean. And one day she decided to tease him by taking away a bone that the butchers next door had given to him. And guess what—he bit her, right there on the chin."

"Your dad bit the cleaner?"

"No, Julie. Sometimes there's just no shutting you up, is there? No, the dog bit the cleaner. He put a little dimple in her chin, right there."

The three women were watching, waiting for the punch line.

"And I've just seen that very same dimple. That cleaner's name ... was Mrs Barker!"

I waited for their reaction, but it didn't come.

Sharon tried her best. "So the dog bit a woman called *Barker?*"

"Yes ... but don't you see? It's thirty-odd years later—almost forty, for god's sake—and Mrs Barker, *the same Mrs Barker*, is still cleaning this very same building."

Julie was troubled. "The cleaner here isn't called Barker."

"Maybe she got married again ..."

And then I remembered. Mrs Barker the cleaner had died sometime in the 1980s.

# 22

*Sticking charges*

I COULDN'T GET IN the car park that morning because there were wagons and workmen in there digging holes, which meant that I had to drive past the end of our street. Glancing down towards the shop I spotted what looked to be a bundle of timber and a long cardboard box in front of the bottom window. But we weren't due for a timber delivery, so maybe I was mistaken and it was something else.

When I got to the shop the window shutter and its steel box were scattered across the pavement, and pedestrians were cursing me for obstructing their progress. The woodwork above the window was shredded where the shutter's box had been ripped away, and at that moment I wasn't so much concerned with how it had happened so much as what to do next, before someone deliberately tripped over the debris and sued us for damages and loss of earnings, loss of memory, whiplash, anxiety attacks, you name it. Call me suspicious, but I didn't want to leave my case (containing the cash float and my sandwiches) on the pavement whilst I humped the bits of shutter into a secure pile, so I opened the shop door. That meant I had to go in and turn off the alarm and, just as you'd expect, a crowd of customers followed me inside, meaning I had to serve them, whatever kind of hazardous obstacle course was outside begging for my attention. One customer gave me a cutting list for timber and plywood (it looked like he was building a rabbit hutch), and said he would wait whilst I cut it out for him.

It was Greville who, with Sapphire's help as she passed on her way to school, brought the bits inside. The landlord of the Malt Hovel came in to tell me that it was a large wagon that had driven on to the pavement and collided with our shutter box as it squeezed past the brewery wagon parked outside his pub. The driver had stopped and the landlord watched him as he wrote his details on a slip of paper and stuffed it through our letterbox. And, right enough, when I checked through the post there it was: a blank scrap of paper.

Sharon went spare, asking how much would a new shutter cost, and how certain people should be castrated for damaging other people's property and not being responsible. Her language that day was somewhat ... strong—no, make that *raw*. I'm sure there were some words that I'd never before heard, yet there was no mistaking to what portions of anatomy they referred.

Greville was sweeping up the half-links from beneath the chain dispenser when Ram Raid Roger came in from the music shop. If his name had begun with a P we'd have nicknamed him Paranoid Pete. As it was, he had an unhealthy obsession with being ram-raided, and for years had been badgering the Council to stick concrete bollards in the pavement outside his shop, when all he kept in the window were some descant recorders for the school kids, an under-nourished-looking drum kit and a non-electric guitar. Now he approached the counter with a different expression: one of sympathy and understanding, and quite inappropriate really. I didn't want any of it.

"Oh, my friend. Don't tell me—they've had you, haven't they? Now they have, I know these things, I can tell. But do you know what? The two of us is stronger than one, and together we can force them slimy-arsed buggers at the Council to give us the bollards we deserve."

"But we've not been ram-raided."

His expression looked like I'd just told him that black was white. "You have! I've seen the damage."

"We haven't."

I watched as his get-up-and-go demeanour simply sagged away. He looked disappointed, forlorn. I almost felt sorry for him. I'd spoilt his day.

"Oh. Well, it's not like the Council won't be able to afford to bollard us," he said. "All the time I've been on at them they've said how short of money they are. Well, they won't be short for much longer, not with these confounded parking charges they're bringing in ..."

His last words seemed to have been said in slow motion, slurred and distorted. I looked up at him, blinking, disorientated.

"Oh, yes," he said. "I'm surprised you haven't heard about it. That's why all the car parks are shut today, see—so they can put the meters and signs in."

"But ... but we were at that meeting back in November."

"Oh, that doesn't matter. They'd already made their minds up. A public vote is only any good if it agrees with them who make the rules. They've shown us who's boss and it's you and me that's stuck with the consequences. And every other poor bloody shopkeeper in town."

He asked what we intended to do about the shutter. We didn't know, but he said he knew someone who works for a big firm of security shutter specialists, and did private work on Sundays as a sideline. He was a pigeon fancier from Doncaster, and he was cheap—cheaper than paying the excess on the shop's insurance policy. I let Sharon make the arrangements.

## On the edge

"My bosses are poking, Chuck. Poking everywhere."

It occurred to me that these days I was asking all our fellow traders how they were doing. Why? Because since parking charges had been forced upon Little Sniffingham, none of the car parks was full anymore, the shoppers' footfall was markedly reduced, and the money had just about stopped flowing.

Ram-raid Roger summed it up when he said, "It's just like somebody's turned off the tap."

"Into every corner, Chuck. You wouldn't believe where they're sticking their big noses. And it's not like I haven't told them what's happened."

"Parking charges?"

"Parking charges. And the attack on America. Between them they've cost us four months' downturn in sales. I've told them it's hardly my fault no one's coming into the shop—"

"Your breath reeking of garlic won't help," Sharon said from across the shop.

Gwendolin didn't quite catch the comment, and carried on. "But they're thinking about either replacing me or shutting down the branch altogether."

"Really?"

"Well, these branches cost a lot to run, you know." And she flashed her eyes at me. "Thousands," she added, confidentially, "tens of thousands."

"Well, they don't spend it on photocopiers, do they?" Sharon said.

"Consumer confidence has been nobbled, Chuck," she said. "And now the parking charges have blown it for us. I've got six girls next door with nothing to do."

Greville suddenly perked up. He had been

assembling another dozen sweeping brushes as there was little else for him to do. The MD was creeping about like a Shakespearian soothsayer. He stopped to deliver his latest premonition.

"Before long, you know, with all these folk getting their own computer-thingies, they'll be buying their own holidays with that new intercourse thing."

"I can't see that happening," I told her, motioning to her not to take any notice of him. "With computers? No, people will always want shops. You'll be okay. We all will."

She signed for her copies and left. I'd never seen her look so downhearted. Sharon came up to me as we watched her go down the aisle.

"Look at her, the trollop, wiggling her hips, strutting out."

"I can't believe this. Only a few months ago, when we were snowed in, you and her were bosom pals."

"Pah! I seen the likes of her before. She can see the end's not far away and what's more, she'll do anything for her next meal. And judging by the eyes she was flashing at you I wouldn't put anything past her. At least you had the good sense to try and make her feel better, before she exchanged her honour for a bag of chips."

"Did you hear that?" I couldn't believe it. "*Thousands*—to run *that* place? That's rubbish. It's not like they've any stock like we have here. Okay, so their takings are down and they're panicking like it's the end of the world. Crikey, our stock holding can easily run into *tens* of thousands of pounds—and most of it is dead at any one time." I turned to Greville, thinking that this was a worthwhile lesson in running a business. "Just look at that wagonload of barbeques we got in last summer. And the weather was lousy and since then we've had to store them all away—all paid for, mind, and bloody un-saleable. If the sun doesn't shine again, or if someone invents a better way of cremating sausages in the back garden—like a solar powered model—"

"Heaven forbid!" called Sharon, but I ignored her joke.

"—then we've lost the lot. We've also had to get used to weathering storms from bad trade winds. It comes with the territory." The MD made some agreeing grunts. "And, would you believe it, our rich trading cousins next door are contemplating suicide? What a laugh!"

Sharon looked at me and she said what she was thinking.

"You're in denial, you are. The travel agents isn't the only ones finding it hard. It's the same for all of us."

"But what's going to happen to us all?"

"People will get used to paying to park and they'll start to come back."

"By which time we'll be long gone. It's costing me nearly forty quid a week just to park the car so I can come to work. It's criminal! It's like robbery with violence!"

She grabbed my arm, squeezing it gently, urging me to calm down, but it only made me feel worse.

"That's what all that bother with the bank was about—those buggers knew what was coming. Oh yes, friends on the council, funny handshakes, winks in the right places, massaging each others' back pockets, pissing in the same pot ..."

"It's okay, Graham, it's okay, it's okay." She rubbed my arm all the harder.

Greville stopped by the tape measures' display stand and looked longingly at one of the hooks. She left me to put her arm around his shoulders.

"Still hankering after the big one, Grev?"

"Huh! The chances of getting that one clipped

to my belt are just about bloody gone," he said.

He was referring to the Stanley PowerLock tape measure that was awarded to staff once they had taken fifty grand's worth of sales. But it wasn't just any old tape measure—oh no, this one was ten-metres long and in a steel case, not a crappy plastic import. Once clipped to your trousers belt you could swagger along knowing full well you were able to report the length of anything (well, almost) that came to hand. It was a badge of office, a sign of a true hardware man (once you'd mastered the technique of wedging a carpenter's pencil behind your ear). It would mean that you couldn't only measure things but could *sell them* as well. Oh yes, only the best measured up to owning such a massive device. Hardware men didn't think about the bulge in front of their trousers; it was the one on their sides that mattered.

"It'll all come right. It always does," Sharon told him, but I could tell that she'd almost exhausted her personal cache of positive platitudes on me.

"Didn't you hear what Gwendolin just said? Even *holiday* sales are taking a nose-dive," I reminded her.

She patted Greville on the head and told him to open the back door to the yard to get some air into the place. "My clothes is fair sticking to me," she said.

As soon as he opened the door he let out a gasp and slammed it closed before staggering back into the shop, making gasping, wheezing noises. The butchers' rotting meat must have been on the move. I have to say that his performance was rather good, and you could have believed that he was indeed choking. I looked at Sharon.

"Well done. Almost good enough for a soap opera," she said.

He staggered towards us with one hand stretched out, pleading for supplication.

"What on earth's the matter?" I asked him, beginning to laugh, desperate for some light relief as he did a lop-sided limp like the hunch back of Notre Dame.

"It's the smells ... the smells ..."

He straightened suddenly when he saw who was standing behind me. I turned to find Gerry's supercilious grin. Sharon looked as if she wanted to smack it right off his face.

"So here's the big man. How ya doing, Pal?"

My face straightened. Between clenched lips I asked him what I could do for him.

"Now then, Squire, what's all this I hear about you selling up?"

"Why—would you be interested in buying if we were?"

"Bollocks, no! I mean, who'd want to trade *from here?*"

"Well, you did once."

"Ah, but times have changed, Squire."

He stood there, making the floor look untidy.

"So what can I do for you?"

"I just heard that you might be on the market, that's all. You never know, I might know someone who's interested. *Maybe.*"

"What makes you think we'd want to sell? We've got a great little business—"

"*Little*—as big as that, is it?"

"—that's been going since the end of the war."

"Ah, well, from what I hear you're *going*, all right—right down the mountain. Make way for the big boys, eh."

Maybe he'd hit a nerve. I began to walk away—for *his* sake, but Gerry wasn't yet done.

"Hey, if your trade is so good, tell me where have all your customers gone?"

I stopped dead in my tracks. I didn't turn around—I *daren't* turn around. Gerry was on a roll and he knew it, and he went on, twisting the knife.

"Shall I tell you where they are? They're all shopping on the outskirts of town."

I turned to face him. "So at least now you admit you're on the outskirts."

"That's where they can park for free." And he tapped the side of his nose. Then he brandished his finger. "And you know what the best news is? The Council has said they have no intention of ever charging shoppers to park in that area. Isn't that fantastic?"

"That's 'cos there's nothing out there," Sharon called to him. "And it's not an area—it's a bleeding wilderness. That's why it's free parking."

Gerry backed off when Sharon and Greville came to stand on either side of me. I could sense Sharon was doing her Macbeth witch's expression, and I sort of hoped he would launch into his routine about being given a license to print money like he usually did because she had told me the next time he did that she would slap him. Instead he backed off.

"I see you've been catching up on your staff training," he said. "Even if it's only your guard dogs." And he left.

We stood there looking at each other, feeling pretty smart that we'd seen him off. But it was short-lived because then he came back to fire a final shot from the doorway:

"Hey! There's a man out here doing wonders for my business." Then, to someone in the street, "Carry on, Pal, you're doing a great job. They need their driving licences taking off them." And he was gone.

We shot down to the door. On the way I said:

"Grev, get a bag of sand and cement—there, that one—no, a *bigger* one ..."

Out in the street the customer that Greville had just served was looking aghast at the scribbling traffic warden.

"Do you want this large bag putting in the boot, sir?" I asked. "It's okay, the boy will do it for you."

He looked at me blankly. Greville struggled the 38 kilo bag around to the back of the car.

"Oh," I said, looking surprised at the warden. "I'm sorry, I didn't mean to interrupt, but this gentleman has just bought this very heavy bag of ready-mixed mortar. Is the boot alright, sir? It's just that it's killing the boy."

The warden sighed, scribbled across his pad and put his pen away. I could tell he didn't like doing that.

"These are double-yellow lines," he said, with a little squeaky voice. In fact, he sounded just like Greville looked at that moment with his face going red and his eyes about to pop out.

"And he's allowed to load heavy items, surely?"

The traffic warden walked away.

I motioned for Greville to take the bag back in the shop and I smiled at the man with the car.

"I shan't be coming here again," he said.

I hesitated, if only for a second or two. "Excuse me, Sir, but we've just saved you from a twenty quid fine."

He waved his hand as if he was throwing me away, got in his car and drove off.


## *Measure for Measure*

Apparently we weren't the only ones who were desperate, which is how we got into trouble with the police—oh, don't worry, we hadn't committed an offence. No, just a cardinal sin, as you'll see. Despite the monthly No Nickers meetings, stock did sometimes find its way out of the door without an exchange of cash. And this particular item was spotted by Sharon.

It had been there when she'd left the day before and, being the highly-priced—and highly-prized, by Greville—tape measure, she'd asked who had earned the cherished Mars bar. I mean, it must have been sold because the boy's numbers were nowhere near high enough for him to win it. So who had sold it? Who would be presented with the much coveted "flogged-it" award—the Mars bar that no one really wanted to eat because of what it would do to your arteries? When she found that no one knew anything about it she went up the wall, as she later put it, saying that it added a whole new meaning to the term *stock-taking*. I heard Greville telling the MD that Sharon wasn't a glad rabbit. He couldn't have said a truer word.

We did a quick scan of the previous day's video tapes. It showed how a young lad had craftily waited for her to go home, then he appeared from hiding behind a tall gondola (so none of us would be alerted by the doorbell), and furtively pocketed the tape.

"I think I recognise him," said the young policewoman as she gazed at the little telly we had set up. "Was his hair fairish but not quite blonde? Hmm, that's the lad I pulled out of the pub over by the canal bridge a couple of weeks ago."

"So he'd been drinking?" I asked.

She shook her head, still watching the lad as he crept down by the tools and went straight for the biggy.

"His father had dumped him in an upstairs room while he got drunk in the bar. The lad scared the life out of the landlord's daughter when she found him hiding in her bed."

"You put the lad in care, then?" Sharon said. " 'Cos if he's coming in here and nicking stuff it's not working very well, is it?"

She turned to face her. When they do that it's the training; they think it gives them the upper hand.

"Yes, I did place him with a family."

"Well, they've done a rubbish job of looking—"

"But only for a couple of nights."

"Oh. Long as that."

The policewoman was beginning to look a bit pissed off, and I didn't want a bitch fight in the shop while we were still open.

"The lad is nearly sixteen. There's not much we can do with him." She got out her paperwork and whatever. "What do you want us to do?"

"Nick him," she said. "Nip it in the bud before he turns into a right thieving bastard."

"Seems like he's had a poor upbringing," I said. "I just want the tape back." I knew we couldn't sell it because now it was effectively second-hand, but we could have saved it for Greville. He wasn't so very far from the goal.

"There's little chance of that. It'll have been sold on—"

"Do you know where he lives?" Sharon asked her.

"I must warn you—"

"Because I'll get the tape back. You just see if I don't. I'll make the little bleeder—"

The policewoman turned to me.

"Yes, the lad has had a poor time, what with his mother running off—"

"Oh, no." I felt stricken to hear it.

Sharon wasn't such a pushover, looking as if she'd heard it all before.

"And leaving little Wayne to look after his two younger sisters. The drunken father was no use," she went on.

Greville, his voice about to tremble like an earthquake, said, "So what happened?"

"The two younger children were taken into care. Wayne couldn't look after them by himself."

Sharon went straight in.

"He was a teenager—of course he couldn't look after them. He'd be buggered looking after himself. So why steal, eh? Answer me that!"

She looked at me, ignoring her.

"Do you want us to pursue this? It's your decision, but I would advise against it. Nothing's likely to come of it, petty theft."

I hesitated.

Sharon was all guns blazing. "Of course he wants you to pursue it. He wants the bloody tape measure back!"

The policewoman sighed, noisily.

I was motioning to Sharon, rocking my hand like a boat caught on a choppy sea. Greville looked like he was about to burst into tears.

"What you both looking at me like that for?" Sharon asked.

I snapped into action. "Can't we just ... you know, ask him not to do it again?"

"Bleeding 'ell, Graham. You don't go *asking* thieves to please not nick my stuff no more. Christ!"

The policewoman sighed once more, then, "Right. I'll need to take the tape."

"The lad's got the tape," said Greville, helpfully.

I stopped the video playback and removed the video cassette.

"I'll give you a receipt," she said. "And I have to seal it now to show that the evidence hasn't been tampered with. It'll require your signature as well as mine. That okay?"

Before leaving she turned to me with an icy stare, just to let me know that she knew that I knew she didn't take kindly to being given extra work. Then she was off.

"Bloody social worker," Sharon called after her.

# 23

THE SHOP DOOR WAS shoved open with an unsympathetic scraping and banging. I knew it was a pram and it would be gouging out great lumps of wood on its way in.

"My, she won't be seeing ninety again, will she?" Sharon was a little protective when it came to the fixtures and fittings, and she watched as the driver of the pram, wearing a fawn mackintosh belted around the waist, and a little black beret with a poky nib in the middle, rummaged beneath her vehicle and took out a carrier bag that she put on the counter as if its value were priceless.

"This is for your man," she said to Sharon in a whiny-squeaky voice. She didn't look at me, and seemed oblivious to my presence.

"My man?" Sharon repeated.

"Your man. And there's this," and she offered to put a carrier-bagged bottle on the counter, but hesitated as if Sharon might have to give a password. "I thought he might like this. I've had it a while, but I don't think I'll ever drink it. Much too strong for me at my age."

"Okay, I'll give it to him ... If you want to leave it with me."

She put the bottle down on the counter.

"It's all I could think of. He said he didn't want anything, but I felt I had to show him just how grateful I am."

"Oh?" Maybe Sharon thought I'd been out changing light bulbs or cutting grass for OAPs or joining bits of cable that people had chopped through with their hedge trimmers.

The old woman leaned forward, confidentially.

"That man of yours is a saint, he truly is. A real saint and a gentleman. You don't know how lucky you are."

"He has his uses," said Sharon. She made no attempt to put the woman straight about our relationship. People would always believe what they wanted.

"I shall always be thankful to him. I will, I truly will." She was on the verge of breaking down in tears. "Your man, the absolute dear ..."

"Yes? What is it he's been doing?"

The woman's bottom lip was trembling so fast it was a blur. "He saved my Peter." And she nodded towards the pram.

Sharon couldn't wait to go round to see. "Hmm, wrapped him up well, haven't you?" and she reached inside, almost as if expecting to find a young child in there. She looked back at the woman and said, "Can I ...?"

"Be careful," she said, holding back the tears.

Peeling back the blanket Sharon immediately snatched back her hand when she felt the long wet tongue reach out to her.

"Oh, you've wakened him! He's been asleep. You shouldn't have done that. Hasn't anyone ever told you not to do such a silly thing?" and she fussed with the pram's occupant, tucking in the blankets, making soothing noises.

Sharon straightened, frowning.

"I'll be off," said Peter's mum. "So give him that stuff and tell him thanks from me, won't you?"

The woman trundled off with the sleeping Peter. Then she turned back to say something else. "And he's a good boy, *he* is."

Sharon looked around. "Boy?"

"Yes—your boy over there. I can see he takes after his dad. Looks the spitting image, he does," and she went out.

"What's he been up to, now?" asked Greville,

talking fluently while holding seven two-inch woodscrews between his lips (his training was coming on a treat).

"Oh, it's just your dad. He's saved little Peter's life."

"My dad? Who's Peter?"

"That's him in the pram. And there's more—that's his mum and she is eternally—"

"His *mum?*"

"—grateful. So much so she's brought your dad—hang on, ah, there we are—"

"I *am* here, you know!" I called from behind the wax polish stand, where I'd been watching on with amusement.

"A frozen pizza? Still, looks okay. Yeah, still in date. What else she got him? Oh, and a bottle of ..." Sharon unwrapped the carrier bag from the bottle. "Three guesses—red or white?"

"That's two. White," he said.

"Oh, you're out of luck," she said. "There's no such thing as white Ribena."


It was Saturday teatime and Greville was writing out the order we would be faxing to Bird's for the Monday delivery. Sapphire gave him her order pad and he stroked her bottom as she walked off, smiling to himself.

"Everything alright, Grev?" Sharon shot at him.

"Er, yeah. Just seeing what Sapphire's wanting."

"More like what Sapphire's wearing," I said.

"I know exactly what *she's* wanting," Sharon muttered, within earshot. "But me of all people's only too aware that you need to be careful. And I don't want the boy getting into bother."

He began to laugh. "Sharon, have you seen this? *Cooper's* plungers?"

"What about 'em?"

"Anything to do with Cooper's droop?" He giggled.

"Have you done that order, yet?"

I thought that Sharon was being a bit hard on him. "He's only young," I said.

"If he's young enough to be laughing at saggy tits then he's certainly not old enough to be touching girls' bums."

Then something occurred to me. "Hang on, didn't Larry say we should have a word with him before we ordered any more? Something to do with the buyer making a mistake and ordering too many? Something about getting us some extra discount?"

"On Cooper's plungers, for god's sake?"

"On *all* plungers. It's a bit out of season, just now. Christmas is the best time, when people have been sticking the fat from the turkey down the kitchen sink. Bird's is trying to shift some of their stock."

"And when was the last time we saw Larry?"

"I don't know. Can't remember. Couple of months?"

"It's more like six."

"Hardly once a fortnight, is it?" I laughed.

"Tell you what," she pointed to Greville, "order them anyway and tell 'em Larry said they'd be doing a special price just for us."

"He said not to do that," I reminded her, not being happy about upsetting apple carts.

"Well, sod him if he can't be bothered to show his face. Oh, and just in case the office bints have never heard of a Cooper's plunger, tell 'em it's a T-handle with a big black rubber disc on the end for clearing out bogs."

"And what is it really?" said Greville.

Well, what he actually said on the fax was *where's Larry?* Or rather, it was more of a little drawing: it was of a Chad—a sausage-headed face with a long nose poking over a brick wall with the words, *WOT – NO REP.*

The following Tuesday Greville got a phone call. It was from old Mr Bird himself. For some reason they had got him down from his shelf and dusted him off. It was such a special occasion, rather like a visit from nobility, that we put on the speakerphone so we could all listen to what he was saying.

"Now then, lad, my office ladies tell me you've been sending cryptic comments referring to our rep."

I could feel Greville go cold.

"No, I don't think—"

"I've got one of them here in front of me," the old man went on. "Yes ... a charming little rendition of the kind we used to doodle during our moments of inactivity during the war. What exactly was the message you were trying to get across?"

Greville looked nervously at us. We sort of raised our eyebrows and looked sort of hopeless.

"Right then, put another way," the old boy went on, "how frequently does our Larry call on you?"

Greville looked scared. He wouldn't want to get anyone into trouble, but then, as Sharon frequently suggested, someone needed to give him a kick up the arse.

"I—I think you need to speak to my b—"

The noise nearly blew me away.

"I'm speaking to you, lad! I don't want your boss! Well?"

"Well, I think Larry is a very nice man—"

I gave Greville a nudge.

"—and he says that we can look after ourselves. We're his best customers."

It went quiet for a second or two.

"That's not what I asked. How often does he call? Just tell me. I have him down as once every two weeks. That right?"

"Er, he calls whenever he can—"

"What on earth is that supposed to mean? I'm a busy man, you know."

"Er ..."

"When was the last time you saw him?"

"Oh, I think he called in—very quickly, mind—about ..."

"Come on, lad, I'm waiting."

"Someone told us he's not been well."

"Not been *well*? Do you mean *ill*? Our Larry's not been ill. Who told you that? Was it our Tracy in the office, by any chance?"

We exchanged glances. And so it went on, with Sharon and I giving Greville scribbled prompts that only got Bird's illustrious rep into even more bother, I'm sorry to say.

"Just between you and me," the old bird went on, "I've had my suspicions about our Larry for some time."

"Oh. Right. Good." Greville straightened as the burden of guilt began to slip from his shoulders.

"But everyone I've asked has covered for him. And to think I nearly got him into my local golf club. I'd have looked a proper fool. Fortunately, he wasn't interested."

"In golf?"

"Aye. But then he's only a rep—"

"Oh, but he *is* interested in golf. There's a big golf club just on the other side of his garden wall. It's very handy for him because he says he can just nip ..." That was Greville trying to be helpful again. Then he stopped and looked at me, then back to the fax machine. It had gone quiet on the other end of the line. And he switched it off.

I began sorting out the dog-eared bank notes in the till. "Fancy a job as a rep, Grev?"

"Why?"

"I might just know where there's one going."

He began making little squirming noises.

"What you gonna do with them grubby bank notes?" Sharon asked me. "They're disgusting, aren't they. They remind me of that thank you gift them sisters from the Old Granary left for you that time."

My stomach almost turned over at the thought. Greville wanted to know more.

"A half dozen pairs in a Netto carrier bag," she said to him. "They'd been festering away for three weeks before we looked in to see what they were."

"And what were they? Hey, don't say they—"

"That's right," she said.

"Why would they do that? Was it a mistake, got the bags mixed up or something?"

"No, they knew what they was doing, all right."

"Ugh! At least they'd be clean."

Greville saw her hesitate and look at me.

"Don't say they hadn't washed them!"

"I fink that's the idea. I binned them before they got up and walked out of their own accord. If we weren't so bleeding desperate, I'd do the same with them notes he's sorting. So, you gonna tell us how you earned the latest hardware perks—pizza and a nice Ribena to wash it down? How did you come to save that dear little soul for his mum dressed in a World War Two mack and beret?"

Greville blew, "Ooh, French Resistance."

"And she won't see seventy-five again."

"Ah," I said. "Peter. The dog. Little white mongrel terrier with black spots."

"Come on, get on with your tail—I mean *tale,* some of us want to get home."

"I was waiting at the level crossing as a train was passing through, and Peter was there with ... his mum. On a walk."

"Makes a change from your usual female admirers. Go on."

"And she'd tied his lead to the barrier while she sorted out her shopping. That's it."

"Is that all?" It sounded as if Greville wanted a blow-by-blow account of some torrid and extremely unhealthy assignation between me and this woman who was old enough to be my grandma.

"Well, the train passed and the barrier went up."

"So?"

"And so did Peter."

"What?" Not even Sharon was ready for this. "You don't mean—"

"That's right, little Peter was hoisted up by the neck. And the more he struggled the more his eyes popped out like an apothecary's drawer knobs."

"Blimey! What did you do?"

"I got out the car and got him down."

"How you get him down?"

I shrugged his shoulders. "I climbed up. It's a trellis so it was easy."

"Did anyone see?"

"The motorists behind weren't so pleased because they couldn't get past until I'd finished. They blew their horns at me. But a little crowd had gathered and they sort of cheered a bit."

The doorbell went and I shuffled Greville out into the shop. A bloke in a suit banged a mortise lock down on the counter.

"Money back!" he snapped.

"What's wrong—"

"It's no good and I want my money back."

Greville picked it up and handed it to Sharon with his thumb pointing out the green price ticket. Ours were yellow.

We told him he'd brought it back to the wrong shop, and that he should go to All Tools.

"It's two miles in that direction." Despite his aggression that was bordering on the violent, we were trying to be helpful.

He looked incredulous and he leaned forward, making Greville stand back from him. Sharon didn't. Then he said all such shops were connected, and no way could we make him take it back to our other shop out in the back of beyond.

And then Greville chimed in with a brainwave. "It's better for you—because you can park at All Tools *for free*. Those are double yellow lines out there and there are wardens about ..."

"It's shops like yours that are ruining this town ..." and before he left he called us some uncomplimentary names, suggesting inappropriate items of physical anatomy—a donkey's, I seem to remember.

People trying to dump duff stock they'd bought, or even nicked, elsewhere was a sign of the times. Those days everyone was desperate. Woolworths' staff outnumbered customers by three to one, some of the shopkeepers sat out in the street on deckchairs, waiting for customers. Even the two pound shops closed down. If customers could go to a purpose-built shopping centre and park their cars for free, why on earth would they pay for the privilege of parking in town? Ram-raid Roger's analogy was spot-on: no one wanted to shop in Little Sniffingham any longer.

# 24

SHARON WAS STANDING IN the shop doorway, nodding to the bloke with the shoe shop across the street, and the video shop manager sitting out on the pavement under his "parachute" (as she called it) drinking the same can of lager he'd had all day, when the policewoman pulled up outside on the yellow lines.

"Vere's never a traffic warden when you want

one," Sharon said, watching her get out and stride across to us.

"Just letting you know how the investigation is progressing. We've apprehended the individual concerned. And I've interviewed him at length."

"What about the tape measure—did you get it back?" I asked, hopefully.

"Ah, I wasn't the one conducting the interview."

"So does that mean that you don't know?"

She sighed. "I would need to ask the person concerned. Right, this young man has been making a nuisance of himself around the local shops." She seemed rather pleased.

"Stealing. Yes, you need to put a stop to that," Sharon said, in case she'd forgotten.

"More like verbal abuse, kicking a ball around in the local convenience store when he'd been asked not to."

"He's a proper little troublemaker, ain't he?"

"We can't have him for that, but we can certainly let him know that it's unacceptable behaviour."

"But why did the little sod steal a tape measure? Bit strange, don't you think?"

"It was a gift for his dad. A plea for attention. What with no mother, neglected by a drunken father ... I've lost count of the number of cases I've seen—"

I was confused. "Sorry, hold on a minute. So this young lad stole the tape measure just so he could curry some attention—"

"Make that *affection*," Sharon put in.

"—from his less-than-perfect father?"

Greville was almost in tears again. The policewoman nodded. I got the impression that I was spelling out something she wasn't at all interested in.

"Right, then," she said brightly, forcing a smile,

"I'll be off. Just came to let you know we're on it."

I wasn't yet finished. "So what happens now?"

"That's not for me to decide, but I'll be recommending that a case be brought against him."

"A case?" Sharon said. "You've changed your tune since last time."

"I'm not the only one working on this. Like you said, we should nip this sort of thing in the bud before it gets any worse. And it will, I see this happening all the time."


Greville answered the phone.

"Someone trying to sell you a woman, boss," he called out.

"Put it on speakerphone, there's not much else to do."

So Greville did. Then we heard the menacing tones.

"So it's *you!*" There was no mistaking the voice, even though over the years we hadn't heard it all too often.

"We've got an order started somewhere, if you want it." Greville was oblivious to the caller's menacing tone.

"Forget it," came the reply. "I've got some bad news for you."

"Don't tell me—the suit's to come off!" Greville laughed.

Larry gave a sarcastic thank you, and rang off.


That teatime I told Sharon that she could go home at five o'clock. It was a mistake; she was bound to be suspicious. And she was still on the premises at a quarter to six, pretending to do some tin-arranging. That particular afternoon her acting wasn't up to much. She missed her bus home. My appointment was late, probably held up in traffic;

241

the ring road had got busier these days because most people just wanted to bypass the town. One woman customer—she had spent hundreds of pounds using the photocopier for the various clubs and institutions she belonged to—had told us that she had no intention of paying to park in such a small town, and would rather pay a little more to park in the larger towns and enjoy a much larger choice of shops. We hadn't seen her since. Sharon pretended to hum something or other, but was getting on my nerves.

"Sharon, you know I can't—"

"Pay me overtime? Pay me anything at all? Yes, I know. But you know me, my love, I always like to keep a tight and tidy shop." She didn't look at me, and I so wanted her to see the look on my face because then she would know—much more than mere words—that she could trust me.

Then the bell jangled and in marched the suit and clipboard. We shook hands and went into the office. Sharon's coat was still hanging behind the door so I thought it better if I took it out to her, but the shop doorbell was jangling and she'd already gone. Maybe she would come back for it, so I left the door unlocked. But it was Gwendolin who burst in.

"Hey, Chuck—is your Sharon all right? She's just bumped into me as I was locking up, tearing past clutching a duster to her chest. Never a word. Not seen her like that before. And one of the girls has just phoned me from the bus station—she's sitting on the ground against a wall, all upset, like."

I mean, what a time for one of the Sunn Joly girls to take a funny turn.

"Oh dear. Do you want me to go with you to see if she's okay?"

There was just a second of puzzlement, then, "No—it's your Sharon that's on the ground ..."

~ ~ ~

There wasn't a queue in the bank. Not even Maggie Newsprint's mum was in there for her amusement arcade slot machine money. I'd never drawn out so much of my own cash before and felt a bit apprehensive walking back to the shop, tripping over the sleeping shopkeepers who had nodded off with their legs stretched out as if on Blackpool beach.

"It's you that's to blame for all this," the MD spat at me. "I've watched you buy all them power tools with hardly any bloody profit on them—not to mention lawnmowers. How many times do I have to tell you it's profit—*profit!*—that we need on *every* single item we sell? And no exceptions." He sat down. I could tell he had plenty more to say but he'd worn himself out.

Outside I caught Sharon moving swiftly away from the door. Greville asked if I was ready for coffee.

"I wouldn't go in there if I were you," I told him.

"But if *I* don't make the coffee, the old boy will try making it himself. I don't want a drink of warm milk."

"He doesn't always forget to put coffee in."

"I'm not willing to risk it."

"And don't call him the *old boy,*" and I tapped him on the back of the head as the doorbell went. "There's a customer for you. Look busy."

A few seconds later Greville skulked back. "I think *you'll* want to see to this one."

At first I didn't recognise the teenager standing boldly at the bottom counter. He was dressed in overalls and his face and hands were filthy. I smiled.

"You the boss?"

"Not necessarily." That was always the safe

option.

He handed me a twenty pound note. "That's for the measure."

"The what ...?"

"I've started a job today so I can pay for it."

It dawned on me. "Right." It didn't seem appropriate to thank him— after all, it was ours— but now I wish that I had.

"I've been working all day so I can pay for it." He swallowed.

Looking at him, there was little doubt in my mind that doing a day's work, and off his own bat, had indeed been a character-building experience for the boy. He went on, with a hint of nervousness:

"Seeing as I've given you the money ... will you—will you drop the charges ... do you think?"

"Are you ever going to steal again?"

"No I'm not. I've got a job, now."

Of course, they'd all say that, wouldn't they?

I phoned the police and the policewoman and her male superior came straight round to see me— and I mean straightaway.

"Do you realise how much time and effort we've put into building this case?" was the gist of their message.

"But the lad came in all filthed-up and paid for what he'd taken—"

"Without your consent, remember. He stole from you. If you'd not had him on camera he'd have got clean away with it."

I felt like I was about to be cuffed and taken in.

"Technically, yes. But now he's paid up so that's that."

"Did you actually say you would drop the charges?" That was the policewoman.

"Of course I did. He gave me money"—I caught the expectant looks on their faces—"for the tape measure."

The boss cop turned to his colleague. "I think

244

we can still go ahead."

She nodded in agreement then said to me, "We'll keep hold of the video tape for evidence and let you know how we intend to proceed. You shouldn't have taken the money."

"*What?* If I hadn't accepted the money and you'd managed to nick him and mark him for life as a hardened criminal, would *you* have come in here to compensate me for a ten-metre Stanley PowerLock?"

They nodded to me and scuttled out of the shop.

Greville appeared, which was what he did when any excitement had died down. "Hey, were they who I thought they were?"

"You mean the Keystone Kops? Yes."

"But you were shouting at them. You can't shout at the police."

"Well, I might've raised my voice a bit."

"What did they want?"

"I've buggered up their case and they're not happy about it."

Greville went to tell the MD. He probably wouldn't be happy, either; it didn't take much. Sharon hadn't looked happy and had hardly spoken to me for three days. What was wrong with her? And I didn't feel happy, either. There was a Bank Holiday coming up and the MD had wanted me to open the shop to catch the holiday trade, but I didn't see any point. The shopping centre car parks would be full because they were free; the town centre ones would be holding just a few cars belonging to semi-destitute shop workers who would be paying over seven quid a day to use. Anyhow, I wanted to get stuck in laying an extension to my drive at home, to make room for the Accountant's car. Call it some sad form of escapism. I'd bought a couple of tonnes of hardcore and 900 block paving bricks and an extended weekend was just what I needed to make some sort of a start. And if I didn't begin to feel a little more optimistic while I was doing it, I could always bury myself beneath it, couldn't I?

By 10 o'clock Sunday morning I was cursing myself for foolishly believing that, singlehandedly, I'd be able to excavate an area of 15 square metres of garden, prepare it and actually get the blocks laid and whacked down with this gadget I'd hired. It felt like I'd been chipping away at the sub-surface sandstone for a lifetime and there was no way I would get this finished even if I went AWOL from the shop for the whole week.

"Excuse me, but do you work here?"

I stood up so suddenly I went dizzy. It was Greville.

"I'm sorry but we're closed," I told him.

And then I saw Sharon and Sapphire walking around the corner from the bus stop. It was good to see them, but I really needed to get on with this job. Sharon was as on the ball as she ever was.

"Looks like you could use an extra pair of hands, my love."

Greville, wearing his dad's old cotton overalls, white ones, naturally, had already begun setting out the edge bricks. I was impressed.

"Sapphire," he called. "See that bucket? I want a three-to-one mix. Where's the sand," he asked me.

"Cement's in the garage, sand's in the back garden."

"D'ya hear that, Sapph?"

The girl, in T-shirt and shorts, yet looking ready for any hard labour, grabbed the big black builder's bucket, emptied out the couple of slugs that had spent the night in there, and went up the side of the house. There was a cry—not a scream, you understand; more like an exclamation. Sharon caught my *Oh my god!* look.

"There's a woman back there," Sapphire said, trying to be discreet. "And she's got nothing on!"

The Accountant was behind her, holding her bikini top to her breasts and scolded the girl for being such a prude.

"I'm not a prude," she said indignantly. Then to Greville she mouthed, "What's a prude?"

The Accountant poked her gently in the shoulder.

"When I think where you've had bits of gold-coloured bling riveted to your body—and, more to the point, the strange practitioners you've allowed to make the holes—I don't see why the sight of my bare bum should shock you."

"Better get the kettle on," said Sharon.

The sun was setting when she joined me in the back garden. With four of us working flat out (even the Accountant), we had dug down to about 10 inches, completed the edge courses and laid most of the hardcore. The removed surface was now heaped in the back garden. That was the biggest and worst part of the job done. I was bloody grateful for the help but at the same I could smell trouble.

"I'm going to come straight out with it," said Sharon.

"Go on, then." I was resigned to coming clean. There was no way I could be expected to keep up the pretence any longer. I'd already compromised the close, open relationship with my staff.

"I believe in plain speaking," she said.

"I wouldn't argue with that. And thanks very much for your help. You could stay the night, you know." That threw her.

"Eh? Stay the ... I don't think vere's room for me in your arse." Well, that's how it sounded. Then she blurted, "Look, love, I'm speaking for everyone. What's to become of us?"

"I don't know what you mean."

"Getting a good price for the premises, are you?"

That was news to me.

"Come on—you're selling up. I know you are. Another charity shop, is it? Or a bookies? Don't tell me it's a bleedin' card shop—another one!"

"What? No, nothing like that."

"So who's this Mister bleeding X that you've been talking with the MD about? I have a right to know!"

Hmm, so she had been listening at doors.

"And where did you find him? What ve bleeding hell does he think he can do in such a godforsaken hole as Little bleeding Snottinham? Works miracles, does he? 'Cos he'll need to."

I explained that Mr X was an investing contact of the Accountant.

"Oh, I see. That explains it, then. Right. I noticed that she managed to get here pretty early this morning."

"But we're not moving out, Sharon. The business is staying put."

"But you just said Mr X is moving in—so what's he after?"

"At first he wanted the shop because, being prime-site, he could start a similar business. But the MD and I were adamant. The shop—essentially—stays as it is. So you see, there's nothing to worry about."

I *almost* had her on side.

"I don't get a good feeling about this. No, there's summing wrong."

"Well, if we don't take his money we might as well close down right away. At least doing it this way buys us some time until the town pulls around." *If it ever will.*

I'd never seen Sharon like this. She wasn't convinced and, after hearing myself speak, neither was I totally, but I had to be confident and in

248

control. Or pretend to be.

"He has a lot of capital and, more important, he's got contacts who can supply him with stock at unbelievably low prices. It seems that we've been paying through the nose for all these—"

"Oh, I see—it's knock-off, you mean?"

"Certainly not!"

"Stock wiv tarmac marks where it hit the road?"

"Sharon, please."

"But *you're* leaving." She began to cry.

I did something I've never done before, and actually put my arm around one of my employees. It wasn't so bad, really.

"Not at all. I'm not going anywhere. Neither is the MD—not that he does a great deal, these days."

"I can't see him staying. He'll be the first to go, just you wait and see if he don't."

"Sharon, look at me—we refuse to leave, so Tel—"

"*Tel?* That his name? Sounds like a right cowboy."

I let that one go.

"—is doing the only thing he can. He's coming in with us, but for a trial period and on condition that ... well, he calls the shots where the new marketing policies are concerned. That's his field, you see. This is the only way we can be more competitive. I mean, watch out All Tools—make way for the big boys." I tried to laugh.

"You mean B&Q?"

"Alright, then—*bigger* boys than ... All bloody Tools." We said that last bit together.

"I don't like change. I had enough of that when I was in the theatre. We'd have a good little troupe going where everyone knew everyone else's secrets and foibles and ven—well ven we was all scattered. You never knew who'd you be sharing your wigs wiv."

I promised her that most things would stay the same. But even I didn't quite believe it.

"Fancy being called Tel," she laughed, sniffling. "Especially wiv a second name like that."

"Like what?"

"X—Tel X. You used to send messages on them."

# 25

*A Midsummer Night's Dream*

I SAT BOLT UPRIGHT in bed.

"My God, what a nightmare!" I gasped. "I dreamt we'd taken on a new partner. He was a right bastard—he'd thrown out all the traditional stock, changed the shop's name and made me repair the roof. I mean—*me!*"

The accountant rolled over. "Not again! That's the fifth time this week you've disturbed me in the middle of the night," she groaned.

I settled down and after a few minutes the shivering began to subside.

"Still, though," I smiled to myself, "five times a week is way past the national average."


The reality wasn't much better. I arrived at the shop to find a new, garishly-painted shop sign with Tel's name and the words OPEN TO THE PUBLIC. Greville was stacking plastic storage boxes on the pavement. They were filled with many of our traditional, if slow-moving, lines—the ones we didn't chuck away when we had the first crisis. I'd lost count of just how many crises we'd had. He didn't see me. Come to think of it, no one did—especially the sundry individuals that were lifting, shifting, stacking, re-wiring, kicking, swearing, insulting, joking ... I felt invisible. Everything seemed to be blurred. I felt myself stagger against a display unit that wasn't there—well, the day before it wasn't. I opened a certain door and stepped inside. It was as close as you can get to complete darkness. It smelled of dust, polish and old sweeping brushes, but for all that it was comforting and familiar. The muffled voices outside had their own world and I still had part of mine. There were clompy footsteps. They stopped outside the door. I froze. It opened and slammed shut almost in the same instant. Then a strangely familiar voice whispered:

"Mr Wide Boy out there says we don't have room for all that old stuff. He suggests you dump it all in the canal."

"Typical," I called. "That bloke is suffering from terminal confusion."

"What's that?"

"He has no idea just who is the boss."

"You need to come out here—"

"Where is he?"

"He's in his office."

"Oh. Where's that?"

"*Your* office."

"Right, that's done it!" I was determined.

"And tell him—"

"I'll tell him—"

"In no uncertain terms, mind—"

"Oh, I shall get straight to the point—"

"Just who—"

"That he is *not*—"

"You'll need to be firm—"

"Oh, I'll be very firm—"

"Is the boss. And it's not—"

"It certainly *is not—*"

"You."

I paused. "But it is me."

"No, you tell him it isn't you."

"What?"

"You say to him, *Look Mr Cowboy, I'm the boss, not you.*"

"But wouldn't it sound better if I said it the other way round?"

"You mean, *you're the boss, not—*"

"No. If I say, you're not the boss—*I am,* that sounds better, don't you think? *I am!*"

"Yeah. Do that."

"Right. I'm going. I am the boss, I am the boss. Thanks, Greville."

"You're welcome, boss. Anytime."

And I stepped out into the unfamiliar stark white of the newly-arranged fluorescents to sort things out. I closed the door to the glory hole behind me, banging poor Greville's forehead. He'd need to toughen up in this new environment. Come to think of it, we all would. The place was unrecognisable. The nocturnal refit was complete, leaving the shop as uninspiring as B&Q. At least it was different enough to make customers believe something had changed—and that's part of the battle in marketing a new image (so I'd read somewhere).

There were more customers in the shop than I'd seen for some time. I had no idea where they'd come from. Wherever I turned there were light fittings hanging dangerously low from the ceiling, and floor-standing lamps littering the aisles.

Tel bustled through, speaking into his mobile phone whilst physically moving customers out of his way (and getting away with it). Pink shirt, psychedelic tie, patterned braces dragging his trousers over his fat belly. It took several attempts to get his attention.

"Yes, young man? If you're after something you'll need to ask one of the staff. There's a young lad kicking around somewhere, not much use, I'm afraid ..."

"I *am* staff! Why have you thrown—?"

"*Three hundred – that's right,*" he said into the phone. Then to me, "The stuff in them boxes is dross—*that's my last offer*—absolute effing crap. I've stepped over better stuff than that down the dog track—*look here, I'll give it to you straight. I'm one of the biggest experts in acquiescence and dismantling of retail merchandise, but I'm telling you right now ... look, look, just listen to what I'm saying*—it's crap and I don't want it in here. Get shut of it all—*I know I'm made of money, remember I told you that, but three hundred is my last offer ...*"

Just then the lights dimmed and flickered. Tel shot forwards, pointing to one of his sundry blokes, the phone still secured to his ear like a limpet mine.

"Too many—you've too many bleedin' lamps on in one go—turn it off! No! Leave that and switch off the one down there—the one with the Ninja tortoises ... *Strewth!*"

Between such rapid sessions on his mobile phone, all I could get from Tel was that the MD had given a thumbs-up in favour of all changes. I detected the proverbial odour of rodent.

"I see you've sorted it, then," smirked Greville as he sidled up to me, weighed down with a selection of traditional seaside tripe (the non-edible variety).

"Where's the boss?" I asked, pointedly.

"He's the one up there with the massive phone bill."

"Not *him*—the MD, the real boss."

"Oh, he's next door having his palm read by Gwendolin. Or his tea leaves."

Right enough, I found the MD seething in Lunn

Poly's staff room. After 54 years he had resigned, dropping me right in it.

"We're always in the shit, it's just the depth that varies," I remarked to Greville when I got back.

When Sharon arrived in the afternoon (her hours were back to where they'd been in Chapter 1), she took one look at the new stock and pronounced it a pile of ... (the terminology left no doubt as to her opinion of its biological integrity).

"If I'd wanted to sell market tat," she hissed, "I'd still be working a stall on the Whitechapel Road. And why is the shop door wide open? It's bloody freezing today." Then she caught sight of Tel. "He don't look much like a hardware man, does he?"

"More like a highwayman. I wouldn't buy a second-hand car from him."

"I wouldn't buy a bag of chips from him," she said, with a particular loathing in her tone. "I seen him before, or the likes of him. They're like cats, always ready to move on. Soon as they find somewhere else they like, they're off. You mark my words, one day you'll come to work and he'll be gone."

"That's if I still have a job here by then."

"Ha! *Open to the public*. Who does he fink he's kidding? We've always been open to the public. Bleedin' spiv."

Greville sidled up. He would be getting quite good at sidling over the coming months.

"So that's the git up there, is it?" Sharon scanned him. "I know his kind."

Greville couldn't believe this. "He's *kind?*"

"I know his sort," went on Sharon. "They're all over the streets of London. It don't matter what type of suit they wear, I can spot a bloke with reptile dysfunction at fifty paces."

"Really?" Greville watched his new boss, trying to spot the tell-tale signs. "Is it how he walks?"

"She means he's a snake," I said.

"So, where's the MD?" said Sharon. "I can't believe he ain't put in an appearance, yet."

I sort of mumbled that he'd gone. This time for good.

"*Gone?* Bleeding hell! What did I tell yer? So it's one down, four to go."

A smattering of customers was examining the new light displays. One or two of the regulars weren't interested in them and banged their heads on the dreadful-looking items hanging from the ceiling, some of them looking like medieval instruments of torture. One man dodged one just in time, but stepped back and knocked over the abrasive papers display, sending sheets of sandpaper wafting all over the shop on the cold air currents blowing in from the street.

Just then the third white van of the day pulled up and the shortest van driver you've ever seen effortlessly humped a dozen cardboard boxes into the shop.

"What's in there?" I asked him.

"None of your business, Sunshine," the cheeky git said.

"This *is* my business," I mentioned as he came out. "Or it was."

He grabbed another box and went inside.

"How's he manage to carry stuff like that?" asked Greville.

"Just lightweight stock," I told him. "You can pick it up anywhere."

Then he spotted some fabric blowing in the breeze from the van's roof rack.

"Hello? What's that?"

I'd already spotted it. "Don't ask."

But he went as if to take hold of it. Sharon popped out just in time.

"Don't touch them," she told him. "You don't know where they've been." And she went back inside.

The driver, his task concluded, strutted on to the pavement. "I see you've been admiring my latest acquisition. Only three nights old."

"Are they a pair of girl's—"

"They didn't come off a girl. That one was all woman. She could nearly show me a thing or two and I'm street-wise."

"More like alley-wise," I heard Sharon say in the background.

"Hey, you, I've had more ..." he was interrupted by a passing car, "... than you've had hot dinners. I can, so I do." That was when he repeatedly thrust his hips backwards and forwards. "Look at that. All man," and he grabbed Greville's cheeks and squeezed hard. "Does exactly what it says on the tin."

Sharon came out and asked him what was inside the boxes. He merely tapped the side of his nose and winked at her, and then he froze when a beefy policewoman stood in his way and pointed menacingly at the plastic boxes on the pavement.

"Is this your vehicle, sir?"

"No," he said, going a very pale shade.

"A member of the public has just complained about restricted access on this pavement," she said.

"I'm only the driver. Been delivering—but not these. Nothing to do with me."

"Really? I can make you open them."

"But I don't know anything about them—honest."

"Do you usually use your roof rack as a clothes line?"

To save his embarrassment I opened the boxes and showed her cartons of loose screws, paraffin heater wicks and other items on which the business had been built in the early days. But I had to give it to Tel—it *was* largely dead stock, a sign of the times. But there was no way I was ready to dump it in the skip, and that night I took it home for safe keeping.


There were one or two surprises in store (no pun intended). I had to admit that the fresh footfall in the shop was most welcome. People suddenly wanted light fittings and I didn't know why, but it was good for our sales of spare light bulbs. We were selling much larger ticket items, which was better use of our time when making, say, one sale of £50 instead of ten of £5. But our original customers still wanted to spend their pocket money on small stuff, some of which had been thrown out. They were the people that walked out of the shop unhappily. The other downside was that we were simply too busy to pay attention to the finer, if unprofitable, details.

"We're selling too many light fittings," said Greville as he flew past me. I'd never seen him move so fast in the old days. He stopped momentarily. "What's it all about?"

"The latest technology—it's caught on, at last. Finally, they're chucking out their old candlesticks."

Greville caught sight of Tel propelling himself from the office, mobile phone firmly in place. When I turned back to him, he'd gone. See what I mean? That used to be me. Many's the time someone would follow me into a room only to find I'd already left.

I opened the office door to find Tel was already at the desk. I had no idea how he got there so fast.

"That lad's coming on, coming on nicely," he said in his gravelly voice, nurtured over the years as an 80-a-day man. "There's still room for improvement. By the time I've done with him he'll be a model." He spoke into his phone.

"A model *what*?" I asked.

He held out his hands—now just how did he do that without dropping the phone?—and motioned for me to sit down. I did want to sit, but at *my* place behind the desk, and not because all the other chairs were piled high with stock.

"Sit down, sit down," he said. "*Hello? Are you there?*" Then to me: "Any time you want a word, even in confidence, just knock on my door. I'm here for you whenever—*hello?*"

"It used to be my door and as far as I'm concerned the MD still has a share in it." *Whatever he says.*

But he was negotiating away at high speed. I threw a box off the chair and sat down. I didn't think he'd noticed the contempt with which I had dumped the box. I was wrong.

"*Hold on a sec,*" he said into the phone. Then to me: "You can abuse my stock about all you want, but it won't change the fact that I've been doing this since my father gave me my first half crown and I went out and bought knitting needles for four old pence a pair and then sold 'em to the girls in my class for a shilling. I sold dishcloths out of me school satchel on the road. I was eight year old—*I said hold on, I'll be with you in a minute*—You've got the premises and you refuse to let go. I don't like that. But *I* know just how much money can be made here. Everyone else is clearing out. You thought you were very smart by not mentioning that to me, but I knew already, see? I've got the skill. You haven't and, more important, you haven't got the cash. But I have."

"But some of the stuff you're wanting us to sell—"

"Hold it there: some of it's crap, I know. I know the difference—why d'ya think I drive a big expensive car? But what you need to realise, and at your age you're a bit late for learning this, is that if punters are willing to pay for shit, then you shovel it up for them, gift wrap it and take their dosh."

He continued barking into the phone (in

italics—sorry, just joking). It was a small room, barely four metres square, and over the years it had seen some good times and cosy chats. But now it seemed the most inhospitable place I'd ever been. I got up to get out of there.

"One minute, you, not so fast! I hear you've got a boat that you're looking to get rid of."

Dare I tell him that it wasn't for sale—not to anyone *he* knew, anyway?

"Yes, I have." Suddenly I felt myself softening towards him.

"I'll keep my ears open for you—*No? Well, can't you go rummaging around B&Q's skip? My dear God, what a bleeding shambles ...*"

## 26

NEW FACES HADN'T BEEN appearing only on the other side of the counter. I returned late one afternoon to find a strange woman leaning next to the staff kettle, her face obscured by a haze of cigarette smoke. I smiled at her just in case she was someone I was supposed to be nice to. She merely smiled back knowingly, like some sultry Hollywood film starlet.

"That's Brenda, the new sales *girl*," Greville laughed.

The smoke cleared momentarily and I saw why. She was five feet tall—with balanced proportions, mind—size 10 (I guessed), tight knitted jumper, jeans, high heels (not a good idea in this shop), bleached fluffy hair and the neck-end of 60. Now, don't get me wrong: there's nothing wrong with being that height and/or that age, but it might be an idea to choose an appearance that didn't remind people of a half-strangled cat.

"She any good?" I asked.

"Nah. Can't sell, can't read, and can't tell the difference between a tub of putty and a Cornish pasty. She was working in Woolworths last week." Ah, that seemed to explain things.

A lady grabbed my arm. "Excuse me but do you work here?"

"I used to—sorry, yes. I do. What are you wanting?"

She saw Brenda sidling behind the counter.

"Never mind, dear, *she'll* do."

She went over and made some disparaging remark about me, and for some reason I didn't care.

Apparently, so Greville told me, Brenda had just lost what would have been her first sale when she offered a top brand oven lamp at £2.99 when a normal 85p pygmy bulb would have done the same job. The customer stormed off, complaining she could get them cheaper elsewhere. Of course she could. The situation had deteriorated rapidly, and Greville had been unable to intervene due to his hiding in the back yard. You see, some things don't change.

When Sharon arrived, I protested that I'd had nothing to do with setting on extra staff.

"Oh, I know all about her," she said, after checking that Tel wasn't within range. "Want to know how she got the job? What her qualifications are, hmm? Let's just say that under those Gucci shoes I wouldn't be surprised to find she's wearing Mr X's socks."


For lunch I decided to visit the Café Rita where I could be assured of sympathy and understanding. Oh yes—and a dose of excruciating indigestion. Rita, being your typical lady from *Country Life* magazine, did not juxtapose well with running a small café in a backstreet in Little Sniffingham.

"Sorry about the cake," Rita said to me. "But I took it out of the oven too early, or put it in too late. I can never get it right," she laughed nervously, leaving me with something that looked like a squashed shoe. I began to wonder what quirk of fate had brought me here. Maybe I was turning masochistic. Maybe my time was up in this world. On the next table was Brad Hall, whom we had nicknamed Brad the Ball. He used to be one of our best trade customers—I say *used to* because we'd not seen him for some time. Although a joiner, he used a ball pein hammer (that's one with a ball opposite the business part) that is usually associated with engineers. Why? To tamp down the tobacco in his pipe. Nothing sinister there, although it may be considered a fire hazard. But he was sitting so still I began to imagine he'd died having eaten some of Rita's cake. I leaned over and asked him how was trade. He seemed surprised that I had spoken to him.

"Oh, not so 'kin bad," he said, his head jerking forwards with every *'kin* thing he said.

"Really? Others have been complaining things have been a lot quieter."

"Oh, 'kin terrible, if the truth be told. I've had a bloody complaint. Gonna cost me a 'kin fortune."

"It's not like you to do anything, you know, not up to scratch." I don't know whether it was the cake or what I'd just said that caused me to almost choke.

" 'Kin third-storey fire escape door, bespoke. 'Kin outward-opener onto a 'kin steel walkway."

I merely nodded. It seemed straightforward enough.

"Should've been 'kin simple."

Brad swilled the coffee around in the mug, looked as if he might take a drink, then thought better of it. Whenever speaking with Brad I always found myself anticipating his nods, and we would sort of jerk in unison. But it required the utmost concentration on his words, trying to accurately predict the jumps. But today he was so off rhythm that we were nodding like a pair of novelty nodding dogs working out of synch.

" 'Kin owner called me out to take a look at the thing. Said I might as well because there was no way he was going to pay for the 'kin job. So I went to see him this morning. There arguing the toss until dinnertime. What a 'kin mess it was."

"It *was?* So had someone else had a go?"

"No other 'cker had had another go—it was *my* lad."

"You have a son?"

"The 'kin apprentice. It should have been a simple enough job. He's been to night school and got summat or other certificate. But no. I found he'd made the door out of split timber and nailed the 'kin corners. When he'd done it was hinge-bound in the middle, didn't fit flush with the 'kin frame, and because he'd lost the latch plate the lock couldn't work so he'd fastened a bit of 'kin string from the knob to the central heating pipe."

I blew out. That was some crap job, right enough. "What a monstrosity, eh? Sounds like your lad has about as much eye for detail as Baron Frankenstein. How long has he been with you?"

"Two months. I owed his mother a 'kin—er, just a favour."

"Two months? Our trainee's been with us for over four years and he's still not fit to be left alone." *Okay, Greville, so you're not really that bad, but I have to pretend I'm sympathetic.* "You can't get the staff, can you?"

"You can't get the 'kin suppliers, neither." He was getting into full swing now. "It was the worst move I ever made when I stopped getting my stuff from you," he called out and explained how his

*GetScrewed Direct* order hadn't turned up as promised. "*Everything for the trade—next day,*" he quoted from their fancy catalogue. "Hah! What a 'kin laugh."

"But you eventually got your stuff?"

"No, but I got the sack. Lost the job." Did he complain to the company? "Yes, but the girl on the phone got right 'kin shirty with me. You should have heard her. A right gob on her, she had." So why did he go there in the first place? Brad seemed a bit embarrassed. "So I could pay by credit card."

I told him that we did credit cards. I detected a faint trace of embarrassment.

"Aye, but with *GetScrewed Direct* I can have the stuff next day—well, that's how it's supposed to happen."

"With us you could have it the *same day* and if not I'd go out and get it myself for next day at the latest."

He thought a moment. "Alright then ... *GetScrewed* has a massive range."

I explained that our wholesalers, many of them local, are as good as if we had our very own warehouses, and the range is massive. I almost had him.

"Bet you don't do PVC pipe solvent and cleaner."

He was amazed when I said that we did. Apparently *GetScrewed Direct* didn't, but sold the plastic pipe thus stealing trade from respectable plumbing merchants. We'd heard it all before. Brad was now looking sheepish so I tried to cheer him up before stepping in for the kill.

"So you've come here to drown your sorrows?" I asked him.

"Nah. I've come here to commit suicide now I've nowhere left to get me stuff from."

He risked taking a sip of Rita's instant coffee and retched.

"It's funny you should mention that," I began.

So by the time I'd finished with him, Brad went out a happier man, and I watched Rita serve some of her hard-as-bullets scones. She apologised to the customers for the lumpy cream because she'd kept it at the back of the fridge, warning them to mind their tongues on the lumps of ice.

"I shall leave these napkins here, just in case you find some bits of glass," she said soothingly. *So now she's passing off broken glass as ice ...?*

"Is there something wrong with the cake, dear?" she asked me.

"No, it was something I ate," I told her. Then, under my breath, "The last time I was here."

## *Tight as Andronicus*

Back at the shop, the three of us spent some time inspecting the new stock and familiarising ourselves with the heinous contraptions that were dangling from the ceiling like alligator traps. Tel was nowhere to be seen, and Brenda seemed to need a fag break every twelve minutes (we timed her). Greville had the bright idea of suggesting to her that she could take as much time as she needed. That way, for one hundred and five minutes per day we could work as we used to do, just so long as Tel stayed in the office planning world domination. Thank you, Greville, for the maths; it could have been more accurate, but it was near enough. So when Brenda disappeared into the cloud of haze that was formerly known as the back yard, we had the shop floor to ourselves.

"That's not a customer," called Sharon, who could tell one telephone ring from another. She was intently gift-wrapping a lingerie set disguised to make it look like a giant claw hammer—don't ask. Lingerie was one area that had flummoxed Tel to the point where he had just walked away, shaking his head and almost dropping his mobile phone. Greville dealt with the call. It was one of the big unmentionable stores wanting to know the price of a particular Flymo lawnmower. Was it that they were short of stock and they wanted to buy one of ours? That could be arranged, I thought (I'd sell to anyone). Or were they perhaps checking our stock for one of their customers so they could suggest they buy the item from us? It was none of those so no surprises there. Instead they were doing a *We will beat any price* deal, and for the first time they were seeing us as competition. We should have felt honoured. We asked Greville what had been said.

"The going price is a hundred quid, so I said we were selling them for fifty." Why on earth did he say that? "Because we don't have any."

"He's right," I said to Sharon. "A big store shouldn't be wasting our time doing their bloody stupid price-promises."

"I know," she said. "That's what I taught him."

"Hmm. He's coming on a treat, isn't he?"

Later that day I was piling up another twenty storage boxes of old stock to take home, when Greville nudged me and spoke in a hushed tone.

"Er, the thing is ... I've got a bit of a problem."

"Come on, Greville, I've not got all day."

"It's a friend. She—*he*, he's lost the key to his padlock. How would I get it open in an emergency?"

"Don't you mean, how would *he* get it open in an emergency?" He looked worried. "Well, it's his padlock, isn't it? Not yours." Now he looked even *more* worried.

I looked over to where I had last seen our set of five-foot bolt croppers that were guaranteed to crunch effortlessly through shackles and links. They were still there. Probably too technical for the new regime.

"Okay. Maybe all is not lost. Tell me what

happened. What sort of fix are you in?"

"That could be a bit painful—*difficult,*" he stammered.

I asked him point-blank to explain his predicament.

"Oh, it's not my lock. Really it isn't. This one's a Woolworths cheapie. You wouldn't find *me* with one of them."

"Well, why didn't you say? That shouldn't be much of a problem."

We were disturbed then because Brenda returned from "taking twelve" and he didn't get the chance to ask me again.

At teatime Sapphire came in and asked Greville, confidentially, although I could hear, if he'd managed to sort anything out. He pointed in my direction and, not without some embarrassment, she came to see me.

"I understand you're locked out," I said to her.

She looked surprised. "Sort of. I wondered if Greville could pick at it."

"At what?"

"The padlock."

"No, you don't pick *at* locks, you pick at spots. Greville's locksmithing abilities involve much picking and not much unlocking, but give him time. The best thing—and the cheapest all round—is to simply chop the bugger off."

"You mean Greville?"

"I mean the lock."

She pulled a face, a painful one.

"Where exactly is this lock? Is it a locker? Is it at school?" I mean, there was some reason why Sapphire hadn't brought it in with her.

She shook her head resignedly. "And it's really, *really* tight."

"Locks usually are, even cheap crappy ones can bust your fingernails. Is it a bag, then? Can you bring it in to the shop?"

Her voice was almost a whimper. "Well, I've got it with me."

"Right, then. Let's get it on the bench out back."

What was it with the current fetish for inserting bits of metal in one's own flesh? I wouldn't have believed how much trouble you could get into with a couple of rings and a padlock. I won't go into detail but, if you're really curious look up the word *infibulation* and the secret will be unlocked.

They're handy things, bolt croppers, although in this instance I wasn't the one using them.


The Accountant was not pleased. Picking her way through the storage area that used to be our living room was not convenient when wearing high heels. She had somehow wobbled over and when I got home she was positioned rather unflatteringly across a box of giant-sized cavity fixings.

"What on earth are we supposed to do with over eighty-three bloody storage boxes now taking up residence?"

I helped her up, she impatiently threw off her shoes and she took me on a tour. Pausing outside the bathroom she asked what I should be able to see when the door was open.

"The toilet," I said.

She kicked. The door refused to go all the way, its passage impeded by a totem pole of plastic containers with part-consumed rolls of sticky-backed plastic. *Blue Peter* would have had a field day with that lot. It was the same with the bedroom, with piles of stock spilling over onto the bed. In the living room, it was now impossible to stretch one's legs from the settee or, worse still, to see the television.

"What on earth made you bring this junk

home?" She was almost screaming. It was a little frightening.

"Me? It was your friend—"

"What are you going to do with it?" she demanded. She was either going to cry or explode.

"Well ... what do you suggest? I mean, you're the—"

"Now hold it just there—"

I looked nervously around. "Where? What?"

"This is *your* stock."

"Not mine *personally*."

"And it should have been sold or thrown away, some of it decades ago. I even stumbled over a bottle of peroxide, for god's sake. It was so old it didn't even have a use-by date."

"They didn't bother with such things during the Second World War."

I thought it was amusing, but she looked quizzically at me, almost questioning my very existence. That's the trouble with accountants: they don't play the game, they only keep the score.

"It belongs to the MD. I'll take it round to him."

"Too late—I've binned it. I realise it's probably illegal and requires special handling, but at least it's out of the way and off the premises."

"Oh. I rather liked the bottle. You can't get bottles like that—"

"Graham, I live here. And there isn't enough room for all this stock and the *two of us*."

"Right."

She paused. "*Right?* Is that all you can say—*right?* I mean, don't you think you should be rushing this stuff out there to the car?"

"Then what?"

"Perhaps I'm not making myself clear. Either the stock goes ... or perhaps you should go. There, how's that?"

"But I lived here first."

"Oh, oh you've done it, now. You have really

done it now," and she sort of shimmied out of the bedroom. "Where's my suitcase?"

"In the loft."

When she got to where the loft hatch used to be visible out on the landing, she screamed. There the boxes were piled to the ceiling and interlocked with others reaching into the second bedroom.

I began to feel hopeless. After all, at home my life had turned into a nightmare; at work it was a bloody laugh.

# 27

SHARON POPPED OUT FROM behind a newly-delivered box of bras. "Got something for you. It's right here."

"Sharon, you can't leave that lying there."

"Why ever not? It's stock and it's legal and honest. It has as much right to be there as a box of sink plungers."

"And pretty much the same shape," I said. "So what have you got for me, then?"

"Ooh, well I don't know what you've been doing to deserve this ..." and she got out a whacking great dinner plate in a Tesco carrier bag which she peeled back teasingly. "Nice bit of Victoria sandwich. Hmm, I wouldn't mind a piece of that, myself."

"Help yourself. Take some home."

"Oh, I couldn't, dear. It's all yours."

"Give some of it to Greville, then. He looks like he could do with a good meal."

In reality, for a long time now Greville had been getting free sandwiches from the women who work in the sandwich shops. He was even cross-eating, by which I mean he could get the leftovers from one bakery and also some more from their competitor. Neither was aware that he was being fed by the other. Somehow the little bleeder got their sympathy, which he lapped up whilst stuffing the sandwiches down his bone shoot.

"Can't do that, love," said Sharon. "His tooth's giving him real gyp. Tell you what, though, you might tell me exactly what you did for the bird what brought this in for you."

"That'll be the fuse wire—either that or the fallen picture. It cracked a woman's hearth, you know. Don't look so disappointed. If any of my little jobs were compensated by sexual favours you would be the first to complain."

"At least I'd have something to talk about."

"Who with?" I looked around and Brenda was having difficulty coming to terms with how to hold a pricing gun whilst using her other fingers to brush fag ash off the counter. She hadn't a clue that I was watching her.

Sharon gave me a hopeless grin. "See what you mean. She'd have difficulty understanding the pricing convention in a pound shop. Anyway, I don't fink it was fuse wire. No, this one didn't look the fuse wire type. She looked like she had all the mod cons with buttons to pop out whenever she fancies. Oh, did I just mention buttons popping out? I actually meant—"

Something occurred to me. "Ah."

Sharon grinned. "Come on, then. And what's all this about you knowing what *the key is for?* What key?"

"I've no idea," I lied. And I think she could tell. She knew about stuff like that.

Sharon reached in her overall pocket and produced a plumbing and wiring detector, which she ran over the cake. It emitted a high-pitched screech. She put her fingers to her mouth in mock surprise.

"Why, I do believe," she did in her best Scarlet O'Hara voice, "there is a foreign body in this cake."

Cue rippling picture as we go into flashback mode ...


It all began a couple of days before when Tel heaved himself out into the shop and Greville looked for a convenient place to hide. Sharon threw down her yardstick. Okay it was a metre stick, but sometimes we felt a bit reactionary. Chucking the stick was Sharon's defiant gesture. She stood back and crossed her arms, squeezing her breasts tight against each other. This was one of her low-cut days. Greville had already said earlier that we would be all set to go diving. It was his little joke—code for "Sharon is wearing a plunging neckline". We waited for Tel to break off from his call.

Greville stealthily made his way towards me.

"There's a landline in there that he could use. Why does this guy always want a mobile hanging off his lug hole?"

"He doesn't trust anything that's plugged in," I said.

Sharon began making threatening noises and muttered, "Come on, dear, we ain't got all bleeding day."

Tel's phone squeaked and he looked at us.

"Key cutting," he said.

"Yeah, what about it?" That was me.

"Just look at all this space it takes up. Them blanks things all over the walls, bloody machines littering the place. Very untidy. I want them out—*you!*" and he pointed at me, "dump them, skip them, take them home with you. I don't care."

It was time to put him straight. "This is a hardware shop—"

"I know what it is—and, I'll remind you to

remember just whose money it is running the place."

"Not all of it." That was Sharon. Tel turned towards her with a nasty expression so I stepped in. "We're supposed to sell locks. And cut spare keys. People expect it. *Customers* expect it."

"It's a bad allocation of space. Keys isn't paying things."

"And what about the call-outs? That's good business—"

"Oh, this gets better with you of all people trying to—"

Sharon piped up: "Nobody's asking *you* to get yer arse outa—"

"How much do you charge, then? Come on. Say I'm locked out of my house. No key. I ring you, you come out in the middle of the night. What's the damage?"

"Depends on the type of lock."

"Cheapest job."

"If it's a mortise lock and it's quicker to drill than pick—"

"Get on with it—how much?"

"Ooh ... fifty."

"You'd charge fifty quid to get me in?"

"Is that too much? We could throw in a new lock."

His expression said it all, so I quickly revised my quotation.

"No, I mean I would charge extra for the replacement lock."

"Well, I should bloody well hope so. I'll tell you what you do—you take ten minutes and charge two hundred."

"*Pounds?*"

"Pounds! Quids! What did you think I mean—Green Shield stamps?"

"With only ten minutes I'd need to drill *every* lock, not just those that can't be picked."

"What's wrong with drilling?"

"It wrecks the lock."

"Look, if some silly bugger has been daft enough to lose his key, then he deserves it. We get him in, we sell him a new lock and charge for the expertise. He's happy, we're happy."

"I'm supposed to be a locksmith. Drilling is a last resort." My sense of pride was beginning to overwhelm me.

Tel grabbed my arm. "Come outside and tell me just where it says we do locksmithing." I resisted. Because nowhere did it actually say that we did. People just knew that we did. "How many callouts do we get?"

"*We?*" said Sharon.

"Not that many. The other shop gets the bulk of the work."

"Them around the corner?"

"Yes, Arbuthnot and Son."

"And why is that?"

"They advertise themselves as locksmiths. But they're not, really. They drill—every time."

"This just gets better. So they get the business, and rightly or wrongly those people around the corner make more money out of this old scrap metal than you do—*and they're the cowboys!*"

"You should know," said Sharon.

"Locksmithing is a mug's game," he called. "Unless you're going to really charge. *Charge! Charge!* That's what all of this is about! Buy cheap, sell dear. You got that? Buy cheap and—"

"Yes, dear," said Sharon.

Tel's phone launched into its annoying ringtone and he danced off into the office.

## *The Turn of the Lock*

That night it was my mobile that rang and not his.

Little Sniffingham is surrounded by hills. These are surrounded by even more hills. If you go far enough in one direction you get to Manchester; in the other you might come across Kingston-upon-Hull. This undulating landscape is littered with ancient farmhouses and fields. Lots of fields. A legend from the dawn of time tells of a traveller whose horse collapsed one wild and blustery night. He made his way for forty days and forty nights towards the light of a distant farmhouse. But he never reached it and died still on his feet. Well, I did say it was a legend. Locals on the outskirts nod their heads knowingly whenever strangers and the unwary ask for directions and they point vaguely towards the hillside where the way of speaking is different. And so are the rules of life. Even missionaries are not safe from being eaten in those parts.

The call had come from a woman trapped in her bathroom. She was calling me on her mobile phone and sounded desperate. I set out and got lost, stuck out somewhere in the back of beyond at ten past three in the morning. I had gone around in the same circle three times, each one five miles, before I found the tiny muck track the damsel in distress had so badly described.

In the dark it was just possible to make out that the farmhouse looked like two houses but with an extra door in the middle of the front wall. That's where I had been told to knock. A faint voice called out:

"Hello? Is that you?"

"Yes. I've come to do the lock."

"Come round to the back. It's the window in the middle. There should be a ladder somewhere."

If I'd been in the army, picking my way around the back of this place would have earned me a medal. To the rear of the property the land dropped away sharply, leaving a black hole so deep-looking that it could have come out in New Zealand. Yes, I found the ladder. The bottom four rungs were rotten and collapsed beneath my feet like soggy newspaper, whilst the uprights bowed silently as I climbed, which was not easy with the tool box. The light from the tiny window was tempting enough though, as I repressed multiple shivers against the freezing night air. The first I saw of the room was the light bulb: a solitary GLS lamp dangling on the end of a yard of thin twisted cable from the 1950s. You'd face a firing squad for selling wire like that nowadays. Another shaky rung further and the room came into view. It was some kind of passage, barely five feet wide, with the front door at the far end.

I hitched myself on to the narrow sill, pulled open the window frame and peered inside. A woman, she was maybe in her thirties, sat on the edge of a rather old-fashioned—almost prehistoric—roll-top bath. I smiled at her.

"I've come about the lock." As if I'd be stuck there for any other purpose at pushing four in the morning.

She stared at me for some seconds. I began to wonder if this was the right window.

"Is there anything for me to climb down on?"

She did look rather ... apprehensive, concerned, frightened maybe?

"It's all right. I'm a shopkeeper."

Then she got up, clutching the towel around herself. She looked around as if to magic up something for me to use, then shook her head.

"No."

Oh great—so how had she managed to unfasten the window? I shoved myself further in to see what kind of a jump it would be and, more important, what kind of a climb so I could get back out if the worst came to the worst and I had to leave her behind. I jumped about six feet on to the uneven stone-flagged floor.

"Well, can you get me out?" From her tone she didn't have much hope. *More to the point, can I get myself out?*

"I take it that's the door in question?" Of course I knew it was; I was trying to put her at ease but she wasn't for talking.

The thick oak-planked door must have been about two hundred years old. Fortunately, the lock was much newer, so at least I'd know what I was dealing with. The brass key was in the hole. At the very least I would have expected there to be some slight movement, but no: the thing was jammed solid. I looked around at the client, sitting on the edge of the bath, shivering violently.

"So, what's the arrangement?"

"You get me out and I pay you."

"No, I mean—"

"Oh, this? It's a shared bathroom with the cottage next door. They're away."

"Oh. And this is the only ..." I looked around. "... means of exit, right. Well, don't worry; you're as good as out of here."

"Look, can you get on with it because I'm freezing. I left all my clothes inside."

I gave her my jacket then began to regret it: the cold coming up through that stone floor was positively Antarctic and with an attitude like hers she didn't deserve looking after. I inspected the lock, turning when I heard the woman shivering over to the window to pull on a cord that jiggled the latch crudely into place. At least she has her slippers, I thought as I inserted a simple hook pick to see if I could detect a collapsed lever. Then I shone a halogen penlight into the keyhole, confirming there was nothing amiss. Which was good news. The door jiggled against the frame, so it wasn't as if it had swollen out of alignment and become stuck.

"It's been very stiff these past few weeks," she said, "but my partner said he'd get you to come and look at it."

"Well, I'm here now." Professionalism, see? You should always put the customer at ease; that's the way to get extra business by word of mouth. I read it somewhere. I was just about to squirt the lock-releasing fluid into the keyhole.

"Can't you just take the lock out of the door?"

"No."

"Why ever not?"

"Because it's fitted in from the edge."

"So?"

"And the door is locked shut. I can't get to it." I thought that would come under the common sense heading.

"Look, are you Mr Arbuthnot or his father?"

The cheeky bitch!

"Er, neither."

"Oh!"

I squirted away with the releasing fluid, directing the extra thin lubricant upwards so it would run down onto the levers and the bolt. We never used oil as such because it attracted dirt and fluff to gum up the works. Not a lot of people know that.

"So let me get this straight—are you from the shop next to the travel agent?" Did I detect a note of suspicion?

"That's the one."

"You're not the one I called."

"Believe me, I am."

"I didn't call you." She stood up, threw my jacket to the floor and backed away towards the window, desperately holding the towel to her chest. "Look, how the hell did you intercept my call? Is this some kind of industrial espionage? And why have you stood up? You should be down there on your knees—"

"Why should I be on my knees?" Was this woman royalty or something?

"—seeing to that lock."

I hadn't realised I had stood up.

"It'll take a few minutes to work."

"Just keep away from me. Stay right where you are," she spat with outstretched arm.

"I'm not moving."

"Don't even think about it."

"Why don't you check the number you dialled? Go on."

Reluctantly she edged forward to the bath. Keeping her eyes on me, she reached blindly for the mobile phone on a narrow shelf beneath a huge, crazed mirror. I could almost envisage her knocking the phone into the bathwater.

"Would you like me to get that—"

She jumped and her brief scream rattled throughout the passage and the phone plopped into the cold water.

"You did that on purpose!" Her shriek was as cruel as the scream had been.

I sighed. "Here's my phone. I'll put it down just ... there, like that? And if I move back to the door, you can come forward and pick it up and check that *you* called *me* and I'm here right now, in the middle of the back of beyond to get you out. And I want to leave, too. Okay?"

"That's not in the middle," she said.

"It's near enough."

I shook my head, cursed under my breath and returned to the door and watched her creep forward towards my phone. She kneeled down and, still watching me like a snake, reached out. That was when her towel fell from around her back. I turned towards the door and heard her slippers clopping hastily to the far end.

The lock was still jammed so I squirted in some more lubricant. I turned to her. With her elbows tightly by her side to hold the towel in place, she was pressing sundry buttons. Then she stopped.

"Right. It's you. I don't know what Phil will say. He told me to call the proper locksmith if I ever had a problem."

"Oh, thank you."

"Well, we're still locked in here, aren't we?"

"That's because I'm trying to save your lock. I can drill us out of here right now if you want, but it'll cost you for a new Chubb five-lever."

"So how long's it likely to take? It's cold in here."

"I have noticed. Wouldn't you have been better bringing a dressing gown or something?"

That threw her for a few seconds. "Well, when *they're* out next door, I like to ... I mean, it's quicker to just come straight in with a towel."

She paused as we heard a car scrunching to a stop outside.

"Oh, that'll be Phil." But she didn't sound pleased. She should have sounded relieved at the very least.

"Phil?"

"My partner."

"Bit late for a business meeting. What line are you in?" Just my little joke.

The heavy thumping on the door made me jump.

"Jill—you in there?" The door handle almost screwed itself off, its screeching sending spasms down my back. "What's going on?" From the sound of his voice he was a big bugger.

Now, this Phil didn't sound the sort to appreciate his girlfriend, or whatever she was, being trapped naked in a passage with a strange bloke.

"Phil? I'm locked in."

Phil swore rather heavily. I got the impression that all of this was Jill's fault.

"Have you left your phone inside, you silly cow?"

"No. I've got the man from the shop here."

"Make that *locksmith*," I whispered to her.

"He's a—a locksmith."

"And he's in there with you, right now?"

"Yes. But it's alright—he's a locksmith, see."

It went silent for a moment, then:

"You haven't gone and left your knickers and stuff inside, have you?"

"I've got a towel."

"Jesus fu ..." Phil seemed unimpressed by a towel's ability to cover his girlfriend's modesty.

I looked at her; he could've been right.

"So how did *he* get in?"

"Through the window."

"This just gets better. Jesus Christ!"

"It's alright. He's working on it."

Then he addressed me. "Hey, Pal."

I tried to sound big and beefy—but then if I'd been as big as I was trying to sound, how on earth would I have got through that small window?

"I heard your firm can get into any lock in minutes. Or are you the trainee? How long have you been here, eh?"

I squirted in some more lubricant that shot out of the other side of the door. It was the least I could do. Phil swore at me.

"Jill? Where is this joker from?"

I didn't really want the door to open at that very moment, but I felt I had to do something so I tried the key. The lock was still jammed solid. I breathed a sigh of relief.

"Jill? *Jill!*" He sounded crazed.

She pleaded with him. "He's trying, Phil. Just let him try. You go inside and wait."

A few seconds later I could hear him: "Hi. My partner's locked in the bathroom and she's called you lot out. Who is this joker you've sent? ... Copple

Mount Farm, Whoreby ... aye, on t' hillside, that's right ... *What?* What you telling me, that you didn't? Then who the hell ...? Right. Get somebody out right now—yes, I'll pay. In fact I'll make this other," (unkind expletive) "pay your bill."

The silence didn't last long. If the thumping on the door was caused by just his fist, I wondered what sort of damage the whole of him could do. I looked at his girlfriend and I sympathised; she was not a big woman.

Again I tried the lock.

"Do you want your coat back? You might need some padding for when he gets you."

*Oh, bloody thanks!* I squirted some more then sat next to her on the edge of the bath. Ten minutes passed; it might as well have been three hours. Jill had been telling me about the peculiar arrangement with the bathroom passage, and I had been admiring the labyrinthine network of brightly-polished copper pipes that fed the tub. A typical hardware man's way of passing the time, looking at pipes. We heard another vehicle crunch to a stop outside. There were mumbled voices, one of them manic-sounding, then another volley of thumping on the door. I honestly thought that this was it: the end. Now might be a good time to be frightened. When it stopped I chanced a peek through the keyhole.

"Bloody typical," I said.

"What's wrong?"Jill crouched down with me. "What can you see?"

"Nothing. It's just Arbuthnot."

"So?"

"And he's got his own ladder, the flash bastard."

"We're coming in!"

Jill shot upright and shook her head.

"Don't you want to get out?" I asked her.

She answered in a quiet voice. "No. How's this

other man going to get in?"

"He'll use his drill and then you'll need a new lock. He'll also charge you extra for fitting it. Night rate, call-out, sundries, you name it."

We heard Phil's voice: "Hang on a minute, mate—just hold it there. What's that you've got? What are you doing?"

We couldn't hear the next bit, despite both of us pressing our ears against the door.

"I thought you stuck in bits of wire and picked 'em."

"It's de-rectanisation of the Foley mechanism," said Mr Arbuthnot.

"What a load of cobblers," I muttered.

"But you haven't even looked at it. How can you tell?"

"Years of experience. I can tell a fault like that from a mile off. It's a complete gonner. Nothing you can do with one of these except force an internal collapse to gain entry. It'll mean a new lock—and they don't come cheap."

"And—but you do have one with you ...?

"It just so happens that I picked one up before I set off. I like to be prepared."

"How much is not cheap?"

Jill asked me what they were saying. I told her the big boys were talking money.

"And what's caused it?" asked Phil.

"Ooh ... any number of things. I bet you've got central heating, haven't you?"

"Yes! How did you know?" said Phil.

I turned to Jill. "I can't believe your boyfriend is falling for this."

Jill started. "What's that sound?"

"He's taking off the bloody handle."

"Is that good?"

"No! He's going to drill."

"No!"

"Yes!" I banged on the door. "Hey! Don't drill.

This job is mine. *You* shouldn't have been called out."

Mr Arbuthnot shouted back. "I'm the one that's getting paid, and it's your bollocks'll be nailed to the gatepost when he gets his hands on you." He laughed sadistically.

"What can we do?" asked Jill. "If we survive this, I'll pay you to change all the bloody locks."

I looked at her.

"I'd even give you a key," she added, almost defiantly. Now it was my turn to be suspicious.

There were a few seconds of uneasy silence where my eyes were locked on hers. That wasn't a pun, honest. I didn't know what to do or say, and I wasn't certain what she meant. Was this a professional or a—dare I even consider the possibility?—personal proposition? Why was my mind racing? Most likely because of the adrenaline due to the threat outside. So no, surely she meant that if I had a key, then the next time this happened I would be able to ... What was I thinking of? That couldn't work because a stuck lock is a stuck lock and a key won't work from either side. Then she abruptly looked away, almost embarrassed.

"Psst!" I got her attention and putting my finger to my lips, I picked up the aerosol, aiming its straw into the keyhole.

"Hello? You in there?" asked the so-called locksmith.

She seemed quite concerned for him. "You're not going to do that, are you? Not when he's looking in."

I shook my head. "Wait."

He crouched down to look into the room through the keyhole and when I sensed that he had turned to speak to Phil—

"I think they've got out. There's no one in ..."

—I fired the spray in his ear. Jill put her hand

to her mouth. He didn't take it well.

"Oh! You could kill him doing that!"

"The only thing that'll kill him is de-rectanisation of the Foley mechanism."

"What's that?"

"Another name for Arbuthnot syndrome. Bullshit, to you and me."

There was talking, gritting of teeth, preparations for dismantling of my body (I'd heard that a lot of that sort of thing went on in those parts). They cleared away from the door so we couldn't tell what was being said, and then a vehicle started up and drove away. The tyres didn't sound happy. Things went suspiciously silent outside. The two of us had our ears to the door. Then there was a slight click—no, it was more of a muffled shuffle. I put the key in the lock, paused to look at Jill. She nodded with a helpless expression. Then I turned it. The movement was as if it were a new lock.

"Are you ready for what could be waiting for you out there?" I whispered to her.

"Are *you*?"

The door opened and the cold night air dumped in. We hadn't realised just how warm it had been in the bathroom. Across the yard a huge bulk of a bloke staggered towards us, his thighs making rubbing sounds with his trousers. He stopped, scrunching some gravel. I don't know what that was all about. He looked straight at Jill and asked if she was okay.

"Yeah— look, Phil, this man here has been a proper Trojan. He's fixed that bloody lock with—"

Phil help up his hand.

"It's okay, sweetheart, I know. That thieving bugger was going charge me two hundred quid." He turned to me.

"I saved your lock," I said.

"All right. You saved the lock. How much you

do want to charge me?"

I told him. One flat call-out fee. No materials. He took out a wad of notes and peeled off a slice or two.

"There you go. I hope that's enough to cover you for the aggro. And for taking care of my girl."

"I can't take all this. I've got some change somewhere—"

"No, mate. You keep it."

Inwardly I breathed a sigh of relief, if that's the word. I just wanted to get home and I turned to the car.

"Say—is it you that's got that boat for sail?"

"Yeah. Twelve foot rowing dinghy. Beautifully made, it is. Utter craftsmanship."

"Sounds a right piece of kit."

"Oh, it is." There was a pause, then I asked: "Do you know anyone ... who might be interested?"

"Me? Nah. Just wondered if it was you that had it, that's all."

# 28

"YOU'RE SPENDING A LOT of time sweeping up these days," commented Sharon, instinctively taking out her duster and setting about those ever-present dust rings around the Ronseal varnish tins.

I told her we'd had an early warning message about the Health and Safety people doing a spot check.

"Can't do with getting into bovver, can we?"

"I'd tell them it was all Tel's fault."

"Ha! Brilliant! So Tel would get castigated for a scruffy shop."

Greville piped up, "Tel's been castrated?"

"Not yet, he hasn't," she said.

Then Tel X, despite the mobile phone in his ear, called out: "Brenda will sweep up. She's nothing else better to do," and he disappeared back inside my office. Or the MD's.

"I wonder what she's done wrong to upset him," mumbled Sharon.

Brenda had been allocated her own counter, complete with cash register, and we looked across to where she was having a battle arranging the boxes of tacks and panel pins in size order. And losing.

"Just look at that," Sharon whispered. "The wheel is still turning but the hamster is dead."

The following morning, Greville's toothache had "kicked in big-time", as he put it. He was moping around the place—slower than usual—and he had taken out of stock a thick wad of mutton cloth (that we sold for polishing) that he pressed to his jaw. It was in times like these I needed Sharon, both to help with serving customers, and for advice, but she wouldn't be in for another three hours. So I asked Brenda, who said that it might be better if he went home—but at closing time.

"I see Tel's been training you," I told her.

So I phoned Sharon (there was no way I was going to try phoning the Accountant whilst she was at the office: that sort of thing might have resulted in her presenting us with a bill).

"I'm stuck here with a woman who thinks a paint stripper is a model for Titian, and an apprentice who's dragging himself all over the place in slow motion. Reckons he's got toothache. And speaking of pictures, I have one to frame for lunchtime—the customer's in a rush—and I've run out of mount adhesive."

"He needs a dentist, the poor lad. Oh, toothache can be so—"

"His appointment is after lunch. That was the

earliest he could get. It's what on earth I'm supposed to do with him now—that's the problem. He's proper painful."

"Of course it's painful—"

"Not his tooth—*Greville*. He's a pain in the—"

"Give him some Paracetamol."

"He's beyond that. He's looking quite suicidal."

"The poor love needs something to ease the discomfort. Have you got any brandy?"

"I'm expecting a delivery of it this afternoon."

"Look in the cupboard by the chimney in the rest room. There's a bottle in there. Have you got some cotton wool?"

"Of course! We use it here all the time."

"Go to the chemist and get him some cotton wool. Soak it wiv a bit—just a dab or so, mind, no more—of the brandy and rest it against the tooth."

"And how do we keep it in place—gaffer tape? He'll look a right pillock."

"*Inside* his mouth."

"Greville!" I called. No answer. "*Greville!*"

There was a bit of rumbling as something was knocked over onto the floor.

"I'm coming," he whimpered, like some obedient three-legged hound.

"So is Christmas. Where are you?"

"I'm in pain."

*Oh, God*, I thought, and told Brenda the shop was hers. She brightened instantly. I never realised her facial muscles could move so fast. "Er, that means that you're in charge." She nodded and I bounded up the stairs two at a time.

"Right," I told Greville, "you need some cotton wool. Splash a drop of this sherry stuff on it and jam it in next to the tooth. I am informed that the pain—if it really *is* pain—will simply go away and you'll be able to work as normal. The customers might not understand what you're saying, but that's nothing different."

Greville merely looked at me with a sort of hopeless expression.

"Oh, bloody hell," and I reached in my pocket for some cash. "Here, and be quick—oh, and get a can of mount adhesive. We've run out."

His drag around town was noted by a number of fellow traders, some of which phoned me to advise of his progress. Under normal circumstances—before the blight on the town—they would have been too busy to notice.

"... the last I saw of him, love, he was heading back towards you," said Maggie. "Just hold on and I'll see if I can still see him—*that's four ninety-five, please, dear ... and five pee change*—hang on, love, I'm still here ... *Mum, who left that frigging box in the way?* ... Yes, that's your Greville, love. I can see him. He's standing outside the travel agent."

The rest of the story I have been able to piece together from first-hand accounts, okay? Just so you don't think I've been using artistic license and making stuff up ...


Greville stood outside *Book'n'Go* and applied the cotton wool swab-like to the bottle of Courvoisier, then thought he'd pour on a more decent measure just to make certain. He rammed it into his mouth and sucked in deeply before experiencing a few seconds of dizziness and wobbling. The world seemed a better place for that, he thought, and then looked around to establish his bearings. Now, where was he and how could he get back to the shop?

Spinning around he found the travel agent with its pleasant and often animated staff of young women wearing smart blue business suits. That was only in winter, of course; in summer they wore either flimsy negligee-type dresses patterned with wispy stripes of brown and yellow and red, or shorts and T-shirts. The thought of the shorts almost had him keeling over. He looked around. Surely there used to be a lamp post just there? It had gone. And the tooth was beginning to give him some more gyp, so he took out the cotton wool, gipping when he saw the state it was in and dumped it in the litter bin that was attached to the lamp post. Taking in another immodest dose of brandy he decided that, whilst in the area, he might as well pop in to *Book'n'Go* to say hello. He made as if to march straight into the shop, but the door refused to budge and Greville's forehead came to a full stop against the plate glass.

He peered inside. The lights were on and the computer monitors were casting light reflections on the back wall posters. But no blue-clad women were at the terminals. He stood up. Perhaps they were on a break. Still, though, surely the company management didn't allow breaks? And if they did, in order to prevent disruption to business, the breaks would need to be ... what was the word? The breaks would need to be ... cock-eyed? No, that wasn't right. Still, if he waited the word might come to him.

Someone in the street said "Excuse me" and pushed at the door, then swore and walked off. Greville looked inside again. It was as before—and then he caught a movement: it was right at the back where a small mirrored window with clear vertical stripes allowed staff in the bureau de change to see out into the shop. Yes, there was definitely movement in there and whoever it was wasn't wearing the company blue.


Liz was crying. She wasn't meaning to, but there was no way she had any control over the tears that were streaming down her heavily-tanned face. She desperately needed the toilet, and the cable ties that bound her wrists to her ankles had ploughed deep painful channels in her flesh. Next to her was Lauren, the trainee. She lay bundled against the opposite corner and had fainted. As far as Liz could tell, she was still breathing. Sitting doubled in two on the floor, it would have been uncomfortable for her to look up to see the faces of the two young men that were speaking too fast to be properly understood. Both were wearing baseball caps and dark T-shirts, and were making aggressive and menacing moves and didn't keep still. One of them was holding a knife threateningly at Claire, the manager.

Claire was not a thin girl, and the room had not been designed to hold five people. She was determined to stay calm, her priority being to get these thugs out of the building as quickly, and with as little fuss, as possible, but all this agitated footwork and garbled speech was beginning to annoy her. In a few minutes, this episode would all be over. She took a deep breath and held up her hands in a gesture of hopelessness.

"Look, please calm down. It's the foreign currency you want, right?"

The only words that she could make out were "give", "quick", "in the bag" and effing "slag". She supposed that was enough. If only he wouldn't keep thrusting that knife with the yellowed blade towards her. And his constant sniffing was beginning to get on her nerves.

"Just take it easy. Believe me when I say that I'm more interested in you getting out of here as quickly as possible than you are. I have two girls down there who are obviously in distress, so calm down and I'll pack everything up for you."

There were more garbled words. Claire merely shook her head and shovelled wads of currency notes into a canvas coin bag, bulking them up with *Post-it* notepads. There were more grunts and aggressive thrusts of the knife.

"You don't need to do that, you really don't. I'm giving you what you want. Is your friend okay? He looks very nervous. And you should take something for that cold of yours."

Claire handed him the bag, which the accomplice grabbed. The knife was thrust dangerously close to her as one last warning gesture, which made her jump back, but only a little.

"And would you like to take the coins, too? The whole lot doesn't weigh very much ..."


Outside at the back of the shop was a low wall, and on it were seven distorted wads of cotton wool laid out in a row like seven dead mice. Greville inserted yet another against his aching tooth and wondered if the police had yet arrived. He had the utmost faith in their ability and trusted they would turn up, in heavy numbers, using what he'd heard on television was called "silent approach".

Then he heard the siren wailing along High Street, intensifying in volume. It stopped and he listened for multiple car doors being slammed shut *Sweeney*-style, but there was none of that, and it was many seconds before he heard just two doors closing as if the passengers were getting out merely to go shopping. At least one other police car should have come around the back because escape was possible from either end of the alley. He winced and pressed the palm of his hand against his cheek, which only made it worse. He was running low on brandy and planned to buy some more as soon as the police had arrived. He wondered if it came in different strengths because this stuff was no longer having much effect.

He froze. There was the rattling sound of bolts being slid aside, and then the clank of a key in a lock. He turned to find two baseball-capped young men lurching out of the back door, both of them overburdened with cloth bags like those he got from the bank. One of them was also clutching a yellow-bladed knife. His accomplice appeared to have a bad cold. Clutching his cheek, Greville marched towards them.

He heard only odd, disjointed words grunted by the first one.

Greville looked down at the knife. There was no way this weakling had the strength to lift the coin bags *and* the knife.

"That's not much of a knife," he said. "I'd more likely die from rust poisoning. I just wanted to thank you."

"What? What yon about?" The murderous expression was not lost on Greville's befuddled state.

"I said thanks."

The thug went to bash his head into Greville's face but he was too late and his own visage was covered in glue from the aerosol can. That was one of them down, screaming on the floor, cloth bags discarded.

The other one looked murderously as if he would throttle Greville. He dropped one of his bags then changed his mind and reached down to retrieve it. That's when Greville squeezed again and delivered another full-face blast of spray mount adhesive.

"*Stagger*," Greville said. "The word is *stagger— staggered lunch breaks*. Must remember that."

He winced and pressed against his cheek.


*Book'n'Go* was closed for the rest of the day whilst the staff were recovering and being interviewed at the police station. Greville was warned that the thieves may indeed take action against him for assault, but he was so far out of it that I was the only one who heard the policeman's warning. I never mentioned it to him again.

When she came to work that afternoon, Sharon took him to the dentist, a rather small and very expensive practice at the bottom of our street. The expert practitioners there didn't realise that by then Greville was well and truly kaylied (a colloquialism for absolutely pissed). They propped him against a panoramic X-Ray machine and, when the camera revolved around his head and back again, he simply dropped to the floor unconscious. They prescribed antibiotics for the abscess, which probably didn't mix well with the alcohol, and it took our little hero three days to recover.

We presented him with the much-coveted 5-metre Stanley PowerLock tape measure in recognition of his bravery.

# 29

"TELL THE COWBOY TO ditch the mobile phone!" That was the Accountant speaking. She had been on at me all week about the massive phone bills that Tel was putting through as business expenses. She wanted him to stop and, standing in her black underwear with her hands on her hips, there was no doubt that she meant it. I'd not seen stuff like this behind the rat poison, and dressed like that she appeared like some kind of warrior from the *Dark Side.* If I didn't get Tel to stop running up huge phone bills, then it wouldn't be him who'd be on the receiving end of her retribution. She was always complaining about her clients and their bad figures, but when she dressed like this her figure was rather special.

"I've got more important stuff to think about," I told her. "Sapphire hasn't been in for two weeks. We've heard nothing from her."

One hand pointed straight at me, the other remained firmly on her hip. She looked fantastic in the early morning half light.

"Just do it!"


There were okay days and there were bad days. Just two things kept me going to the shop: the staff and my determination to pay off the bank loan, which was almost done. Oh—and another: I must not let down the mystery benefactor, feeling that I must, at all costs, justify their trust in me. Despite Tel's influx of fast cash, we were still trading on the financial bump that the temporary gift had provided. It had, after all, allowed us to get this far, still trading, still doing what we wanted ... or maybe not, come to think of it, because the old buzz was all gone, the thrill of not knowing what item we'd be asked for next, the expectation of a big sale, the satisfaction in sorting out a customer's seemingly insurmountable problem, and the knowledge that what made the business stronger also made us—*its staff*—that little bit better for whatever else was thrown at us. For us, making a sale wasn't only about an exchange of stuff for money; it was also about making something happen for the customer: stopping a leak, sorting a squeak, fitting a rail, hitting a nail ... These were like little stories, each with a beginning, a middle (usually where *we* came in), and an end (where we would envisage the resolution to the original issue).

Now all that was gone. It was like working a treadmill; nothing more, no light at the end, no special reward for making things work right. Everything we sold—and believe me, there was some absolute shite—was just a commodity; just that, nothing more. Even we were commodities, there to assist bundles of cash along the conveyer belt to some unknown destination. Okay, so we were being paid—nothing marvellous, maybe the going rate, but something. It was just enough to keep us treading away forever.

## *The good days*

They came in threes.

There was the one when a customer, whose lawnmower we had been servicing for some years, sheepishly came in one Saturday afternoon, carrying a large package.

"Er ... didn't get this from you, I'm afraid," he said, with a sheepish expression.

"No, you got it from Argos. I can tell from the box." I sounded perfectly pleasant, joking even; it didn't sound like a put-down.

"Well, you don't do petrol mowers, do you?"

"You know damn well we do. I showed them to you last year." *Whoops!*

"Ah. Well, they didn't put any engine oil in this one. And when you buy it, it's all in bits in the box ..."

Had someone, namely Greville or me, not been willing to handle merchandise sold by the competition, then this man would not have been able to cut his grass that weekend. It was Greville who pointed that out to me. See what I mean about sales having little stories with satisfying endings? Compensating for the deficiencies of the multiple retailers was just the icing on the cake, yet I was under no illusion that small shops could ever win in the great scheme of things.

And just when Greville and I were certain that we had completed the *Hardware Man's Pocket*

*Guide to Cocked-up Nouns*, there was another customer who asked for some special glue to stick up his *dildo* rail. And there was the man who asked Sharon if she had some of that incest spray. Oh, and the one who asked Brenda, "How much for a little screw?" I kid you not.

Another memorable day was when we received an email from Bird & Son—or rather, it was from the boss's secretary, addressed to Old Mr Bird. I assumed that she had intended to send it through the firm's internal email system, but she'd managed to accidentally send it to everyone in her address book. I could tell because their email addresses, over one hundred and eighty-six of them, were listed at the top of the message, and included all of Bird's customers as well as their suppliers. Interesting, from an industrial espionage point of view.

What fooled Tel was that there wasn't a text message as such, the actual content of the email being in the attached photo. I looked around to see if he could see what *I* could see. He was negotiating some deal over a warehouse-full of Chinese lampshades, so I breathed a sigh of relief.

Sharon burst in to hang her coat on the back of the door. Tel didn't like her doing that.

"Get Greville," I whispered. "Just get him before I delete this."

"Crikey!" said Greville. "That's not just a *private* message, is it?"

Sharon blushed. "It certainly ain't. That's a *really* private message."

We looked at the photo. I gave my expert opinion. "That's not been done with your average run-of-the-mill fifty quid digital camera, that hasn't."

"Perhaps it's just a little over-exposed," said Sharon. "Just a little bit of cellulite—just there, look, at the top of her thighs."

"*Cellulite?*" Greville was at it again. "Haven't we got something on the shelves for that?"

"That's *cellulose*, you twit."

"We've all got it," said Sharon. "Noffing wrong with that."

She peered at the photo. "You can tell she ain't happy. That's a gesture of defiance if ever I seen one. Look at the way she's thrusting her bum towards the camera. She's saying 'Here, take that, you bastard!' And the way her hands are pulling down her underwear—she's framing it with palms outstretched towards the intended recipient. Do you see? That's body language."

"I hadn't noticed her hands," said Greville.

"She's being open and honest wiv him."

"She's being open, right enough."

" 'There,' she's telling him, 'you can have this—in yer face!' "

"And you can tell all that just by looking at the way she's standing?" Greville was impressed.

"I know all about posture—"

"That's not to be confused with *posterior*," I put in.

"It's all to do wiv how you present yourself before the camera."

"And if you're in any further doubt," I added, "that big writing on her left bottom cheek should confirm it."

She had written *KISS THIS* and an arrow pointing where, just to avoid any confusion.


*The bad days?*

Like when Tel installed his daughter, Trace. For once I had some sympathy with him. I had forced myself —well, psyched myself up—to have it out with him about her. I was standing by the office door, waiting for just the right moment to go in (it was all a question of finding the right moment, you understand, the optimum point in time). But maybe I was procrastinating a little too much because the Accountant's image was suddenly projected on the white paintwork: hand on hip, the other pointing at me like the Spirit of Christmas Yet to Come. And her menacing words trembled into the ether ... *"Do it ... tell the cowboy to ditch the mobile ... ditch the mobile ... mobile ... bile ..."*

Greville saw me. "Surely you're not going in there? Rather you than me."

"I have to," I mumbled. Then, "Why not? It's my office."

Greville laughed. "Not any more, it isn't. Don't forget to knock."

I was about to knock when the black lingerie began to materialise, so I went straight in to escape it.

"Come in," said Tel. "Just park yerself there. My office is always open—"

"Trace hasn't been paying for all the Duracell batteries," I spluttered. The Accountant was beginning to haunt me in her black underwear. *Okay, I'll get to the phone in a bit.*

"Oh? What batteries?"

"And she's not been turning up for work."

"Neither has your girl Crystal, or whatever she's called."

"That's because you've as good as given your Trace Sapphire's job. It's no wonder she no longer feels wanted. Anyway, Trace has been helping herself to very expensive batteries by the handful. She's reducing stock levels so that we're losing sales to paying customers."

"We'll put it down as wages," he said. *He's always got an answer!*

"But she doesn't do any bloody work," I said. "And who's this Jessica?"

"I thought your girl was called Sapphire."

"Trace is taking batteries for someone called Jessica."

"Oh, that's Trace's rabbit," he spluttered.

"Greville's got loads of rabbits but none of them need batteries," I said, but he got back to his mobile phone.

I felt myself beginning to tremble, but there was nothing else for it: I would wait there and deliver the Accountant's wrath and ... and pretend it was mine.

He terminated the call with a flourish, rubbed his hands together and announced the impending arrival of a few hundred roller-type exercise gadgets.

"You should see 'em! Twin-wheeled, plastic handle grips, comprehensive instructions in ten languages," he smiled as if he was trying to flog them to me. "And that's not all—*full colour boxes*."

I could barely contain my excitement.

"We'll triple our money, you'll see. I can shift a couple dozen of 'em at the next meeting of the Lodge. There's plenty of fat gits there. Have to let 'em go at cost, though. Still it's only fair. They've done all right by me."

Back on the shop floor I sensed an uneasiness; it was almost like a faint buzzing niggling away, but there was no denying its menacing aspect.

"Can *you* hear that?" I said to Greville.

"Yeah, it's only Brenda lighting up again."

The exercise roller thingies arrived an hour later.

"You don't expect me to model these fings in the window, do you?" Sharon asked, holding one of them at arm's length.

I pointed to Trace who was sitting in the window, gorging on a salad teacake, her backside pressing against the glass showing her butt cleavage to the passing public.

"Get her up to the attic and pack some kapok

down and up and wherever else you think suitable."

"Ven what?"

"Give *her* the part. It'll make a great story—pudding girl turns to Twiggy, right before the customers' eyes."

Don't get me wrong: it wasn't that we were blind to Trace's talents; quite simply she didn't have any. Many's the time she would see the shop filling with customers then plonk herself in front of her computer and pretend there was some urgent task to perform. And every time she got an error message on the screen she screamed. Very loudly. Greville would cringe, Sharon would whisper some expletive and I would wish I were somewhere else. Only Brenda wouldn't notice anything out of the ordinary.

And then there was the day when it was Sharon's turn not to be happy. It was all to do with Brenda's frequent breaks. I was sorry I had promised Sharon that nothing much would change, when in reality the old atmosphere had been replaced by a grey haze that she hoped one day would mean the building had caught fire. You see, Sharon didn't care anymore.

"It's your fault," she said out of the blue and quite disapprovingly. "You're a Libran and all too willing to accept Mr bleeding X's viewpoint. You should have been a Virgo because a Virgo would kick the bastard out."

"I can't kick the bast—*Tel*—out. We can't afford to—he's got the turnover up."

"And does that make you happy?"

"No—yes—no."

"Make yer mind up."

"This bloody council—those idiots have wrecked this town."

"And as for that pitiful excuse for a female over there—"

"Oh, please, not Brenda again."

"Well, let me put it like this, if she had just one more brain cell, she'd be a plant."

I motioned for Sharon to lower her voice. "*Sharon* ... Brenda fulfils a vital role—"

"You mean she keeps the other side of Mr X's bed warm. I don't know how she manages because at work she doesn't move fast enough to raise a sweat in a heatwave. What does she do all day long except take a fag break every ten minutes?"

"Twelve minutes. At least we can set our watches by her. It passes the time of day."

I reminded her there was a time when she would not have harboured such unkind thoughts, but Sharon was no longer a glad rabbit.


The timber companies had taken to sticking labels on their sticks of wood. All timber we had for sale now had bloody big labels well-and-truly glued on. I guessed this was to make life easier for the workers in the sheds—the ones that couldn't tell one size of wood from another. And it also enabled the timber to be recognised by a bar code reader. The problem was that these labels could not be removed and could potentially ruin fingernails and cause a worldwide shortage of *Brillo* pads. They were on forever. Not a lot of thought had gone into that one. One of the consequences was that customers would need to waste those portions because, quite simply, you just couldn't see the wood for the labels.

One lady was extremely annoyed and blamed me for the waste. Now it was part of my training to disarm an irate customer by 1) listening (or giving the appearance of), then 2) apologising, and 3) grovelling. During step 1, I sneaked a tenner to Greville and told him to go to the chemist.

"You know what for," I nodded to him knowingly.

He returned during step 3 with a packet of

condoms, which didn't go down too well because by then I was already on my knees before the customer.

But Sharon just happened to have a bottle of neat acetone in her handbag which, she said, every latex-covered alien should carry. If only Dr Who himself had known that little trick. And it's very good at removing the sticky from stubborn labels too.

Monday evening, having left early to play tradesman, I'd expected Tel and Brenda to lock up and secure the shop. It rained that night. Tuesday morning I found fifteen 25kg bricks out in the yard, each bearing a soggy wrapping mistakenly claiming it was Portland cement. Greville and I stared at them.

"Well, I can't think what's happened to them," coughed Brenda. "Maybe they were faulty."

"Thank you, Brenda." Whenever I said that, she sort of posed for me, put her head ever-so-slightly on one side and smiled. Sharon said she had developed some kind of disarming survival instinct.

"Brenda, you know that new BMW of yours?"

She giggled. "The one that Tel bought for me?"

"That's the one. Tell me, was it an expensive birthday gift?"

There were always a few seconds of noisy thinking time.

"No? That's my reward for working in the shop."

"Good. Then perhaps you and Tel would like to use it to transport those bags of hardened cement to the tip."

Brenda quite surprised me by recognising the insult so soon and she shut herself in the office for the rest of the day. Needless to say, the bags ended up in the back of *my* car.

When I eventually caught up with Tel about his mobile phone usage, he turned it around and said I should get rid of the photocopier.

"And what about all the work it does for the travel agents?"

"Tell them bleeders to get their own."

My protestations about it bringing in a different type of customer, creating impulse sales, as well as the few hundred quids' worth of turnover every month, fell on deaf ears. It was no wonder they didn't work very well, with that blasted mobile poking them every minute of the day.

By Wednesday the week had got worse. Sharon was off for two days in London for an audition. There were road works all down our street. The Council had decided to do away with the tarmac pavements and replace them with cruddy concrete slabs. Our street would be closed to all traffic for six weeks and deliveries would have to be carried from across town. These in-town road works turned out to be merely a camouflage for the Council altering the traffic flow so that the third lane on the ring road would automatically deposit the unwary in the new Tesco's massive car park.

As a hardware man you learned to take stuff like this in your stride: shopkeeping was not for the squeamish.

# 30

*The Force be with you*

THURSDAY AND I WAS snappy, paranoid—so much so that I completely missed the fact that Sapphire had turned up minus the hardware. It didn't even occur to me that she was actually on the premises. She was noticeably prettier for her de-perforation, but not to me. Not then. I even snapped at her for turning up when it wasn't a Saturday and I made some clumsy comment about her not wasting the staff's time by talking to them. I remember her looking at Sharon. Even Brenda seemed put out. That was when they knew something was wrong.

Two blokes staggered in, one grasping the other's hand that he slammed palm-up on the counter, with the forefinger a crimson dark blue, impaled on a 6mm drill bit (whoops! Sorry, I meant to warn you).

"Have you got some pliers to get this out for him?" was the request.

"That's not one of our drill bits, is it?"

"What? I just want it taking out of his finger. He says it hurts."

I peered at it, but not too closely. "I thought not. The tips of ours are all dipped in blue paint."

Sharon tried to point out that masonry bits (for drilling into walls and stone) have painted tips, and this one was obviously a high speed steel bit, which are not painted. I left everything to Sharon and Greville. The ambulance couldn't get near because of the line-up of JCBs outside, but somehow they cleared the shop of all casualties, including an old lady who'd fainted and banged her head on a 5-litre can of floor varnish.

Sharon collected me from Sainsbury's where I had applied for a shelf-stacking job. When they turned me down, I tackled them about how, when they had opened the store in this town, the management had forbidden its staff to use the store's own car park; instead they were instructed to fill up the town's car parks with staff cars, thus forcing the public into theirs, and thus into their store. It was then they realised who I was and gave me a lecture about how valuable was the service I provided for Little Sniffingham, that I should be proud, and that they frequently sent their customers (against company policy, they claimed) round to my shop for things they didn't sell. The town couldn't cope without people like me, they said. But it sounded to me like begging.

Friday, yes Friday. Tricky one, that. The Accountant had been administering earache by the tonne and what was worse was she now made sure she was fully dressed when she did it. That morning Tel hadn't turned up and there was no sign of Brenda. Even she was better than nothing. Greville was on holiday, not that he'd gone away anywhere, which I resented at the time. I had to take in a delivery of the crud whilst trying to watch the customers because they would soon walk out rather than wait to be served. So I phoned Sapphire. And she came to help out, but when she walked into the shop I could tell she was wary of me. I didn't know why and I couldn't give a damn.

The customers were getting served but I was constantly snapping at Sapphire for her not knowing where recently-moved stock now lived.

"If you bothered to bloody turn up more than twice a year you'd know where everything was," I snapped at her. That was in front of a customer, and not something I would usually do.

She smiled at me and playfully smacked my arm. It completely escaped me what she was doing.

And then a woman came in with a five-pound note that was torn but repaired with tape.

"You just gave me this in my change and it's been refused in another shop," she said.

"Which shop?"

"Well, it's a stall in the market. I want another one."

"I don't have another one just like that," I replied.

"Don't try to be funny with me. I want another one. I don't know what you think you're playing at."

"That was the only fiver we had." I opened the

cash register and the fivers' slot was empty. Tel took care of the float, these days. We were also short of every other denomination.

"I want you to change this," the woman demanded. "Your problems don't concern me. Just change it."

"There's nothing wrong with that note. It can be spent."

"It's not legal tender and you shouldn't have given it out. That's illegal."

"Rubbish. I took it off someone and if I hadn't I'd have lost a customer."

"Well, you're just about to lose one now."

As soon as it went quiet I realised that our voices had been raised. Other customers were staring. Some were drifting out of the shop. I had been unaware of them and I had allowed the woman to get the better of me in a public place. I knew something was wrong, but I couldn't quite get at it. Sapphire began speaking, trying her damnedest to retrieve some normality. Another two customers walked out. The rest pretended to be busy looking at the stock to escape the embarrassment. I went around the aisles telling everyone to leave.

"Out you go, come on, get out, every one of you ..."

The last one got out of the door and I had it locked in less than a second. I slammed over the *Closed* sign and wiped everything off the top shelves as I went back up to the counter. Tins, bottles, tools, packets, trays ... everything was toppled indiscriminately to the floor. I even kicked at a 5-litre can of varnish, remembering the one that the old woman had brained herself on earlier that week. I seem to remember someone calling blasphemously at whoever he believed was responsible for this sick situation. But I didn't recognise it as my own voice. As I went behind the counter and sat on the floor Sapphire, who was already hiding there, gave a little scream.

"It's okay," I said in hushed tones. "I've locked them out. Every one of them. We're safe, now."

"*Who's* safe?"

"You and me. We'll be okay. Just got to sit it out and see what happens."

"Oh. What's likely to happen?" I got the impression she didn't like to ask that question.

"Well, I don't know."

A minute or so passed and then she asked, "So what do we do now? We can't really stay here, can we? Not like this?"

There was a knocking on the glass door. I froze. Sapphire carefully turned and looked over the counter and drew in a sharp intake of breath."

"What is it?" I asked, whispering.

"It's a woman! And she's looking in!"

I could hear, faintly, a woman's voice calling to someone, "... and I think he's got a girl in there ... I thought I saw someone at the far end."

"Get away, you nosy old bag," I called.

Sapphire told me to shush, then, "That mess is gonna take a load of clearing up."

"The mess. Yeah, the mess." *So what! Do I care?* And in that very moment I realised where I was and what was happening. More to the point, I saw what I had just done to the shop.

"I'll give you a hand, if you like."

"Thanks, Sapph. I don't know what the hell came over me."

"You've been queer all week—sorry, *strange*, you know what—"

"I know what you mean. And you're right. It's as if I've not really been here at all. So where exactly have I been?"

She shrugged her shoulders and I saw that her usual facial adornments were gone and when I looked in her eyes I was aware of the thousand years' worth of wisdom that women are born with. And there was I, old enough to be the father of a young woman who already had the world sussed.

"Shall we get started?" I asked. I was about to apologise to her when—

*BANG! BANG! BANG! BANG! BANG!*

Both our heads looked cautiously over the counter and both of us instantly dropped back to the floor.

"It's the police!" Sapphire squeaked. "Now what?"

*BANG! BANG! BANG! BANG! BANG!*

"*Police! Open the door! Police! Open the door!*"

She looked at me, grabbing my forearm tightly. "What are we going to do?"

"Armed police officers! Open this door!"

*BANG! BANG! BANG! BANG! BANG!*


"Anyfing exciting been happening?" Sharon breezed in, seemingly not noticing the smell of white spirit that was stinking the place out. We had used loads of it to clean up the mess.

"Not really," I said, lifting half a dozen cans of linseed oil onto the top shelf.

She turned in an instant.

"You're a bleeding liar," she spat at me. "That's not what I've heard. Myrtle's told me everyfing."

"I bet she hasn't."

"She has."

"She heard it on the pipe?"

"The whole bleedin' town heard it! Armed police? Silent approach? Road blocks at both ends of the street? Cordons taped around the place? Marksmen on the gas board's roof? Does none of that not sound exciting to you?"

I shrugged my shoulders.

She turned suddenly. "Hello, Sapphire, love. Surprised to see you here."

"So at least Myrtle doesn't know everything, then."

I saw it dawn on Sharon that I'd not been alone.

"Are you alright, love? I heard all about it." Sharon turned to me, the vicious tone hacking down my back. "What ve bleeding hell did you fink you was doing? I'll tell you this much—I don't know if I want to know you any longer. You want your head sorting out, you really do."

Of course, I was suffering from what is colloquially known in the trade as "bad HED" or, to be precise, a severe case of Hardware man's Embitterment Disorder. It can be serious, but dealing with power-mad section heads at the Inland Revenue and watching traffic wardens scuttling around desperate for the bonus to buy the Sunday joint tends to ease everything back in proportion. Sooner or later. In my case the recovery had been brought about by the frightened look on a young woman's face; a young woman who should have felt she could trust me with her life; a young woman who should have never been forced to doubt that I would protect her.

Later that day, once the second contingent turned up, there were smiles when I said I had noticed the little holes in Sapphire's skin.

"Oh, they'll heal," she said. "They'll not leave big black marks."

"No, just little black marks. Can I ask you a ... delicate question?"

Completely off her guard, now the excitement of the day was over, she nodded.

"Has *all* of your pierced jewellery been removed?"

She hesitated.

"Just so we know to keep the bolt croppers

handy," I smiled.

I heard Sharon whisper, "It's okay, luv, I fink he's back to normal."

# 31

"CAN I GIVE YOU a lift?"

The old boy was propped in the corner of the bus shelter on the estate and he sort of jolted as if he'd been on the receiving end of a cattle prod. He walked stiffly over to the car and peered in through the passenger window.

"I thought you were never going to ask."

I watched as he expertly manoeuvred the dead otter on his head through the door. I think he'd been practising.

"Town?" I asked.

"I've been waiting at that same bus stop, now, for ... well, it must be over five years—"

"Nearly ten."

"Has it been so long? Goodness me. Eight years."

"No, ten years. I had no idea that the local bus service was so bad," I said. "You been waiting there all that time?"

He hadn't heard me. "And every time you've looked at me and driven straight past."

I felt a bit awkward that it had taken me so long to get around to offering him a lift.

"Why have you been looking at me so intently? I mean, it's not as if you know me. We're not related, I hope."

"I didn't mean to stare. I just wanted to be certain that ... well, you see, you didn't seem to move. From one day to the next."

"I see, and you thought I'd died, is that it? Well, if I had, surely someone would have done something. I mean, they don't just leave bodies lying around, you know."

"But they might leave them standing up."

"What was that?"

"Town—are you going to town?"

"No, I'm going to the seaside."

"Are you serious?"

"Of course I'm going to town. I go every day, except Sundays. That's why I buy *two* tins of cat food on a Saturday."

"But you'd like to go to the seaside?"

"We'd all like to go to the seaside. My parents used to take us there when we were children. Those were the days. A long time ago. There's nobody left now, except me."

"What about your own family?"

"Haven't got anyone. But it'd be nice to get back there, one last time."

Something began to vibrate in my pocket. It was Greville calling my new company mobile phone.

"Special request for you," he said.

"What is it now—battery in a remote control? Barking dog next door? Drowning gnome in a garden pond?"

"... aye, everyone should have a day at the seaside ..."

"You'll like this one—hey, who's that with you? Have you picked up a bird?"

"No, just a dead otter."

"A dead what?"

"Get on with it, Greville. I've not got all day."

"It's a very special customer."

"Mrs Lipstick."

"Mrs Lipstick with one eye paying, the other on its way out? How did you know?" I groaned. "Anyway, a bit of good news. She might just know someone who wants to buy your boat."

"Might? Only *might?*"

"Just joking—it's a sale! Definite. It's someone going on holiday and they want it straightaway. Cash. Can you be there by twelve noon?"

"Hey—hey! You bet I can."

"That's when they're setting off. No boat by twelve, no sale, that's the deal."

I scribbled down the details and set off.

"Whereabouts can I drop you off?" I said to my passenger. "I'm in a bit of a rush. Got a twelve-foot boat to deliver—*yes!*"

My passenger had assumed the rather stiff expression he'd been using at the bus stop for the past ten years.

"Excuse me, but where would you like me to stop?"

Still keeping my eyes on the road, I nudged him gently. There was no response. Something dawned on me and a cold spasm shot down my back. I needed to stop but the rear view mirror showed a big wagon that was unhealthily close, and the traffic ahead was slowing to a standstill. I stopped anyway and the dead otter slumped forwards. The car in front moved on a few metres. The wagon behind blew its klaxon. I grabbed the man's hand and fumbled to find the pulse, trying to remember where to put my forefinger. Couldn't find it. Checked my own: still alive. Checked his: nothing.

"Of course there's no pulse," I muttered. "If he's ... *Hello! Hello?*"

The klaxon sounded again, longer, the wagon's engine revving impatiently. I closed up the gap in the traffic, reached for the handbrake and instead got the lifeless hand.

I pulled up at the police station. Well, actually it

312

was about a hundred metres away because of the double-yellow lines. In that day and age I could see myself getting a parking fine for delivering a corpse. It would have made entertaining reading in the newspapers, but no one would have paid the fine for me. When I got to the main door it was locked and in a small glass-fronted display case was a notice showing the opening times: weekdays 10 am to 11.30 am. But there was an emergency intercom, with a note stressing the *emergency* aspect. At that moment in time I firmly believed that my predicament would justify my pressing the button. There was no sound when I did, and that sort of thing makes you wonder if you're on the same planet as the idiot that designs or maintains this junk. After a couple of minutes, in which I was nervously looking at my watch, a rather breathless woman answered.

"Yes." It wasn't a question. She must have run all the way from the other end of the building just to answer my call.

"I've got a body."

Pause. "Would you repeat that?"

"I've got a body."

"You've got somebody ...?"

"Not *some* body: a *body*. Just the one."

Pause, then: "This station isn't open until tomorrow morning at ten."

"But can you help?"

"I'm just the duty officer." I took that as a "no".

The intercom clicked off abruptly. I pressed the button again.

"What do I do with this body? I'm in a bit of a hurry."

"What kind of body are we talking about?"

"A dead one."

She coughed. "I can't help you."

"Well then, how about I want to report a death. Can I do that here?"

"No. You'll need to go to the main police station."

There was a click and then silence. The nearest main station was five miles away and it was now 10.22 am. An ambulance screamed passed. And then another—what was I thinking of? Of course, the hospital! So I got back to the car, noticed a dog-walking couple who were pointing my way. My passenger had slumped forwards again. I pretended to wave to him and talked as I got in and pushed him back into the seat. But he didn't want to stay there. Not even the seat belt would hold him back—until I set off with a grid start, when he shot backwards with a groan.

Things at the local Accident & Emergency department were fraught. On the journey I had given way to five ambulances and the customers' car park, when I got to the hospital, was full. I had no change with me so I couldn't have paid to get in anyway. The only thing I could do was find a spot outside a house three streets away. I didn't block anyone's drive—honest—and a woman knocked savagely on her window, but I didn't have time to put her picture on the wall or whatever else was her problem. No, I had a boat to sell. And a body to deliver. *Mustn't forget the body.*

It took me fifteen minutes—over, in fact—to nick a wheelchair and get back to the car. It was almost ten past eleven and it wasn't looking good. But if I could deliver my passenger to what used to be known as Casualty, then I might be in with a chance.

But no: loads of nurses and porters and not too many doctors were running around all over the place seemingly not knowing where they were supposed to be. And the receptionist was having none of it.

"We don't take bodies," she said. "We have enough on at the moment. There's been an emergency, you know."

Quick change of tack.

"Oh, I don't think he's dead—well, not yet, anyway. Or rather he wasn't last time he spoke to me—" Which wasn't a lie.

"Our doctors have no contractual obligation to attend someone who's dead."

"But I don't think he's actually *dead*." That was a lie.

"Well, he doesn't look well." *Oh, an expert.* "Look, just wait in the queue. I'll get someone to come and take some details as soon as I can. But it'll be some time." And she answered the phone.

I looked around. The wounded were being manhandled by porters into a corner of the waiting area. The electronic display showed that the average wait was four hours thirty minutes. I could have walked out, but somehow it didn't seem fair on those people who were bandaged up and bleeding and aching and moaning. A group of young—I took it they were recently-qualified doctors, men and women—rushed past the end of a corridor, shoving a trolley. They sounded quite excited. A few minutes later they ran past in the opposite direction. The receptionist watched them before turning to a nurse.

"That's the crash team, lost again," she said.

Next stop: the mortuary. It might as well have been the local nick. They weren't interested: no paperwork, no identification, no success. And they were concerned about the fact that I had moved the body after death. No, they were not happy about that.

"Okay," I said, looking at my watch. "What do you suggest? I'm supposed to be somewhere else in ten minutes."

"This should be reported to the police. We wouldn't be happy about getting involved in what the coroner might decide are suspicious circumstances. Yes, the police should be informed."

"Okay. Right. Will you call them?"

"It might be better if you went yourself. That way you could explain what's happened."

I looked at the man slumped in the wheelchair and straightened his hat.

"And what if it was me who murdered him?"

The door slammed and we were alone on the ramp.


It was twenty minutes to one when we finally pulled up with the boat and its trailer. Telling my passenger that I shouldn't be long, I got out and rang the bell. It sounded depressingly empty inside.

"There's no one home," called a head-scarfed woman from across the street. "They've gone on holiday. You've just missed them. They've been hanging on for somebody. You can't rely on anyone, these days."

"They're no longer in the market for a boat," I told my passenger. "Not this one, anyway."


I didn't know why Tel was giving Greville a telling off. The lad was unable to get a word in edgeways to defend himself or offer any morsel in mitigation. But something in me snapped and before I realised what was happening I was at the top of the shop.

"Oh, yes I *can* fire you," Tel was bawling. "You're only here right now because I inherited you from the previous bleeding shower. But I wouldn't set on someone that looked like you. You're about as much use as a wank mag to the Pope."

The next thing I knew I was in the office on top of the desk, with Tel underneath me. He seemed to be experiencing some difficulty in breathing. The babble of voices were not recognisable to me, but firm female hands peeled me away from the desk; they were not Sharon's, who wasn't due in until later.

"You remember, Mr Cowboy—you leave the boy alone, d'ya understand? Leave him alone."

I was out in the shop. My heart was pounding, the bright lights whiting-out the fixtures and fittings. The hands that had guided me there gave final reaffirming squeezes. The voices were Brenda's and another. I spun around.

"Oh, take it easy, love, just calm down." And then, to someone else, "Jesus Christ, I think he'd have killed him. Who *is* that bloke?"

Her face swam into view. It was the girl from the butcher's across the yard. I'd never really seen her before, but I recognised her voice from the toilet. Right now she seemed a nice lass, and suddenly it occurred to me that I could need all the friends I could muster.

"You okay, Greville?" I asked.

He grunted, not certain what to say. I thanked the butcher's girl, grabbed Greville's arm and led him out of the shop to the car. He saw the boat on its trailer.

"Where are we going?"

"Far away."

"Have we left?"

"Yes."

"What—for good?"

"He can't get rid of us that easily. We'll be back."

"So where *are* we going?"

"Kingston."

"*Kingston?* Isn't that down south?"

"Upon Hull."

Greville mouthed the words to himself.

Thirty-five minutes later we were steaming along the motorway approaching Selby. We had left behind the dark satanic mills and areas of multiple chimney pots and this was now open countryside:

gently undulating landscapes of refined agricultural paradise.

"You're not having another attack, are you?"

"You mean of HED? Nah." I turned up the music and we headed towards the noonday sun and the East Coast.

# 32

"WHAT ARE WE DOING here?" asked Greville, having just awoken. "It's the sea—look!"

"Yes, Greville. I'm glad you recognise it."

"But ... what do we do now?"

"We find somewhere to park up and put the boat in the water."

"What? You're having me on."

"I'm having you on."

"What the hell is that?" He spotted the ornate stone edifice on the promenade. Two stone pillars on either side of a gothic arch, all intricately carved. As we got closer we could see that each pillar contained a room with a small window looking out on whoever would have passed—but to where? The pier was long gone and now there was just a shingle beach and timber groynes reaching out into the sea. Okay, so we had travelled further than Hull, but out there it just seemed the right thing to do to keep going past the huge oil refinery and on towards the coast. When we found it, the little seaside town was not busy for mid-week and there were loads of parking spaces on the front.

"Right Greville, I've brought you to the seaside. It's your turn to pay to park. Go find a machine."

"Where is this?"

"Haven't a clue, but isn't it great? I just wish

we had Sharon and even the Accountant with us. We could make a right holiday of it. Get a parking ticket, off you go."

I was admiring the block-paving on the promenade. It hadn't been there long and didn't end abruptly where the money had run out, but seemed to go on forever. And to think that all this concrete had been manufactured in a quarrying village only a short distance from our shop and yet here we were, a million miles from home. Between the sea and the heart of the town was a landscaped crater with bandstand and kiosks. I could imagine that, in times gone by, that might have been a boating lake. I could be wrong, but to the family holidaymakers of the 1930s it would have been superb for sunny afternoons by the sea. Heaven on earth.

"We don't have to pay," Greville said, leaning forwards on my door. "No charge."

I got out, looking around to check that we were still in the cash-greedy UK.

"Straight up," he said. "Nice bird over there selling ice cream. Told me everything. This fancy thing here was once the entrance to the pier. Look at it—it's fantastic. I've never seen anything like it before, especially around our way."

"Well, there's not a lot of call for piers inland," I told him.

"So what's it to be, eh? I didn't ask you before because I thought it might be a surprise, but I'm asking now. What are we doing here? You're not thinking of opening a hardware shop, are you?"

"What, here? No—"

"Because if you were, that would be fantastic. A hardware shop by the sea. Think of it—the salty air, the seagulls, the holidaymakers, the nice young women."

"It's not exactly Greece, you know. You wouldn't get packs of young women swimming naked in *that* sea, would you? It's brown and horrid.

They'd come out with scales."

He stood up and looked around, seeing the line of amusement arcades and chip shops.

"Still, though ..."


The young woman, dressed in T-shirt and exploded sawn-off denim jeans, tripped down the side of the house and showed off the expanse of their "dwarf plus" stockholding. She turned and smiled, tossing her long wavy hair over her shoulder. Greville thought she was smiling at him, but he was mistaken.

"Dwarf what?" he asked her.

"Dwarf plus. That's any figure three feet and bigger. They're mostly from the Snow White collection. We've got gnomes in three different sizes—they're our best sellers—and just over there we have some classical Greek ladies, with or without urn, with or without inbuilt water feature, and all options clothed and unclothed." She smiled at him, but his imagination was on already.

"Wow." Greville's eyes couldn't have tried to pop out on their stalks further if Vanessa had been talking *real* women.

Inside the workshop, with its breeze-block walls and its inadequate corrugated steel roofing (hardware men notice these things), she showed us aisle upon aisle and rack upon rack of frogs, birds, squirrels and other concrete wildlife. There were numerous designs of birdbath and various water features such as fish fountains, untrained Yorkshire terriers (indiscriminately urinating) and kneeling naked ladies with trickling bowls on their shoulders. It wasn't just about garden gnomes: here was a whole new line for us to sell, and one with previously undreamed-of profit margins.

"It's amazing just where you find new suppliers," I told Vanessa's mum, Doris, who spent ages hand-writing great lists of invoices like some ancient Greek scribe. How she kept her concentration whilst chatting away, I could only wonder.

"So you actually write out the invoices by hand," I observed. "A bit like *Gnomer*."

"So, who told you about us?" She didn't laugh and she didn't look up. "We're a bit off the beaten track here."

"We were just passing," I said.

"A couple of lads on the razzle," said Greville.

"Good Lord!" She looked at me very questioningly indeed, then took up where she'd left off on the page. "I won't have one of those computer things in the place. If I do it this way, then *I* know every item that anyone has ordered. I keep it all up here," and she tapped her head. "Would you like to take some things back with you, now?" There was eye contact with that remark. Clever.

"Do you have—"

"We don't deliver. That's how we keep our prices low. Whatever you want, as long as we have it in stock, you just take it away with you."

"Ah, so we definitely need to come and collect it. It's over three hundred miles for the round trip."

"Well, if you don't come and pick it up yourself, it's not going to get to your place on its own now, is it?"

"So none of your stock has a *gnoming instinct*." I smiled. No response. "Well, Greville, how about it?"

He could detect the threat of there being some carrying of heavy items to do. "Hang on, I thought we came out here to escape, not as a buying spree. And what if Tel doesn't like any of this stuff? I wouldn't want to be in your shoes when you turn up with this lot."

"It won't be as bad as that. There'll be two of us."

He looked aghast.

"You walked out too, remember."

"I was dragged—on my will."

"*Against* your will." I looked at Doris. "Kids, these days, tut. Look, Greville, we can get back with a car load of stock and let the sales start *ticking* away on the run up to summer—like a *metrognome*." Again, there was nothing.

"Where will we store it all?"

"How about *Gnome-man's* land?"

He looked at Doris. They shook their heads ever so slightly.

"And how are you going to pay for it?" He was beginning to sound like me: all responsible, like. Well, after going AWOL with the newest recruit and finding this seaside town where the local council isn't run by a set of bastards suffering from terminal financial ineptitude, I was beginning to feel that a little irresponsibility might not go amiss. I'd deserved it.

"Leave the eco-*gnomics* to me," I said. "I'll use my own money and sod the new bloke."

"And what if Tel kicks us out?"

"Then we'll wander around flogging our stuff—a bit like *gnomads*."

The shriek of laughter came from behind us where Vanessa had the good manners to appreciate my pathetic attempts at humour.


We travelled back into the seaside town slowly.

"We'll need to be careful on our way home," I said, more for my benefit than Greville's. "All this weight affects the steering. Makes it light."

"She's a grand lass, isn't she?"

"Who is? Brenda?"

"Nah, Miss Seaside Concrete. Vanessa."

"I hadn't noticed."

"I like her dress sense."

"She's hasn't got any."

"I know—bloody hell, those shorts!"

"What shorts?"

"Crikey—you can see her—"

"Greville!"

"Well, you can. And the stuff she can lift. You'd think she was built like a brick—"

"Greville!"

"Well, you know what I mean."

"She's fitter than her dad. That was him tinkering with the cement mixer one minute and then rubbing his back the next."

"Old man's back trouble, eh?"

"What he needs is a good *gnomeopath*."

"He's nowhere near as fit as his daughter."

I thought for a moment. "Yes, she's got that one hundred and fifty watt look in her eyes, don't you think? You know, the sort of person that knows how to think. I would give her a Saturday job."

"And I'd give her one, too."

"I asked her dad if he uses a special additive in the concrete mix."

"What for?"

"To make it go hard faster. Just wondered."

We left the car and trailer parked on the front again, this time with the bodywork resting on the tops of the tyres, and went to explore the town.

"Look!" cried Greville. "A hardware shop!"

"There are one or two still surviving, you know," I told him.

Of course, we *had* to look inside: it was every hardware man's right to see what fellow traders were getting up to. And Greville seemed to enjoy himself looking at the stock and prices and how the layout was appropriate to the shop's trade emphasis. Out on the pavement, I told him to keep quiet about what we had been up to, otherwise our work colleagues would think we were a couple of sad gits.

The amusement arcades dominated the town and although their entrances looked like little shop fronts, once inside they mushroomed out and occupied the whole block. We played the machines, rubbed shoulders with a smattering of holidaymakers and had a good time.

Greville was hungry. Well, we had missed lunch and it was approaching teatime so we queued for fish and chips. It must have been the sea air and sunshine that made the smell of them being fried seem like some exotic delicacy. We sat on a bench on the beach and began eating them.

"Look at the size of this fish," he said, holding out the tray to me. "We don't get them this big around our way."

A couple of minutes later he began to gip.

"God! What ...? This fish as got *bones* in it."

"That's why I didn't have fish. They don't bone fish around these parts. I thought you knew."

"How would I know that? I've never been this far away from home before."

"You'll probably find they've also left the skin on."

"*What?* Oh, my God! I've eaten some of that—ugh! Why do they do that?"

"It stops the fish shrinking when they fry it."

He smacked the tray on the bench and folded his arms.

"Well, I'm not eating any more, the idle sods."

"Just eat your chips. It's a long drive home. If Tel gets his way, after today you won't be able to afford to eat."

"How do you mean? No one starves. Not these days."

"No, I suppose you could always suck some leftover fish bones—"

"Don't!"

"Or make a nice fish bone soup—"

"You're turning my stomach over."

~ ~ ~

The sun was heading dangerously close to the sea and brushstrokes of pink had been randomly applied to the sky.

"It's gonna be a nice day tomorrow," said Greville.

"Yep."

"You didn't sell the boat."

"I didn't sell the boat."

"Thanks."

"Why, do you want it?"

"Thanks for fighting for me, with Tel."

"You're welcome."

"Have we still got a job?"

"Tel's not daft enough to get rid of you and me. We're far too valuable. We can fix things, we can mind-read, we can do sums, we can operate equipment, talk to people from various walks of—"

"And Tel's a git."

"Mind what you're saying, he's still your boss."

"No—y*ou're* my boss. He told me that as a salesman you're as much use as a chocolate teapot."

"You're right—he is a git. See that line of posts out there? Those brown sticks stretching out into the sea? It's called a groyne."

"You're having me on."

"Straight up. A groyne. Tel's groin will be softer. But you'll still need your boots on."

The sea scratched away at the beach, the waves making unremitting progress as they gained ground. I watched Greville's silhouette as he gazed, almost mesmerized.

"Nice here, isn't it?" he said. "You know, I've never seen a sunset before, not over the sea. My mum always said she'd take me to the seaside, one day. But she never did. She used to go off with her girl friends from the factory, always Blackpool. On a coach trip to play bingo on the front. She never offered to take me with her, not there, not then, with her mates. I asked her once, but she came up with some excuse or other. Not enough money. Not enough Co-op stamps in the book."

"So, this is the first time you've been—"

"It's great, isn't it?"

"Yeah, it is. Everyone deserves a day at the seaside."

"What?"

"Oh, just something someone said to me."

A squabbling flock of seagulls circled overhead. They must have heard Greville's disparaging remarks about fish skin. Keen ears, seagulls.

Greville drew in a deep breath. "Do you know what? I don't want to go back. I want to stay here where I can watch the tide come and go whenever I like, and breathe in all this ... *air* that makes me tingle. You know what I mean? And where I could just go out in a boat and sail. I know where there is a boat." He looked at me. I believed he was serious. He went on: "Well, no one's going to buy it, so why not? Why not just go out there for a bit of a sail, test it, see how she handles?"

"There's someone using it right now," I said.

"How do you mean?"

"A sitting tenant."

I looked at my watch: it was ten to nine.

"It's getting dark. We need to be getting back and we've a tonne of concrete to drop off at the shop."

Greville sat back, reality's grip reaffirming its tenuous hold on his spirit.

When we left the beach there was just one solitary occupant. He was sitting on the very bench where the apprentice and I had watched the restless sea as it washed our thoughts and randomly scattered our hopes and dreams and disappointments. He sat perfectly still, wearing a fur hat that looked like some ridiculous stuffed otter. Oh yes, and with a part-eaten tray of fish and chips on his lap.

# 33

THAT WASN'T QUITE WHAT happened, although I do wish I had actually taken the old man for a last day at the seaside. But writing it down that way has provided me with a better lasting image and I hope that you don't mind.

It was nice to be appreciated and, apart from Christmas cards and the odd Easter egg, there were very few ways by which our customers could express their affection. Most of them didn't really want to.

Greville had no problem with this aspect of consumer relations as every weekday at four pm a gang of ever-changing fifth and sixth form girls descended upon the premises to bestow upon him compliments and attention. In my day I remember that the boys did the chasing. That's progress for you.

On this particular day nearly every customer had trudged up to the counter with that *guess what I want to buy* expression.

"Well, I don't know what you call it, but I'll know it when I see it," they said.

Sometimes I would ask what *they* would call it, but that could be considered an intimidating question. You had to guess, it was all part of the ritual; selling stuff wasn't meant to be easy.

One woman had refused to pay 35p for a sink

plug because she lived in a rented house. If it wasn't hers, why should she spend any money on it, she said.

"What do some of these people live in," Sharon once said. "A tent with no chair?"

This particular day there were still two hours to go. I was by myself. And I didn't like it. Tel was in the back, but he didn't count as *active* staff.

I smiled as a lady at the copier handed me the money, then she took me by surprise.

"This is a good service you offer. I can see you keep your machine regularly maintained."

My God! She could actually *see*. Did she want a Saturday job?

"And it's a pleasure to deal with someone like yourself."

"Why, thank you." She took her change then made eye contact. "And I love you too."

Her confident form disappeared into silhouette as she headed towards the door and I turned to the next lady customer. I barely recognised her but, if anything. it was the look in her eyes that caught me.

"It's you," I said. "You're the ... you usually wave to us through the window."

"Yes, when I'm passing."

"Our apprentice—"

"Granville?"

"Greville—he was saying that we've not seen you for a while."

"No. Had a spell in hospital. Didn't she tell you?"

*The Accountant?* "I've not been ... all here. She might have done—well, she's bound to have mentioned it," I mumbled, feeling awful. I must really have been up my own ... well, never mind where exactly.

"Would you like me to carry on waving when I'm back at work?"

*Salvation!* "Oh, yes please, by all means. Thanks. Something for us to look forward to. We're not, erm, *appreciated* by that many people, you know."

"Oh, surely not. That last lady seemed to appreciate you."

"Yeah. Did she really say that?"

"That she loved you, too? I'd stand up in court and testify to it."

"It's a long time since anyone said that to me."

"Well if you like, I'll say it to you when I go out," she smiled.

She knew exactly what she wanted and I handed her the change. Just then another couple came in, making straight towards the counter, doing the *Guess What Shuffle* and I knew we were back to normal for the day.

"On second thoughts," Jane whispered, "I'd better not. They might get the wrong idea. I'll see you again," and she winked at me. By the time I had basked in her smile, she was gone.

A distant door creaked open. Anyone would think we didn't sell oil for hinges.

"Hey, lad!" called Tel. I didn't move, which meant that he'd be forced to embark on a search and destroy mission to find me. Which he did. I made it easy for him.

"I've been calling you."

"I've been serving."

He slammed down a box of assorted springs.

"I want these pricing. Should make eight hundred per cent on them."

"Fantastic."

"That's how you do it, you see. That's where you and that old bugger have been going wrong all these years." He tapped the side of his nose.

"I hope that's not catching."

"What?"

"That itching nose. Your mate with the van has

got it as well."

He slammed down his drinking mug. That meant he needed both hands ... and there was no sign of the mobile.

"Get the boy to do it when he gets back." And I watched him drag himself back to his inner sanctum.

The voice behind made me jump.

"Ooh, love, that's a nasty pot."

Myrtle, immaculately permed hair, bright red lipstick and a face like crumpled cardboard—corrugated at that—peered into Tel's mug. Anyone else's stomach would have turned over. And Myrtle knew a nasty pot when she saw one.

"You'll need something very strong for that," she groaned.

"You know all about dirty pots, don't you, Myrtle?"

"I can smell a lavatory that hasn't been flushed from across town." She regarded Tel's coffee mug once more. "I've seen worse, much worse than this."

I nodded eagerly. "Yes, I know."

"I could tell you some real stories—"

"It's okay, you already have done."

"It's a bad 'un, is this."

"Drain cleaner?"

"Strong as you've got, love."

"Caustic soda?"

"Nothing stronger?"

"Even caustic soda's classed as a poison. New European Union regulations."

She shook her head in despair. I wanted to steer her away from recounting the latest about what she'd seen, what she'd heard and other things "on the pipes". She usually came in at lunchtime and often she had called me out of the office when Greville and Sharon had mysteriously disappeared. The things she said could put you off eating for 24 hours.

"Afternoon off, Myrtle?"

"That's why I'm here to see you, love." She sounded quite sorry for herself. "To say goodbye. I'll not be in again."

"Oh, dear."

"I've been given the push," and she slapped the counter. "Council doesn't want me no more."

Even I found it hard to believe. "You've been given the flush?" Slip of the tongue.

"Forty-seven years I've been in them loos—*forty-seven years*! And the goings-on that I've seen, you wouldn't believe—"

"I would."

"—if I told you."

"You have. Many times."

"I started on two pounds twelve bob and eleven pence a week."

"As low as that?"

"Oh, don't get me wrong, it wasn't a bad wage for a young woman at the time. In them days it was either the bogs or the streets. But for the things I had to do and the things I had to see, oh, you wouldn't believe—"

"I would."

"—if I told you."

"Really, you have." I nodded. A lot.

"And do you know what they're going to do with them?"

I shuddered to think. "Renovate them, I should think."

"No. Oh, no. They're making it into a *baker's shop*."

"You mean—*food?*" It wasn't one of my better days.

"In them very walls. And when I think about the stuff they've witnessed, the things I've seen—"

"I know."

"You wouldn't believe—"

"I would."

"—if I told you—"

"Oh, you have."

"—it'd make your hair curl."

"Yes, I believe it would."

"But the vacancies of my profession forbid me from saying exactly what I've seen."

"Thank god."

"I could have made a fortune selling stories to the papers. But there was no point in prostituting myself, was there? I'd have been sacked."

"But now you have been sacked—"

The bell went and some people bustled noisily into the shop. Greville was one of them. By the way he walked I could tell he hadn't had a good day, either.

"Well, I'll be off then, my dear," Myrtle said and then, having caught sight of the ancient couple negotiating their way up the slope, whispered confidentially:

"Watch out for that one—she's only got one passage." And Myrtle trotted out of the shop for the last time, giving the woman a wide berth.

"I've only got one passage," said Greville.

"That's all you're supposed to have," I said, without thinking.


Greville was coming along nicely. His training was still incomplete but it occurred to me that, at some point, it might be an idea to allow him a little responsibility. I was brushing down the heavy deposits of alloy and brass dust and swarf that had formed little pyramids and deserts on the key cutting bench, and at the same time watching him serve ... smoothly—yes, *smoothly*, calmly, in control. And then a teenage lad walked up to the counter. Something wasn't as it should be; it was his body language and it reminded me of a schoolboy walking across a stage: it wasn't natural.

"A packet of Stanley knife blades, please." As soon as he said it, I knew.

Greville spun around and took a card of blades from the display, but stopped before placing it on the counter. He asked the boy how old he was. At that moment the lad held out a five pound note, thus tempting Greville to take it. Instead he turned to me with a questioning look. I said to the lad:

"Does your mum know that you're buying knife blades? How old are you?"

He answered without any hesitation. "Sixteen. They're for me dad."

"So why doesn't he come in and get them himself?"

"He can't. He's working."

"So who's that man standing down by the door?"

Like flicking off a switch his face dropped almost to the floor. I gave a warning look to Greville and shot down to the bottom of the shop and grabbed the man's arm. He made a few grunting noises and struggled to get out his identity card but I wasn't interested.

"In America this sort of dirty underhand trick would be classed as entrapment."

"We're obliged by law to check up on retailers in this—"

I called for Sharon. She came running down.

"I'm not allowed to manhandle this slimy git," I told her. "But you can have a go at him if you don't mind getting your hands dirty."

As I went back up the shop I thought I heard her telling the creep from the Trading Standards Department just how much he should be ashamed of himself ...

"... for stacking the shit against one of your own."

*What?* I did a rapid about-turn and found Gerry pinned up against the window with Sharon's finger well and truly thrust into his quivering chest. When she saw me she told him to go back to his grotty little stall on the hillside, but not in so many words.

"Right, Greville, you've shown just how responsible a person you can be. I'm proud of you."

"Why? What would have happened?"

"If you had flogged those blades to that twelve-year-old schoolboy, you'd have got a telling off and the owner of this business—if they could have fathomed out just who that is—would have got a five thousand pound fine or six months in prison and a criminal record."

"Really? As much as that? Just for selling Stanley knife blades?"

"Yes, to a kid, which is illegal. So what made you suspicious of him?"

"He used to live next door-but-one."

"Oh." I think I was disappointed.


*A right old pun-to-mime*

It was December and Tel had been absent for some weeks. Sharon had been right. He had taken everything with him except his girlfriend. In order to further finance his aunt's affairs, he had sold the house from over Brenda's head, under her feet or behind her back (take your pick)—or rather she awoke one morning to find a FOR SALE sign in the garden. So that was the car and the house he'd taken back. Now she was turning up late and had taken to smoking roll-ups as thin as matchsticks. But it wasn't like the old times and we were not sure where we stood or even who owned what part of the business. The present was uncertain enough; the future was known only to the few remaining soothsayers—speaking of which, we had not heard of the MD for some time.

Trade had been hotting up early for Christmas.

The Burtons, who lived in the local folly—a Victorian sham castle perched on a flattish plateau overlooking the town—ordered automated curtain rails for all of their downstairs rooms. Nice little profit margin on each of those. I smiled at the thought of Chateau Belle Vue putting a strain on the National Grid every evening when the curtains were drawn. It seemed that there were more and more drains on electricity than ever before. That would have been a nice spot of commission for the Swish rep if she'd not stopped calling to see me.

"Aye, well one day there'll be windmills all over the place," the MD had once said.

"Windmills? Making stuff to make bread with?" asked Greville. He was thinking fairy tales again.

"No, not *big* windmills. They're bound to be smaller—but it's the wind, you see."

"It always is," I thought aloud.

"The wind is very powerful—and it's free, that's the whole point! So why not harness all that energy and make electricity? It stands to reason it'd work."

We hadn't believed him.

Another good sale came about when a local manufacturer of metal food containers had purchased a machine from China. It was in fact a copy of an ancient contraption that had previously been dumped in the Orient by some unscrupulous British machine trader, like the locks I mentioned. The Chinese had set up a new industry to make spare parts for these machines and sold copies of the machines back to us. The problem, though, was that the Chinese had also copied the old Whitworth fastenings. By the early 21st century there hadn't been any call for old-fashioned Whitworth spanners for over forty years. Did we have any that would fit these obsolete nuts and bolts? You bet we did! They were at my house in one of the infamous storage boxes. This was top quality tackle, some priced as high as 9/11d (49p). The MD would be proud of me for not chucking them away, what with inflation and everything.

Later that day Brenda was not trying very hard to get eye contact with a lady at the counter and I knew I'd have to step in. I recognised the look of hopelessness tinged with desperation—the customer's, that was. It had been a sad story about her husband's illness and a reluctance to allow him to be admitted to a specialist care facility. I'd lost count of the number of times she'd asked for help with problems ranging from wiring a plug to sowing a lawn. In a perfect world I'd have had plenty of time to deal with her; but then in a perfect world her husband wouldn't have been stricken down so cruelly.

On my way to her I called out to ask Greville if he'd managed to get us tickets for the Travis concert that both of us wanted to attend.

"Sold out," he grimaced. "Within an hour of going on sale. Huh!"

I felt gutted, but turning to my customer I realised how fortunate I really was. Apparently the doctor had said it might help if she played old home videos to her husband, but she'd dropped this particular one and accidentally trodden on it.

"The big electrical store said I should throw it away, but it's the only one I have of our last holiday." She placed a bag of loose bits on the counter, almost too embarrassed to ask me if I would try to help.

"Leave it with me," I heard myself saying, sounding like some character from *Postman Pat*. If I could just re-house the tape in another body, I could then copy it to DVD. Otherwise, she could need a miracle.

The following Saturday was exceptionally busy. It was customer—sale! Customer—sale! Customer—sale! However, Tel had turned up. He didn't speak to Brenda or even acknowledge her presence, and caused her to mope around like some love-sick schoolgirl who was just dying to share her chewing gum (and then some) with the head boy.

"What do you want?" I demanded of him, but sort of half-heartedly because we both sensed that his time with us was at an end; he had given his best shot at running a retail business, but a bullet heavily labelled with £ signs was not enough. Looking back I realise that we all knew that chucking a load of cash at a problem was merely a temporary approach; it might plug the leak, but wouldn't fix the tank and Tel's time with us was transitory.

Thanks to him, Brenda was having one of her *dysclumsic* days and was dying for a fag. Someone wanted a drill bit like this one and handed it to her, but it shot from between her fingers into the air. It had landed before she realised what day of the week it was. She was flustered for about a minute before some customers shouted, "It's behind you".

"Oh! Where?"

"It's behind you!" a few of them joined in.

Brenda picked it out of a wall display and then dropped it in the till where it became lost under the penny coins.

Things were getting hectic. Adrenaline was flowing. Greville plonked eight tins of paint on the counter and told the customer:

"There you go: one litre non-quick-drying white gloss and seven small lilacs. Or should I say, *slow white and the seven mauves*?"

Sharon suggested we have a working break to keep us going, and offered to buy each of us a Snickers bar. Sapphire called in to ask if she could have her Saturday job back. I was about to tell her to take her coat off there and then, but Tel wandered through carrying his pot plant and said that no way was he having that girl back in his

(*his?*) shop when he already had a very capable girl of his own. Brenda beamed at him, almost blossoming, then realised she was holding the hammer by the wrong end.

The customers had gone silent, apart from a laughing one who must have heard how very "capable" Tel's daughter really was. I reminded Tel that originally he'd set on Trace to fill in for Sapphire's *temporary* absence. He denied this, using a fair amount of expletives.

"Oh, yes you did," called Sharon.

"Oh, no I didn't," he maintained. Then the customers jeered him and he retreated to the office.

At closing time, coats on, lights out, ready to go, we reflected on one hell of a week. I went first.

"The drill in the till." I said.

Brenda gave me one of those blank stares she usually reserved for the customers.

"The spanners for the canners," Greville laughed.

"The curtains for the Burtons," added Sharon. "In the chateau on the plateau."

"I sold some pliers," said Greville. "For the wires?"

"The snail in the pail." That was Brenda.

We looked at her and she admitted leaving a pile of buckets outside overnight and selling one the next morning complete with livestock.

Then Sharon said, "The Snickers in my ..." There was a pregnant pause. "... pocket."

"Phew, that's a relief," said Greville.

Sharon hung about after everyone else had left. Outside the darkness was oppressive when I switched off the window lights. It seemed appropriate.

"Well, that could be the last we ever see of Tel," said Sharon.

"We'll see him in court—"

"In court?"

"When he fights us for his money."

"You can always give him back his naff stock. Look at it, piled high and collecting dust. Solar-powered hair curlers for the woman abroad! What a pile of crap! He's been a right bastard to Brenda."

"I thought you didn't like her."

"She's coming on nicely, she is. Spending time with us, somefing was bound to rub off, wasn't it? The snail in the pail?"

"Or the sale of the snail."

We laughed, briefly. A minute or two of silence as we grew uncomfortable with the darkness around us. Not even the faint buzzing of the fluorescent lights provided any comfort. Not now.

"Nothing stays the same, Graham. You know vat, don't you?"


"What you writing down?" Greville was reading over my shoulder.

"Just some diary notes in case I ever want to write about the adventures and uncertainties of running a hardware store. The people, what they want, the stuff they say."

His grunt told me that my wanting to remember certain aspects was perhaps something to do with my age. I'd just got down the story of the curtains and spanners.

"Is that it?" asked Greville, reading over my shoulder. "It's not much of an ending."

"Happy endings don't really exist," I reminded him.

"Found this on the counter," he said, dropping an envelope on the keyboard. "It's addressed to *The Nice Man*, so it can't mean me, and it certainly doesn't mean Tel. It'll be an early Christmas card."

"Thanks."

"Well, aren't you going to open it?"

I felt the envelope and yes, it did feel like a

card.

"It's a bit early. Wait until we get some more," and I put it down.

"No! Open it now. The way things are going this one might be the only card we get."

He had a point.

Inside the envelope was a thank you card, unsigned. And with it were two tickets to the Travis concert in Manchester. We couldn't believe it.

"How someone has managed to get hold of these, I don't know." I wasn't certain what to do with them—I mean, they were so rare. And the fact that someone had somehow acquired these and given them to us, and wanted to remain anonymous ... Surely it wasn't the mystery benefactor striking again ...?

The phone rang. "It's me," the Accountant said.

"Oh, hello. You'll never guess—"

"With some bad news." She paused. "You remember Jane, don't you?"

"Oh, yes. She was in here only a few weeks ago. What is it?"

"She's died."

I froze. "But she can't have. She used ..."

"Yes, I know."

"But I was talking to her ... She almost told me that she ..." My voice trailed off.

"Forty-three, two children. Breast cancer."

# 34

*The winter of our discontent*

RITA PRESENTED ME WITH a specially frothed coffee that she knew I liked and then, surprisingly, she sat down next to me.

"Excuse me, dear, but I did hear a rumour and wondered if there might be any truth in it?"

I looked nervously at the counter where three tourists were waiting to be served. Let's face it, they had to be unsuspecting strangers, didn't they?

"I happened to hear—caught it on the grapevine, so to speak—that a certain *person*," and she looked around suspiciously, "has sold up and ... vacated the premises."

"Yes, Maggie and her mum have sold up and moved away to start a new business. A bingo hall, I think."

Rita brightened. "Oh, dear, I shall miss her."

"You didn't know her."

"Ah, but I knew *of her*." She straightened. "So how *is* business, dear?" Then, looking beyond me as the doorbell tinkled away, "Oh, hello. I haven't seen you for some time. Are you well?"

The next I knew the MD had plonked himself on the chair beside me. He leaned forward confidentially.

"I knew that bugger wouldn't last long."

"I'll bet you did, with your all-seeing eye." It was no wonder there were no spare parts for crystal balls if the MD had stockpiled them all. "I wish you'd told the rest of us, then we'd have had something to look forward to."

"You had a cushion. I made certain of that, but

I can wait a bit longer to get it back. Come on, we need to get back up the street and get cracking."

Did he say *we?*

"There's Christmas just around the corner."

"Is that another of your predictions?"

"From what I can see, that clever git of a friend of yond woman's—"

"He was never a friend of the Accountant—"

"From what I've heard," he said, raising his voice, "he's left the place an utter bloody mess. Well, I'm ready to get going."

"*What?*" He must have been the neck-end of ninety.

"Oh, yes. I've done it before and I can do it again. I don't expect your mother will be all that pleased. She'll just have to lump it like we did when I started it up just after the war. So come on."

"Hang on a minute—what's this cushion you mentioned?"

"Oh, just a bit of summat to help tide you over. So come on, let's roll up us sleeves and get cracking."

He was on his way to the door. I was suffering information-overload.

"But we really need to talk about what we're going to sell. It's all changed while you've been gone. Things are different."

"Look, lad, I'm not bothered about that. Not any more, I'm not. We'll sell ladies' underwear if we have to."

"Ah, we've something on the shelves for that," I said. following him.


### *All's Well that Bends Well*

The MD's new-found testosterone was all very well, but the town centre trade was well and truly ... I shan't use the naughty word, and we were sort of half-existing in what seemed like a drug-induced state. And it wasn't just our shop but all the local traders.

At Christmas the town was presented with a bent tree. We usually chained the festive lights just to the top third to prevent the bulbs from getting nicked, but this thing was so out of plum that, looking like an inverted sink trap—or U-bend—its top reached over so far that the lights scraped the tops of passing cars. At the No Nickers meeting we agreed this would be the last time we'd accept a free gift from the king of Norway. At least the council surprised us that year by forking out to get the lights switched on by a celebrity who *used* to be famous. He'd stopped by on his way to the *Celebrity Big Brother* house.

But following the Council's insistence on charging for *every* conceivable parking space, needless to say the shoppers joined a mass exodus. If I'm truthful, the best of them went as soon as parking charges were originally introduced, leaving us with the pensioners without cars, and the social security supportees. Now, I mean no disrespect but it stands to reason that you can't make much of a living out of those sections of the population—after all, if you don't have much money, you can't spend it. I should know.

So overall it was the Council's fault. Part of the problem was that, being merely a satellite town, Little Sniffingham was charged the same business rate per square metre as the big central town that got all the council resources like street cleaning, visiting recognisable celebrities, tourism, huge road signs saying "Good stuff this way" and festive lights. Oh yes, and a straight Christmas tree.

The 34$^{th}$ Rule of Non-retention states:

> *Blessed are the flexible, for they shall not be bent out of shape.*

This little gem had indeed saved us from premature demise on a number of occasions. But this last December's takings were down and, council mismanagement apart, the feeling in the shop was that we had lost our direction. But it was impossible to pinpoint the actual ingredient, missing or otherwise. Whatever, the effect was like the last nail in the coffin, the final straw (or bag of it) on the camel's back. We sold bits of this, not a lot of that, and even the picture framing service began to suffer. Once we had thrown out Tel's crap, it was too late and he had already lost us our hardcore of customers. I think the problem with being too flexible was that we had lost all recognisable shape.

At least Tel didn't disappear without Trace, his daughter. We were confident that she would not return with her amazing fingers that could put a smile on a bloke's face, yet couldn't actually spell the word "smile". The bad news was that he wanted his investment back. All of it, and he was demanding interest.

I took Sharon and Greville on a walk around the town—and I don't just mean the usual rush from A to B; this time we actually *looked* at the empty shops, the types of fly-by-night businesses that moved in one minute and disappeared without trace the next. It was depressingly apparent that the core of the town's shopping centre had been allowed to erode and die.

"I fink we've been here too long. Just look at it," said Sharon.

"Crikey," said Greville, "I had no idea. That used to be a posh shoe shop. Where do you buy shoes, now?"

Sharon pointed out others along the street. "Book shop. Electrical shop. And look over there—the butcher's is gone! This high street now has more empties than a milk float."

"The town's well and truly shagged," grumbled Greville.

Sharon made as if to smack the back of his head, but stopped herself.

"Things are better elsewhere," I said. "Not all little towns are shag—*finished*—as me and Greville found out a few months ago."

Greville turned to Sharon, then to me, a look of bewilderment on his face. "What's happened to it?"

"You've grown up," I said. "That's what five years serving these people has done to you. You've worked bloody hard, provided a priceless service, taken the crap and smiled throughout. You're not the apprentice any more. And all the while things have been changing around you. People have got more mobile and greedy despite becoming better off. They don't starve any more, but some of them don't mind if *we* do."

We walked back silently to our street. Outside the shop we watched a traffic warden slap a fixed penalty notice on a car that had parked without displaying a ticket. The driver, not seeing him, rushed out of the shop, thanking Brenda for the change, and fed the meter. Then he saw the warden's evil grin. Shaking his head, he got in and drove away. Probably forever.

We stood across the road from our shop, the windows well-stocked and brightly lit in the failing afternoon light. I noticed a couple of bulbs had been nicked from the Christmas lights and there was some recent graffiti on the rendering beside our window. We had something on the shelves for that.

"I'll get the Graff Zapper," Greville said.

I stopped him.

"Don't bother. I think this is it, Grev."

He paused, wary. "You don't usually call me that," he said.

Sharon sighed and momentarily looked down, blinking her eyes, trying to stop the tears. But I knew her too well. Then, for the first time ever when addressing me, she said the eff word.

"What the flipping hell do we do now?" she asked, trying her damnedest to appear unperturbed. She was a good actress (been in *Dr Who*, you know), but I could see through her current performance.

"It's not the premises," I said. "I've spent too long tramping up and down that concrete floor to be the least bit sentimental about it."

I looked at each of them. Greville held Sharon's hand.

"It's the people—people like you, *both of you*. If we packed it in, I would miss working with you, being with you, being able to talk with you. It's as if we're ... *related*."

"Well, my love, I suppose we could all sign-on the dole at the same time. But we can't stay together, can we." It wasn't a question.

"Well, it's funny you should say that ..."

Greville looked puzzled. I went on:

"I think we should stay together ... and expand."

"You mean have babies?" he said.

Sharon spoke with an element of excitement. "Of course—so that's where you've been disappearing off to! The new industrial units!"

"That's right," said Grev. "Cheap rent, bigger premises—and free parking!"

Sharon smacked Greville playfully. "Babies indeed."

For the first time in months I could feel a buzz of excitement between us. We must have lit up like Christmas lights.

"How big are they?" Greville was becoming animated. He didn't know just then, but I had big plans for him.

"Oh, *massive*."

"Big as Woolworths?"

"Not far off."

"How many cats' worth?" (Translation: how many cats could you actually *swing* in these new premises?)

"You'd be able to swing a number of them in the unit I've got my eye on. *And* ..."

They waited for the crunch line.

"It backs on to the mere."

"Oh, great! What's a mere?"

"It's a lake, Grev."

"Right—*right!* And I just happen to know someone with a *boat!* When can we see it?"

"The MD can have his own office—"

"Can *I* have a van?"

"We'll have room for ... bathroom tiles ... large power tools ... a dedicated showroom for the concrete garden ornaments—we could call it *The Petrified Forest*."

"What about underwear?"

"Sharon, we don't need underwear."

"Oh, don't we indeed! We'll see about that ..."

We laughed across the street and went into the shop. There was much to do.

THE END

# The Christmas Poem

'Twas the week before Christmas
    upstairs out of sight
Our Saturday Girl's
    in one heck of a plight:
Sitting stark naked,
    wearing only a blush
And holding one end of
    a chimney sweep's brush.

The apprentice was with her
    learning his trade
She'd got stuck with her tights
    and he'd gone to her aid.
They sat there and simmered,
    squinted and stared
With clothes on the floor
    and bodies now bared.

Then horror of horrors
    "Could that be," they cried,
"The boss on the landing
    and peeping inside?"
The hinges creaked open
    and faces turned red;
The boss in the doorway
    was scratching his head.

"What the hell are you doing?"
    (He hadn't a clue)
"A chimney sweep's brush
    when there isn't a flue?"
They got dressed in a rush
    and elastic went *twang!*
So for someone, at least,
    Christmas went with a bang.

**Before you go …**

Thank you for reading this book. If you enjoyed it, I would appreciate you helping others enjoy this book too. Please help by recommending it to friends, readers' groups and discussion boards, and tell other readers why you liked this book by reviewing it online – a sentence or two is all that's needed.

Visit me at grahamhigson.com
and click **Keep me updated**

# Also by Graham Higson

*The team returns for another episode!*

*Hammers, Rammers, Jammers, Scammers*

The most famous hardware man in the world (well, maybe) returns with his eclectic bunch of staff and dysfunctional customers in this short "equel" to *How Much for a Little Screw?*

As if things aren't bad enough running small shops in a tiny town, a gang of roaming conmen and women descend upon Little Sniffingham and threaten to strip and plunder, sparing no one.

Feeling helpless, he is determined to find a way of combating these despicable rogues. But no one knows who they are, nor how and where they will strike next, and it isn't long before the victims begin dropping like flies.

*"Readers who cherish idyllic ideas about English village life will have those notions challenged by Higson's gritty portrayal..."*
    Louise Titchener, author

Amy's world is a cold and inhospitable one of treacherous cliffs and lethal tides that can trap the unwary. The hostile villagers think that she doesn't understand much, but she knows more about that coastline than anyone else there.

The unpredictability of the sea brings both loss and discovery into Amy's life that changes it forever. The storm takes the one person she truly loves and yet brings her a stranger that transforms her childhood innocence into the passionate reality of a young woman.

The danger is, the year is 1915, England is at war, and the stranger is German.

Includes links for the following:

- High-resolution map
- Further reading
- Interview with the author
- Reading Group Guide

# About the author

GRAHAM HIGSON lives in an outlying Pennine village and shares this blustery environment with a growing collection of books, his understanding wife and a workshop piled high with offcuts of oak. Their two grown-up children are among his best friends.

Having been interested in writing since he was at primary school, he began interviewing celebrities when he was 15, going on to write professionally on wide-ranging subjects for various magazines over the following years. *Oak Seer: A Supernatural Mystery* was the first of his published novels, followed by *Flither Lass*, a historical novel set during the First World War. His fictionalized memoir *How Much for a Little Screw?* stories are based on many years working as a hardware man. His biggest critic is his technical manager, Gerald the cat.

He's a member of the Open and University College Falmouth alumni, and his hobbies include woodworking, reading, watching lots of screen drama, publishing books for the Walmsley Society, and searching for that elusive moment of self-discovery, though he says he'll keep trying.

www.grahamhigson.com